Making Blended Finance Work for the Sustainable Development Goals

OECD

BETTER POLICIES FOR BETTER LIVES

This work is published under the responsibility of the Secretary-General of the OECD. The opinions expressed and arguments employed herein do not necessarily reflect the official views of OECD member countries.

This document, as well as any data and any map included herein, are without prejudice to the status of or sovereignty over any territory, to the delimitation of international frontiers and boundaries and to the name of any territory, city or area.

Please cite this publication as:
OECD (2018), *Making Blended Finance Work for the Sustainable Development Goals*, OECD Publishing, Paris.
http://dx.doi.org/10.1787/9789264288768-en

ISBN 978-92-64-28875-1 (print)
ISBN 978-92-64-28876-8 (PDF)

The statistical data for Israel are supplied by and under the responsibility of the relevant Israeli authorities. The use of such data by the OECD is without prejudice to the status of the Golan Heights, East Jerusalem and Israeli settlements in the West Bank under the terms of international law.

Photo credits: Cover © Stephanie Coic (OECD) and Pierre-Yves Perez-Queyroi (Studio Pykha).

Corrigenda to OECD publications may be found on line at: *www.oecd.org/about/publishing/corrigenda.htm*.

Foreword

Donor governments face increased demand to finance the 2030 Agenda and increased pressure to link financing with development results. Blended finance - defined as the strategic use of development finance for the mobilisation of additional finance towards sustainable development in developing countries – is gaining traction as a way to grow development aid. Initial OECD studies show that blended finance has generated over USD 81 billion for development goals in four years and a survey of OECD Development Assistance Committee member countries demonstrated that the majority are participating in some blending.

Going beyond finance, blending can deliver much more than capital for achieving the Sustainable Development Goals; diverse actors from the public and private sector working together leverages strengths from each sector that can be applied in new ways to solve persistent development challenges. Public sector engagement brings trust, transparency, and a mandate to help those most in need. Enter the private sector with innovation, risk-taking, and a results-driven approach. To achieve and sustain poverty eradication by 2030 demands a collective effort and a broad scaling-up of blended finance has the potential to maximize impact and produce shared results.

However, as this report demonstrates, not all blended finance is necessarily quality blended finance. "Quality" means one thing at the OECD: achieving the core mission of the Sustainable Development Goals to "leave no one behind." Ad hoc projects will not be sufficient to reap the untapped universal benefits of blended finance and to deliver the trillions necessary to achieve the SDGs. Governments and the private sector need broad, ambitious, and coordinated strategies to mobilise additional resources beyond official development assistance (ODA) for developing countries.

The OECD Development Co-operation Directorate (DCD) is playing a role to help align increased blending activity and growing SDG challenges, by providing a roadmap to donor governments informed by data-driven evidence. To do this, the OECD DCD has developed an ambitious blended finance work programme that aims to provide policymakers with standards for advancing quality blended finance policies. This publication aims to set out a common understanding of blended finance, defining the key actors, instruments, and mechanisms. It also outlines initial lessons learned from the growing body of evidence on blended finance, informed by a diverse set of case studies and surveys of the market and donor governments.

There is a shared responsibility amongst donors as well as commercial financial actors to make the impact of blended finance match the ambition of the SDGs. To mobilise private sector resources, donor governments are challenged to operate differently, both in terms of the development finance instruments used and the risk profile of instruments, as well as the sectors and economies where blending is applied. Donors must put in place the right incentives in order to encourage private sector engagement. For financial investors to deepen engagement with development finance – often opening access to growth markets in developing economies – investors' structuring skills and understanding of risk should be applied. Together, these efforts can create the environment that will bring quality private sector participation to scale and attract additional institutional investors.

This report was developed in parallel to the OECD Blended Finance Principles *which were adopted by the OECD Development Assistance Committee during its High Level Meeting on 31 October 2017.*

Together, this publication and the Principles are a strong signal of the importance that the OECD attaches to driving new actors towards the Sustainable Development Goals and our long term ambition for activating new innovative levers like blended finance that can accelerate much-needed progress on the 2030 Agenda.

Jorge Moreira da Silva
Director, OECD Development Co-operation Directorate

Charlotte Petri Gornitzka
Chair, Development Assistance Committee

Acknowledgements

This report was prepared by the OECD Development Co-operation Directorate (DCD) under Jorge Moreira da Silva, Director. It was managed and edited by Naeeda Crishna Morgado, Policy Analyst, with guidance from Paul Horrocks, Team Leader and Jens Sedemund, Senior Advisor, Blended Finance, and the strategic leadership from Haje Schütte, Head of the Statistics and Development Finance Division, DCD.

The report was drafted by a core team from DCD: Chapter 1 (Naeeda Crishna Morgado), Chapter 2 (Dan Preston), Chapter 3 (Jens Sedemund, Wiebke Bartz-Zuccala and Tamer Teker), Chapter 4 (Naeeda Crishna Morgado, Paul Horrocks, Irene Basile and Ashima Bali), Chapter 5 (Wiebke Bartz-Zuccala and Dan Preston), Chapter 6 (Floriane Maman, Bérénice Lasfargues, Owen Hill and Soren Andreasen [EDFI]), Chapter 7 (Wiebke Bartz-Zuccala and Dan Preston), Chapter 8 (Wiebke Bartz-Zuccala) and Chapter 9 (Irene Basile). Valentyna Vozna and Bérénice Lasfargues provided editorial and substantive support.

The analysis of funds and facilities in Chapter 6 benefitted from, and built on earlier surveys conducted by Commons Consultants and as part of the World Economic Forum/ OECD ReDesigning Development Finance Initiative. The entire report, and Chapters 3 and 8 in particular, benefitted from the inputs of the OECD work on tracking amounts mobilised from the private sector by Julia Benn, Cécile Sangaré and Tomáš Hos from DCD and Raphael Jachnik from the Environment Directorate.

The authors would like to thank the following OECD colleagues who took the time to review and provide comprehensive feedback on the draft: Karen Wilson, Emily Bosch, Hans Lundgren, Kathryn Nwajiaku, Mags Gaynor from DCD; Lorenzo Pavone and Rodrigo Deiana from the Development Centre; Raphael Jachnik, Rob Youngman and Kathleen Dominique from the Environment Directorate; Joel Paula and Timothy Bishop from the Directorate for Financial and Enterprise Affairs.

The report benefitted from in-depth peer reviews by Paddy Carter (Center for Global Development), Cordelia Lonsdale (Development Initiatives), Cherie Nursalim (GITI Group), Simona Santoro (UNCDF), Dr. Anke Philipps (KfW) and Winston J. Allen (USAID). An early draft in 2016 also received comments and feedback from Joan Larrea and Chris Clubb (Convergence); Neil Gregory and Kruskaia Sierra-Escalante (IFC); and Laura Atienza (European Commission). The funds and facilities survey in Chapter 6 and the case studies in Chapter 7 received specific contributions and feedback from Dan Barton (Asian Development Bank); Pierrick Balmain (Blue Orchard); Kristy Graham (Department of Foreign Affairs and Trade, Australia); Paul Lazaro (Development Bank of the Philippines); Yves Ehlert (European Commission); Milena Bertram (Finance in Motion); Tom Bui and Martin Normandeau (Global Affairs Canada); Megumi Muto (JICA); Morten Koch, Kurt Strasser and Anirban Kundu (KfW); Julia Prescott (Meridiam); Johannet Graemers, Reinoud Linschoten, Bjorn Kuil and Rosemarijn van der Meij (Ministry of Foreign Affairs of the Netherlands); Mats Slotte and Charles Wetherill (NDF); Harald Hirschhofer (TCX); Agnes Dasewicz and Jeffrey Paretchan (USAID).

The report was reviewed and discussed by the OECD Development Assistance Committee in September 2017. An early draft was discussed at an informal meeting of the OECD Advisory Group on Investment and Development in October 2016. The research underpinning this report has greatly benefitted from insights collated at three meetings of the OECD Senior Advisory Group on Blended Finance Principles held between March and September 2017. Development of the report recommendations have also benefited from the work of the Blended Finance Breakthrough Taskforce of the Business and Sustainable Development Commission.

The report was prepared for publication under the direction of Henri-Bernard Solignac-Lecomte and Stacey Bradbury (DCD) with editorial support from Susan Sachs. Pierre-Yves Perez-Queyroi (Studio Pykha) did the layout and design for the report, and Stephanie Coic (DCD) prepared the cover image. Anne-Lise Prigent from the Public Affairs and Communications Directorate provided editorial and content oversight. The authors would like to extend a big thank you to Clare Lannigan and Susan Hodgson (DCD) for administrative support.

Table of contents

Part II

Insights from blended finance in practice

Tables

Figures

Boxes

Abbreviations and acronyms

AAAA	Addis Ababa Action Agenda
ADB	Asian Development Bank
AFD	Agence française de développement
AfDB	African Development Bank
AIF	Africa Improved Foods Holding
AUD	Australian dollar
BOAD	West African Development Bank
BMZ	Federal Ministry for Economic Cooperation and Development (Germany)
BPP	Business Partnerships Platform
CAD	Canadian dollar
CEFPF	Clean Energy Financing Partnership Facility
CFPS	Canadian Climate Fund for the Private Sector in Asia
CIFs	Climate Investment Funds
CIV	Collective investment vehicle
CRS	Creditor reporting system
CTF	Clean Technology Fund
DAC	Development Assistance Committee
DBP	Development Bank of the Philippines
DEG	German Investment Corporation
DFAT	Department of Foreign Affairs and Trade (Australia)
DFI	Development finance institution
DFID	Department for International Development (United Kingdom)
EBRD	European Bank for Reconstruction and Development
EC	European Commission
ECA	Export Credit Agency
EDFI	Association of European Development Finance Institutions
EIB	European Investment Bank
EIP	External Investment Plan
ESG	Environmental, social and corporate governance
EU	European Union
EU-AITF	EU-Africa Infrastructure Trust Fund
EUR	Euro
FMO	Netherlands Development Finance Company
GAC	Global Affairs Canada
GCF	Green Climate Fund
GDP	Gross domestic product
GEEREF	Global Energy Efficiency and Renewable Energy Fund
GEF	Global Environment Facility
IDA	International Development Association
IFC	International Finance Corporation
IFI	International financial institution
IMF	International Monetary Fund
JICA	Japan International Cooperation Agency
JPY	Japanese yen
LDC	Least developed country
LFI	Local financial institution

LMIC	Lower middle-income country
M&E	Monitoring and evaluation
MDB	Multilateral development bank
MENA	Middle East and North Africa
MFI	Microfinance institution
MIGA	Multilateral Investment Guarantee Agency
NDF	Nordic Development Fund
NGO	Non-governmental organisation
ODA	Official development assistance
ODF	Official development finance
OECD	Organisation for Economic Co-operation and Development
OPIC	Overseas Private Investment Corporation
PFIs	Private financial institutions
PPP	Public-private partnership
PWRF	Philippines Water Revolving Fund
SDG	Sustainable Development Goals
SEK	Swedish krona
Sida	Swedish International Development Cooperation Agency
SME	Small and medium-sized enterprise
SPV	Special purpose vehicle
TCX	The Currency Exchange Fund
TOSSD	Total official support for sustainable development
UCO	Universal credit organisation
UMIC	Upper middle-income country
UN	United Nations
UNFCCC	United Nations Framework Convention on Climate Change
USAID	United States Agency for International Development
USD	United States dollar
WBG	World Bank Group
WEF	World Economic Forum
WSPF	Water and Sanitation Pooled Fund

Executive summary

Delivering the Sustainable Development Goals (SDGs) and the Paris Agreement will require more resources than are currently being spent on development outcomes, not least in developing countries. Blended finance, an approach that mixes different forms of capital to support development, is emerging as a solution to help achieve the "billions to trillions" agenda. Scaling up blended finance without a sound understanding of its potential and its risks, however, may have unintended consequences for development co-operation providers. This report presents a comprehensive assessment of the state of blended finance and priorities for action to improve its implementation, drawing on surveys, case studies, interviews and desk research. It argues that while blending has potential to scale up commercial finance for the Sustainable Development Goals, its deployment by the development finance community needs to be based on a common framing and principles, as well as additional evidence and analysis. While this report is meant primarily for a development co-operation and finance audience, its findings and recommendations are useful for a broader range of policy makers and practitioners pursuing sustainable development in developing countries.

Key findings

Blended finance has potential to help bridge the estimated USD 2.5 trillion per year investment gap for delivering the SDGs in developing countries. Taking stock of financing for the SDGs two years into the Addis Ababa Action Agenda, the Inter-Agency Task Force on Financing for Development (2017) reports that growth in capital for these investments largely has not materialised. Public development finance alone, from governments and donors, will not be sufficient to achieve the sustainable development agenda; it needs to catalyse and mobilise other sources of financing for development. While there is no shortage of capital worldwide, a lack of risk-adjusted returns constrains commercial investors from investing in projects in developing countries. This is where blended finance could make a difference. By deploying development resources to improve the risk-return profile of individual investments in developing countries, blended finance can attract commercial, private financing, help to demonstrate project viability and build markets that ultimately are able to attract further commercial capital for development.

A critical first step to effective blended finance is a common definition. There is much ambiguity and variety in the ways blended finance is defined, even among members of the OECD Development Assistance Committee (DAC). This report and the OECD DAC Blended Finance Principles, which were endorsed by the DAC High Level Meeting in 2017, present a definition and framework to support donor governments in designing approaches that mobilise and better target commercial capital towards the SDGs. Blended finance is *the strategic use of development finance for the mobilisation of additional finance towards sustainable development in developing countries.* Additional finance is commercial finance that does not have an explicit development purpose and that has not primarily targeted development outcomes in developing countries, and development finance is public and private finance that is being deployed with a development mandate. This framing of blended finance distinguishes finance by purpose rather than by source, moving away from the emphasis on public/private actors to highlight development/commercial finance flows. It is broader than those used by multilateral development banks (MDBs) and development finance institutions (DFIs) in that it does not depend on concessionality as a pre-requisite for blending and considers blending in the context of both public and private investments. Blended finance occurs within the context of a specific transaction, and differs from public support for policy and regulatory reform which also has a role in unlocking commercial capital in developing countries.

Donor governments and other development finance providers increasingly use blended finance. At least 17 members of the OECD DAC now engage in blended finance, although they are at very different stages in terms of the range of instruments used and how blending is carried out. MDBs and bilateral DFIs also engage in blending, both as facilitators of blended transactions and using their own finance. Between 2000 and 2016, donor governments set up 167 dedicated facilities that pool public financing for blending and the number of new facilities grew every year, according to surveys by the OECD in 2017 and the Association of European Development Finance Institutions (EDFI). This growth is a sign of increasing donor interest but it also demonstrates increasing fragmentation in approaches and vehicles used. Attracting commercial capital at scale will require some degree of standardisation in terms of both access to development finance and instruments used.

Development actors are using blended finance as an innovative way to mobilise capital. The instruments used extend beyond the more traditional loans and grants to include the use of guarantees, securitisation, currency hedging and political risk insurance. Structured blended finance funds are one example where donor governments use concessional finance in a first loss position and provide a risk cushion which help to attract commercial investors. Another blending model garnering interest is impact funds, in which development finance providers and private actors invest with the aim of generating financial returns and measurable development impact. Across the different models, engagement with local public and private actors, and efforts to build local financial markets, can support the long-term sustainability of the project.

While interest in blending is increasing, the evidence base on blended finance is still quite limited. Different efforts have aimed to map the blending landscape but have not produced a single, consistent and comparable estimate of the blended finance market that covers the entirety of flows. The OECD is engaged in work on tracking the volume of private finance mobilised by official development finance interventions that will be institutionalised in the reporting system for OECD DAC members, representing a useful advance in this regard. Significant shortcomings in existing monitoring and evaluation systems also contribute to gaps in the evidence base that have implications for blended finance. Developing these systems for blended finance is particularly challenging because they must satisfy the needs of quite distinct and diverse stakeholders. Initial evidence shows that monitoring and evaluation of blended finance funds and facilities are less developed than for other development co-operation activities.

Policy recommendations

Development finance providers need to move towards blended finance 2.0. This report finds that while blended finance has potential to support financing for development, donor governments need to guide its deployment to ensure it meets the needs of the SDGs. Blended finance is not a silver bullet that will solve the myriad challenges associated with mobilising investment for the SDGs. It is one pillar in an array of development finance approaches that will have to complement each other in order to deliver the resources needed. The report recommends that donor governments need to move towards 'blended finance 2.0' i.e. to ensure that blended finance mobilises commercial resources that are not currently supporting development and better target blended finance to a broader range of development issues (i.e. SDGs) and contexts. In this regard, the OECD DAC Blended Finance Principles, developed concurrently with this report, identifies five areas for action:

- Anchor blended finance use to a development rationale (Principle 1)
- Design blended finance to increase the mobilisation of commercial finance (Principle 2)
- Tailor blended finance to local context (Principle 3)
- Focus on effective partnering for blended finance (Principle 4)
- Monitor blended finance for transparency and results (Principle 5)

The proof of blended finance for the SDGs ultimately will ultimately depend on how it is deployed. As an approach to mobilise investment, and to bring development and commercial actors together, blended finance has potential if the development community acts together to ensure its application is based on mutually agreed standards and guidelines. This report and the OECD DAC Blended Finance Principles are a significant contribution to on-going joint efforts to establishing a common framework for blended finance by key stakeholders. The SDGs call for concerted action, bringing together all actors, to drive forward progress in developing countries. Ultimately, how well blended is deployed will determine how far it goes in supporting this global agenda.

BLENDED FINANCE FOR THE SUSTAINABLE DEVELOPMENT GOALS

BRINGING DEVELOPMENT AND COMMERCIAL FINANCE TOGETHER

Blended finance could help bridge the investment gap for the Sustainable Development Goals in developing countries. Donor governments need to ensure blending approaches attract commercial sources of finance and directs these to development outcomes.

MORE FINANCING NEEDED TO MEET THE $2.5 TRILLION INVESTMENT GAP FOR SDGS IN DEVELOPING COUNTRIES

Sources of external finance to developing countries

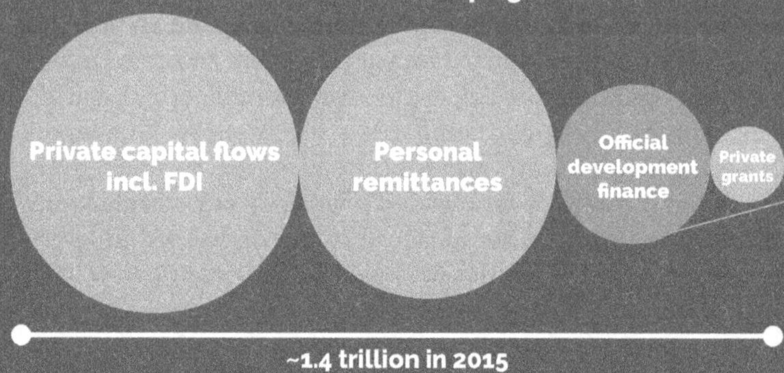

To raise resources required, development finance has to mobilise more finance and better target commercial finance to SDGs

...BLENDED FINANCE COULD HELP BRIDGE THE INVESTMENT GAP...

What is blended finance?

Blended finance is the strategic use of development finance for the mobilisation of additional finance towards sustainable development in developing countries.

Additional finance = commercial finance

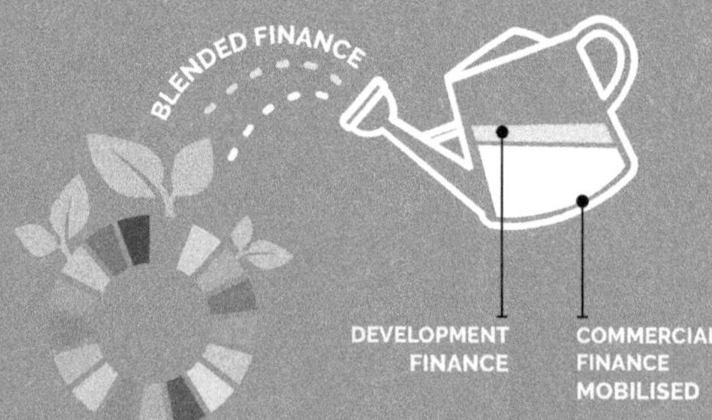

BLENDED FINANCE CAN SHIFT THE RISK-RETURN PROFILE OF PROJECTS IN DEVELOPING COUNTRIES TO ATTRACT COMMERCIAL INVESTMENT.

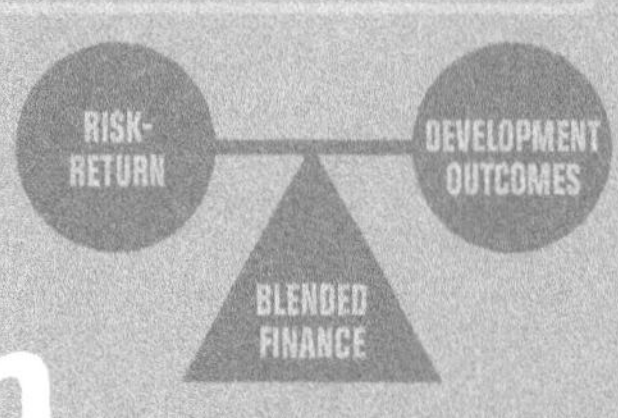

$81 billion **private finance mobilised** by development finance 2012-2015

BLENDED FINANCE IS GAINING TRACTION AMONG DEVELOPMENT FINANCE PROVIDERS

17 **of the OECD Development Assistance Committee** members now engage in blending

167 **facilities launched,** 2000 - 2016, to pool finance for blending

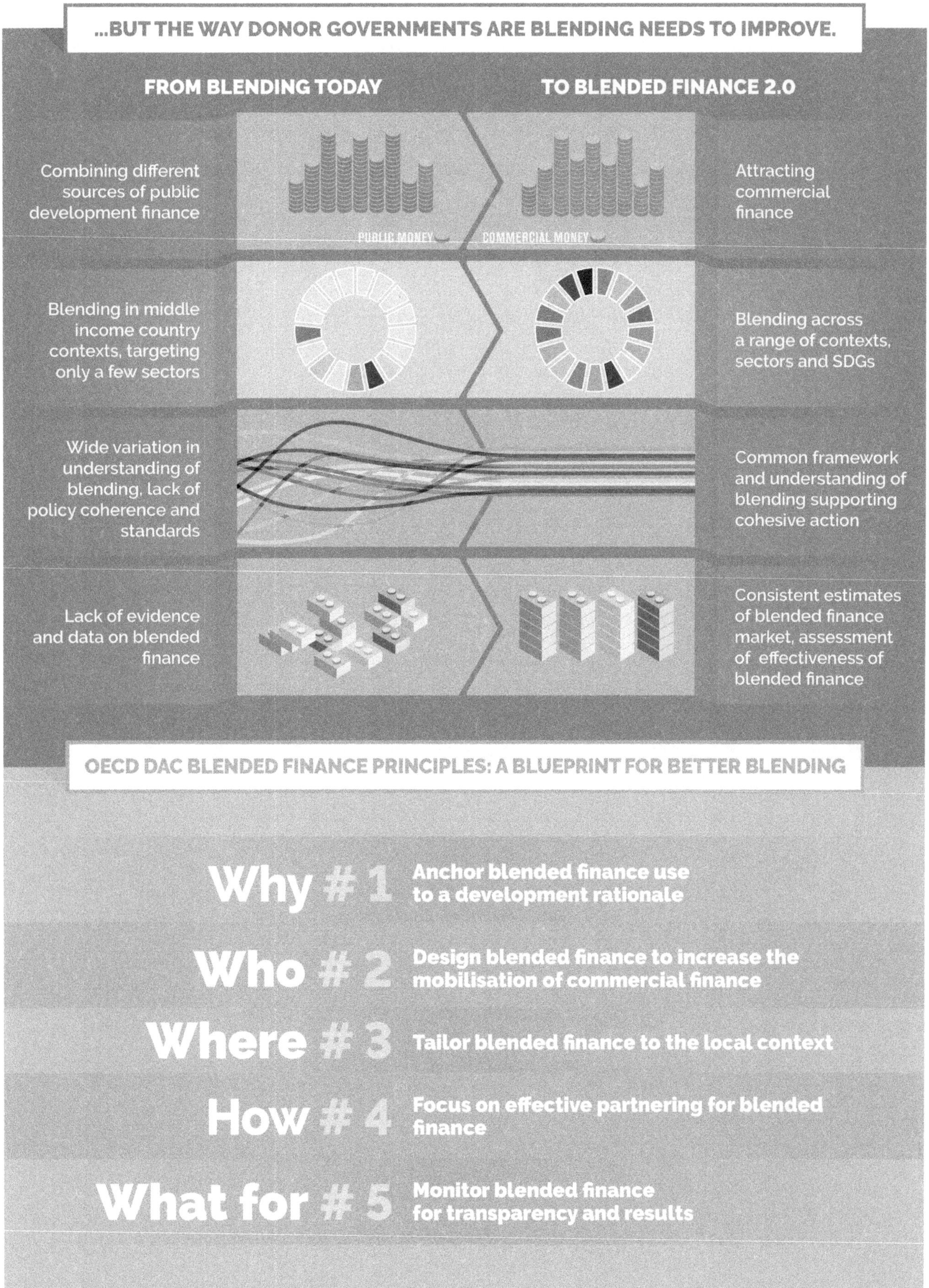

Source: OECD (2018), *Making Blended Finance Work for the Sustainable Development Goals*, OECD Publishing, Paris, http://dx.doi.org/10.1787/9789264288768-en.

Making Blended Finance Work for the Sustainable Development Goals

Chapter 1

Overview: What will it take to make blended finance work for the Sustainable Development Goals?

Blended finance is emerging as an approach to help bridge the financing gap for the Sustainable Development Goals. This chapter contains an expanded synthesis of the report, highlighting the challenges and opportunities for blended finance and outlining key policy recommendations. The chapter presents an overview of the main building blocks of blended finance – concepts, definitions, blended finance architecture and instruments – and highlights important gaps and challenges that need to be addressed. It presents policy recommendations for the development co-operation community and outlines the OECD DAC Blended Finance Principles to improve blending efforts. It highlights an agenda for action for research work in this area going forward.

HIGHLIGHTS

Blended finance has potential to help bridge the investment gap for implementing the SDGs in developing countries by using public support to mobilise commercial investment. Blended finance can address the risk-return profiles of investments in developing countries and help attract commercial investors.

While blending has potential, a lack of a common framework for blending hampers the wider awareness and understanding of this approach. This report presents a definition of blended finance designed to support donor governments in moving towards more effective blended finance.

The development community is increasingly using blended finance. The majority of OECD DAC members are blending and development banks and development finance institutions are integrating blending into their operations. A number of financial instruments and structures are emerging as innovative ways of attracting commercial investors.

However, in order for blending to deliver on its potential, issues and challenges around blending need to be addressed. Blending efforts need to focus on attracting finance that is not already addressing development efforts, i.e. commercial finance. They also need to target a wider range of issues, based on careful analysis of what works in different contexts.

The report recommends that donor governments need to advance towards blended finance 2.0 with a greater emphasis on mobilising commercial finance and targeting the SDGs. The OECD DAC Blended Finance Principles present a standard to help them get there.

Going forward, further research will be needed, including on the size and scope of the blended finance market and on applying blending to different issues and contexts. Policy guidance on how to apply blending effectively and, in particular, how to measure impact, will be important.

Key facts

- Annual investment gap to deliver the SDGs in developing countries is estimated at USD 2.5 trillion
- 17 of 23 DAC members who responded to a survey for this report are engaging in blended finance; 10 of those report having well-established programmes that have been in operation for a number of years and/or cover a range of instruments
- Between 2000 and 2016, a total of 167 facilities that engage in blending were launched, with a combined size (as measured by commitments) of approximately USD 31 billion

Introduction

The global community has spoken loud and clear – more resources must be mobilised to end extreme poverty and mitigate the effects of climate change. Two years on from the agreement of the Addis Ababa Action Agenda, overall investment is not growing sufficiently to set developing countries on the path to meeting the Sustainable Development Goals (SDGs) and goals of the Paris Agreement. More concerted action is urgently needed to enhance long-standing mechanisms of development finance and create innovative ways of channelling investment for sustainable development. Against this context, blended finance is increasingly considered within the development community as a way to help move development finance from "billions to trillions".

At the same time, important concerns have been raised about blended finance, focussing on associated risks and unintended impacts that could arise if this form of financing is scaled up without appropriate policies, checks and balances in place. Among the important questions being raised are whether blended finance can be used to address different development outcomes, to what extent it can be used to attract commercial capital into difficult markets (such as countries transitioning from conflict or facing forms of fragility), how blended finance can be applied so as to not distort competition and crowd out other actors, how blended finance can be aligned with national priorities, and what safeguards are needed to ensure that blended finance does not negatively impact the environment or vulnerable communities (Development Initiatives, 2016; Carter, 2015; Eurodad, 2013). In addition, there is a lack of information and evidence on how blended finance is being applied and how it could be applied better. The lack of a clear and common understanding of blended finance is partly responsible.

This report provides a comprehensive overview of blended finance today, discussing concepts and definitions, blended finance architecture, instruments and innovations, tracking and data, monitoring and evaluation. Chapter 1 presents a synthesis of findings from the report. It highlights the main challenges and opportunities for blended finance and outlines key policy recommendations. The report then is divided into two parts. Part I introduces blended finance: background and context (Chapter 2); definitions (Chapter 3); role of development finance actors (Chapter 4); and instruments and mechanisms (Chapter 5). Part II presents insights from blended finance facilities and funds (Chapter 6) and project-level case studies (Chapter 7); discusses the challenges of tracking blended finance (Chapter 8); and outlines issues around monitoring and evaluation of blended finance and their implications for growing development financing overall (Chapter 9).

The research presented in this report builds on several analyses. These include a survey of Development Assistance Committee (DAC) members to understand the status of their blended finance activities; specialised surveys of blended finance facilities and funds that were conducted by the Association of European Development Finance Institutions (EDFI) in 2015 and by the OECD in 2017 to gain a picture of the market for pooled financing vehicles engaging in blending; and case studies of ten projects utilising blended finance and encompassing a range of sectors and issues. This report also draws from the OECD work on measuring the mobilisation of private finance as a result of official development finance interventions. The report benefits from additional recent efforts to map the landscape of blended finance including by the OECD and World Economic Forum ReDesigning Finance Initiative (OECD/World Economic Forum, 2015) and Convergence (2017).

Blended finance is emerging as an approach to finance the SDGs

The 2030 Agenda calls for new approaches to finance development

The ambitious 2030 Agenda and the Paris Agreement will require significant investment as well as new forms of partnerships to increase investment and stimulate collaboration on sustainable development. If investment remains on its current trajectory, it will not be sufficient to achieve the SDGs in developing countries. The gap now is estimated at USD 2.5 trillion a year (UNCTAD, 2014). More financing that targets development outcomes in developing countries is coming from private businesses and individuals than before. But to narrow the investment gap, developing countries will have to mobilise additional financing from the private sector domestically and externally and from other actors not currently investing in developing countries.

In the development finance community, blended finance is emerging as one solution with significant potential to help meet this challenge by using public support to mobilise commercial finance. The logic behind the approach is simple. Commercial investors, businesses and project developers respond to and are constrained by the risk-return profiles associated with investments. Investments in developing countries with important public good dimensions may possess good business models and positive projected returns, but associated risk and uncertainty deter commercial investors from providing financing. In many cases, very shallow and immature local financial markets, coupled with information asymmetries and market imperfections or failures further discourage private investors. Public support through blended finance approaches can help address these issues by improving the risk-return profile of investments in developing countries and thus attracting commercial financing.

Presenting a common framework to understand blended finance

Despite increasing interest in blending, there is a lack of a commonly accepted framework for understanding blended finance which hampers its effective use. While most actors in the development finance landscape agree that the objective of blending should be to mobilise finance for the SDGs, blended finance is understood differently, even among DAC members. In this report and in the OECD DAC Blended Finance Principles (OECD DAC, 2017) blended finance is defined as **the strategic use of development finance for the mobilisation of additional finance towards sustainable development in developing countries** (see Figure 1.1). Additional finance, in this definition, refers primarily to commercial finance that is not currently deployed to support development outcomes. Commercial finance includes both public and private sources — for example investment by public or privately owned pension funds or insurance companies, banks and businesses — as long as their primary motivation is commercial. Development finance here focuses on external finance to developing countries and includes development assistance from donor governments and development finance providers as well as private funds from philanthropic foundations that are deployed for development purposes.

Blended finance refers to the use of development finance to mobilise commercial investors within the context of a specific transaction. It is not the same as public support for policy and regulatory reforms, which also help to unlock commercial capital, and which will be the focus of the upcoming *OECD Global Outlook on Financing for Development.*

The following tenets underpin this definition:

- *Finance mobilised is additional to what would have been available without blending:* Blended finance is based on the need to mobilise finance for the SDGs that would not have otherwise been allocated for development.
- *Development finance catalyses the additional investment:* In blended finance, there should be causality between the two sources of finance with the development finance contribution resulting in additional finance mobilised.

- *Finance is distinguished by purpose rather than source:* Development finance or commercial finance could be deployed by both public and private actors. Private development finance is deployed by philanthropic foundations, and public commercial finance could be deployed by state-owned enterprises or financial institutions including state-owned pension funds.
- *Concessionality is not a pre-requisite for blending:* While many blended finance examples to date have been based on concessional development finance, concessionality is not always needed in order to mobilise commercial resources. Development finance providers bring other benefits to a project that may have a direct financial value to commercial financing partners such as reputation, expertise in development issues and, networks in developing countries.
- *Blended finance is closely related to but does not replace private sector development:* All development finance provided at market rates to private companies is not blended finance. Some of this activity serves a different, and valid, primary purpose such as developing a healthy private sector in developing countries and thus may not result in additional (external) commercial finance being mobilised.

Figure 1.1 **What is blended finance?**

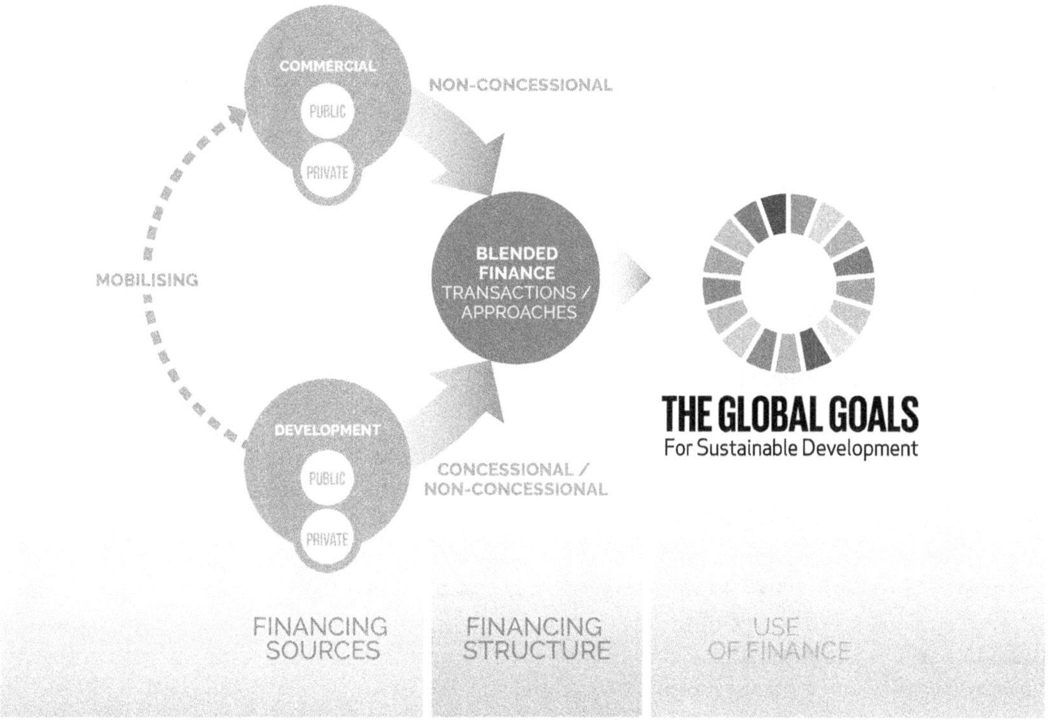

Source: Authors' compilation

Development actors are increasingly using blended finance to mobilise capital

Donor governments are initiating and scaling up blended finance interventions

The majority of OECD DAC members engage in blended finance in some form, although they are at very different stages in terms of the range of instruments used and how blending is carried out. Of the 26 DAC members responding to survey conducted for this report,

17 are engaging in blended finance; at least ten of these members have well-established programmes in place that have been in operation for a number of years and/or cover a range of instruments. Survey responses suggest that DAC member countries define blending in different ways. The extent of established policies and guidance governing blending operations among donor governments was also not clear. Only 6 of the 17 DAC respondents who reported engaging in blending reported having an explicit strategy or guidance in place. Only four of the DAC respondents reported that they actively monitor blended finance activities separately. However, donor interest in blending appears to be growing (see Chapter 6). According to the 2017 OECD survey and 2015 EDFI survey, 167 dedicated donor facilities to pool public financing for blending were set up between 2000 and 2016 (Figure 1.2).

Figure 1.2 **Increase in the number of blended finance facilities launched, 2000-16**

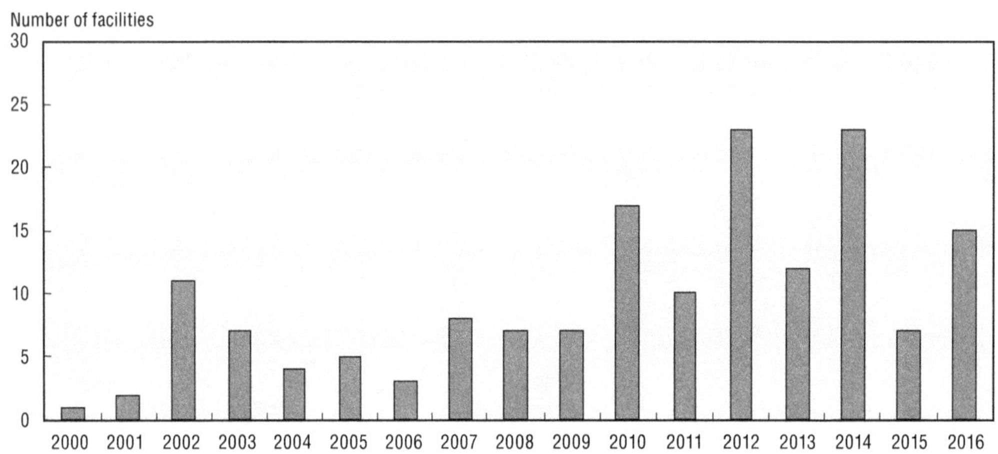

Source: OECD 2017 and EDFI 2015 surveys of blended finance funds and facilities

StatLink http://dx.doi.org/10.1787/888933648176

Multilateral development banks and development finance institutions are actively engaging in blending

Multilateral development banks (MDBs) and development finance institutions (DFIs) are important actors in blended finance as both facilitators of blended transactions and providers of development finance that is used to mobilise commercial capital. MDBs are beginning to integrate blended finance into their overarching service offering to development countries. The World Bank Group's "cascade approach" is an example. It prioritises blending where possible over the use of purely public development finance to cover financing needs of development projects, while blending in turn is an intermediary step towards meeting financing needs fully through private financial markets.

Private sector-oriented DFIs (including EDFI members) support development outcomes by taking a pathfinder and market leader role, especially in countries where there are few alternative sources of financing. While DFI activity is essential in supporting the objective of blended finance to overcome market failure and accelerate market evolution, DFI investments that do not have the effect of mobilising additional commercial capital would not necessarily be considered blended finance. DFIs take an intermediary role in blended finance by managing donor governments' blending activities and are seen to invest in the middle (mezzanine) tranche of subordinated funds to provide an additional risk cushion for senior investors. They also invest in impact funds and, with other impact investors, mobilise further commercial capital.

A range of financial instruments and mechanisms are being used to support blending and target different risks

One of the main barriers to commercial investment in development is that investors often associate investments in developing countries with an unfavourable risk-return relationship. While financial risks are associated with any investment, they are usually exacerbated in emerging markets. This can be due to the nature of the investment, for example cross-border investments are inherently associated with foreign currency risk, or the country itself, which may have a poor credit rating. A range of approaches can be used in blended finance to alter risk-adjusted returns of investments. These include the use of financial instruments to crowd in commercial finance (e.g. equity, loans, mezzanine instruments, guarantees or grants), and mechanisms to structure or intermediate instruments with the same purpose (e.g. funds, syndication, securitisation and public-private partnerships).

Although a number of instruments can be used for blending, donor governments are relying to some extent on instruments that traditionally have been used in aid programmes such as grants, loans and guarantees. Donor-supported blended finance facilities are examples. European Union blending facilities, for example, have provided loans and grants that go towards blending at the project level. Greater diversification through the range of instruments that are available and being piloted could support better targeting of different risks in order to attract commercial investors. This is illustrated by initial evidence on the mobilisation effect of different instruments. An OECD assessment of five instruments — guarantees, syndicated loans, credit lines, direct investment in companies and shares in common investment vehicles/ funds — highlights that different instruments are being used to mobilise private finance in different country contexts and to target a range of sectors (Figure 1.3).

Figure 1.3 **Private finance mobilised by selected official development finance instruments, by sector, 2012-15**

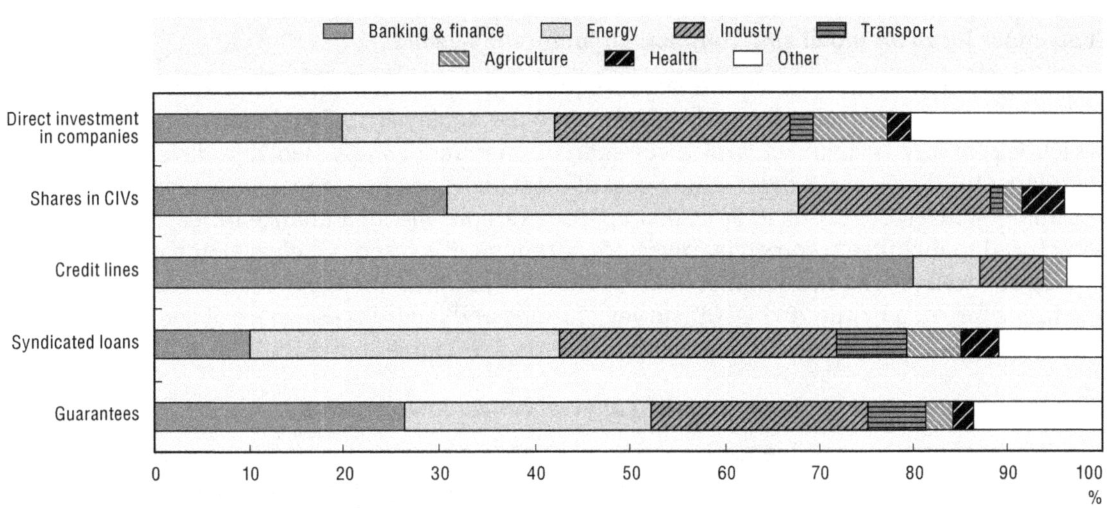

Source: Benn, Sangaré and Hos (2017), "Amounts mobilised from the private sector by Official Development Finance interventions", http://dx.doi.org/10.1787/8135abde-en.

StatLink http://dx.doi.org/10.1787/888933648195

Pooled financing in facilities and funds offer opportunities for testing, targeting and scaling up blending

Collective vehicles bring development and commercial actors together to pool financing and offer opportunities for scaling up blended finance. This report considers two different pooled models: donor government facilities that pool public resources to support blending further downstream and blended finance funds that blend development finance from donor governments and DFIs with commercial finance.

While facilities do not engage private capital in the facility itself, they enable donor governments to support blending for specific issues or regions. For example, the OECD and EDFI surveys show that half the commitments from donor governments towards blended finance facilities target specific issues (e.g. climate change, food security, etc.) across several or all continents. These facilities have also helped MDBs and DFIs to scale up blending involving concessional development finance.

Blended finance funds offer a way for development finance actors to blend their finance with investors within the fund itself and, in some cases, to target this blended capital to crowd in further commercial capital into projects or companies. Such funds are well suited to attracting additional commercial investors. For example, in the case of the Microfinance Initiative for Asia, donor governments take a first-loss position and provide a cushion for private investors who take a more senior share in the fund. In interviews that contributed to the research for this report, stakeholders suggest that funds offer more potential advantages to mobilise commercial finance compared to facilities. These include an acceptable return rate, an investment grade profile due to low volatility, significant vehicle sizes and the potentially higher liquidity of their assets. Alternatively, funds may offer development and commercial investors the same exposure to risks and returns but can crowd in private impact investors or commercial capital through a signalling/demonstration effect and/or technical assistance. In addition, blended finance funds can also be used to support further blending, as is the case of the Global Energy Efficiency and Renewable Energy Fund (GEEREF), which is managed by the European Investment Bank (GEEREF, 2017). It is a fund of funds that provides equity for funds that in turn invest in clean energy projects.

Blending in practice highlights issues and challenges that need to be addressed

A stronger focus on mobilising commercial finance is needed

Mobilisation of finance at the scale required to meet the SDGs demands a focus on finance that is not already part of the resources deployed to development priorities, which essentially is financed with a commercial mandate as opposed to a development mandate. While this is the overarching goal of most blended finance today, participation of commercial investors needs to be scaled up. For example, blended finance funds are being structured to mobilise commercial investors, although it is often not clear that the capital shares of development and commercial investors fully exploit the scope for crowding in. In the funds targeted by the 2017 OECD survey of funds and facilities the share of commercial investors is still quite limited when compared with development investors.

Blended finance needs to target a wider range of issues and contexts

While efforts to map blended finance in this report have not necessarily painted a complete picture of the market, they do coalesce around one main point: blended finance needs to be more strategically targeted if it is to meet the challenges of supporting developing countries to meet a wider range of SDGs. The amounts mobilised by official development finance through five instruments (guarantees, shares in common investment vehicles, credit lines, direct investment in companies and syndicated loans) in 2012-15 demonstrates this clearly (Benn, Sangaré and Hos, 2017). The majority of financing (77%) was mobilised in middle-income countries (43% in upper middle-income countries and 34% in lower middle-income countries) as opposed to low-income countries and least developed countries. Moreover, the mobilisation of private capital is most pronounced in the finance and energy sectors. The high concentration of capital mobilised in upper middle-income countries deserves more reflection - while there is a need to mobilise capital across all income groups, blended finance applied to upper middle-income countries needs a clear exit strategy. Donor governments will need to sustain a dynamic evolution in the way blended finance is deployed, identifying opportunities to apply blending to new markets and contexts. More work is needed to understand, what blended finance instruments and structures may work best in low-income and least developed countries, as well as in specific contexts such as countries transitioning from conflict or facing forms of fragility.

Blended finance also is not targeted across all Sustainable Development Goals. The 2017 OECD survey of blended finance funds and facilities assesses their alignment with different SDGs (Figure 1.4). The SDGs most targeted by funds and facilities are those focussing on economic growth and jobs (SDG 8), infrastructure (SDG 6, SDG 7, SDG 9, SDG 11), climate change (SDG13), and goals that cut across most others (SDG 1, SDG 17). In contrast, the SDGs least targeted by funds and facilities were related to biodiversity and natural resources (SDG 14 and SDG 15). This pattern reflects the tendency for blended finance to go towards sectors for which the business case is clearer and the potential for commercial gains more apparent. Blended finance many not be the right tool to apply in all contexts, but it would be helpful to understand if there are opportunities to use blending to mobilise private finance towards different goals. Going forward, it will be important to ensure there is a clear case for achieving development results in the use of blended finance, calibrating the use of concessional finance and balancing the risk-return relationship for individual transactions as needed. Beyond this, and while blended finance may not be applicable to all sectors at a given point in time, it will be important not to limit the outlook and focus on particular sectors but rather to continue targeting new solutions and public-private approaches as they emerge. The use of blended finance (and its exit) needs to be adjusted on an ongoing basis to keep pace with rapidly changing market conditions and technologies.

Figure 1.4 **How blended finance funds and facilities target the SDGs**

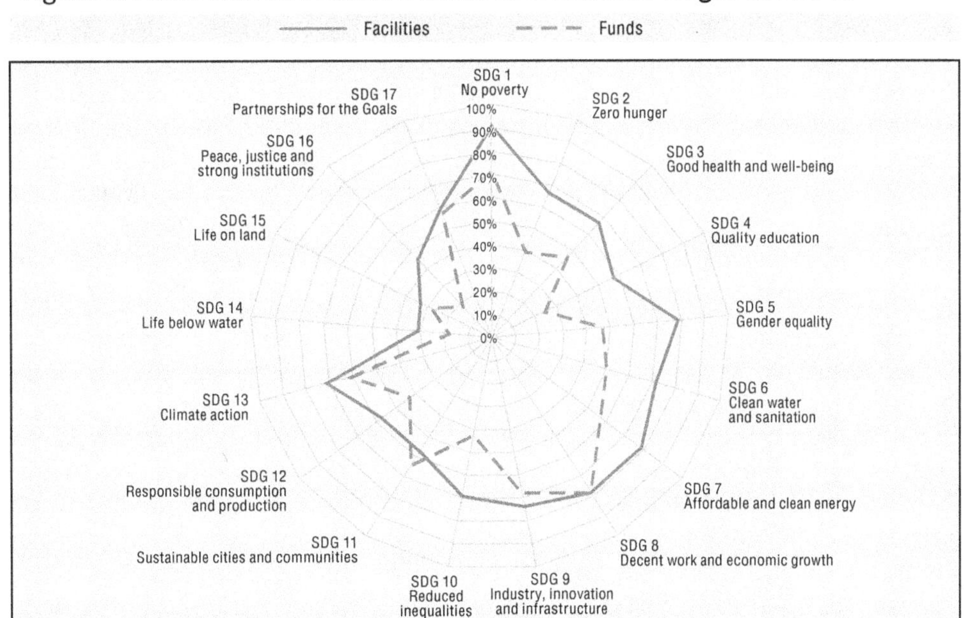

Note: Survey respondents were asked to what extent their development strategy was linked to the SDGs. Three possible responses were presented and respondents could choose only one. The possible responses were 1) "the SDG is explicitly mentioned in our strategy; 2) "We have similar objectives, but the SDG is not explicitly mentioned"; and 3) "the SDG is not at all relevant in our strategy. Figure 1.4 represents the combination of the first and second responses.

Source: OECD 2017 Survey on blended finance funds and facilities

StatLink http://dx.doi.org/10.1787/888933648214

Addressing increasing fragmentation of blended finance development and governance will be important to ensure its effectiveness

The number of new blended finance facilities being set up suggests a risk of increasingly fragmented approaches in the way blended finance is being developed and governed. In terms of governance, some donor governments engage in blending directly but most blending is still done through intermediaries, either MDBs or bilateral DFIs, or private actors (especially in the case of blended finance funds). These institutions usually fall under the remit and responsibility of ministries or government departments with political responsibility. They generally also have their own governance frameworks, are usually financially self-supporting, and are not dependent on recurrent budgetary support. While the intention is to reflect a deliberately private sector character, by implication the policy direction from donor governments tends to be less direct as their development financing moves down the chain. In other cases, donor governments pool their support through multi-donor blended finance facilities that in turn invest in blended finance. Often, financing from facilities can be further invested in a standalone fund or fund-of funds before it is invested in projects. The increasing layers of intermediation have implications for tracking development finance flows in blended finance interventions, for monitoring progress, and for the evaluation of impacts and results. It also has implications for how safeguards policies and standards set by donor governments can be upheld through the chain to the final beneficiary of projects supported by blended finance. In addition, an increasing number of approaches and vehicles can cause difficulty for commercial actors who have to engage with an increasing array of modalities, terms and conditions when engaging with development counterparts.

Achieving local ownership is critical to long-term sustainability

Engaging and involving local actors in developing countries in blended finance can help build ownership and long-term sustainability for the project. Interventions have taken a variety of forms. In the Indian state of Tamil Nadu, for example, KfW funding was combined with government equity to a special purpose vehicle that subsequently raised support from investors through bonds (Box 1.1). The project enables local municipalities to access much needed financing for infrastructure. In Rwanda, the Netherlands Development Finance Company (FMO) invests alongside the Rwandan government in the Africa Improved Food Holdings project, a local enterprise that produces nutritious food products channelled through the World Food Programme and subnational governments. The equity contributions by FMO and the Rwandan government served as anchor investments for additional public and private investors. Both of these cases are discussed further in Chapter 7 and Annex C.

Another sustainability consideration relates to deploying blended finance in a way that is consistent with the goal of, and where possible reinforces, the evolution of local financial markets. This could include providing financing in local currency and seeking opportunities for participation from local financial investors. Doing this helps to mitigate the risk of exposure to currency fluctuations that arise when the project revenue streams and refinancing are in different currencies. Moreover, local participation, denomination and intermediation all provide stimuli for developing and deepening local capital markets and the investor base in addition to enhancing the prospect for follow-on investments in this project as well as others. For example, in the case of the United States Agency for International Development (USAID) securitisation of loans provided by universal credit organisations in Armenia, the issuing of bonds in local currency enabled local pension funds and investors from within the country. Despite the benefits, local currency financing is still limited amongst blended finance funds and facilities. The majority of respondents to the 2017 OECD survey (60%) reported having less than one fourth of their portfolio in local currency.

Box 1.1 **Case study: Enabling municipalities to tap capital markets to fund infrastructure development**

The Government of India and the German development bank, KfW, established an innovative blended finance scheme to help municipalities in Tamil Nadu state tap into capital markets to finance local infrastructure projects. KfW provided a EUR 10 million concessional loan to the Indian government to fund the subordinated tranche (35%) of a special purpose vehicle, the Water and Sanitation Pooled Fund (WSPF) that is designed to disburse loans to urban local bodies. Tamil Nadu Urban Infrastructure Financial Services Limited manages the Fund, which is an asset manager that the state had already set up and is jointly owned by the government and private financial institutions. The Government of Tamil Nadu provided equity support as cash collateral of 10% to provide an additional cushion against potential losses. The combination of the KfW concessional loan and interest on the bonds (the first bond issued at 10.6%) permitted on-lending on a revolving basis to municipal projects at a sustainable level.

The intervention achieved meaningful outcomes, with the ex-ante assessment showing a strong expected development impact of local infrastructure projects funded with loans from WSPF. Likewise, over the long term, the issuance of bonds via this special purpose vehicle enhanced the local market. In sum, the project contributed to delivering SDG 9 (industry, innovation and infrastructure) and SDG 8 (decent work and economic growth) by providing access to finance to municipalities.

Source: This project is one ten case studies analysed for this report. See Chapter 7 and Annex C for more details.

Intermediaries are essential facilitators for blended finance activities

Intermediaries play a critical role in blended finance by structuring the transaction, bringing together the actors and facilitating the blending. For many donor governments, intermediaries offer a more efficient way of blending as these organisations have the capacity, track record and skill sets to be able to engage with commercial actors that staff in governments or aid agencies lack. MDBs and DFIs commonly take on this role as they are mandated and organised to work with the private sector. However, private fund managers, local financing institutions and even non-governmental organisations (NGOs) also can act as intermediaries for blended finance. The 2017 OECD survey of blended finance funds finds that private fund managers manage 68% of blended finance funds. In the Elazig Integrated Health Campus project in Turkey, Meridiam, an asset manager, took a leading role in co-ordinating with the European Bank for Reconstruction and Development to structure the project financing including a guarantee by the Multilateral Investment Guarantee Agency. This made the resulting bond offering attractive to investors. In another case, Global Affairs Canada works with the international NGO MEDA in a project with Tree Global Inc. to implement blended finance in support of Ghana's tree crop supply chain. Chapter 7 and Annex C provide details of these cases.

The role of intermediaries is important not only in the structuring of the transaction but in many cases the intermediary is instrumental in bringing commercial investors to the table. The majority of respondents from blended finance funds to the 2017 OECD survey of blended finance funds and facilities stated that the fund manager engaged with and brought private investors to the table with no additional interventions from public investors. As donor governments increasingly engage in blending and will face the need to build their own capacity in working with the private sector, intermediaries provide a way forward in engaging in blending and bringing investors to the table.

Further data on the blended finance market is crucial for transparency

There is an increasing need for transparency on blended finance flows. Information especially is needed on the magnitude and concessionality of development finance being channelled towards blended approaches and what is being mobilised as a result; how is this financing being allocated in terms of countries and sectors; what impact is being achieved through blending; and which instruments are most effective in mobilising commercial finance and addressing different SDGs, among other issues. The bedrock of such analyses is robust data on blended finance flows. Different efforts have sought to map the blended finance market, but none of these has managed to cover the entirety of the flows in a consistent and comparable way. Much of what is known about blended finance has been based on standalone surveys that have focussed on either funds or facilities or both, and while these have provided insights on the public finance deployed and the commercial finance mobilised, they do not provide a picture of what happens outside of the funds or facilities. Project databases, either publicly supported or commercial, are another source of data that can provide proxy estimates of blending. But they vary in their breadth, coverage and comparability.

An alternative to standalone surveys is tracking blended finance through existing statistical and reporting systems for development finance, such as the OECD or the multilateral development banks' task force on tracking mobilisation. The OECD's work on tracking the volume of private finance mobilised by official development finance interventions is an important step forward with regard to measuring blended finance and data from initial surveys have supported some standalone assessments of blended finance. While the number of instruments considered is limited — currently, amounts mobilised as a result of concessional loans or grants are excluded — methodologies for these latter instruments are being developed. Reporting according to these methodologies in the DAC statistical system in 2017 will make available project-level data of the public contribution and the amount that was mobilised, which will enable a broader assessment of blended finance. However, caveats remain. Due to the current boundaries of the methodologies used, estimates of blended finance will be conservative when compared with the definition of blended finance in this report.

Monitoring and evaluation systems for blended finance need to be strengthened to ensure its effective use

Several specific challenges distinguish blended finance from other development co-operation instruments when it comes to monitoring and evaluation (M&E). Blended finance is a partnership pulling together different mandates and purposes. As a result, the M&E system must respond to the needs of quite diverse stakeholders. This in turn may trigger diverse expectations on the content and quality of data produced and on the effort put into measuring and learning from development impact. For example, responses to the 2017 OECD survey of blended finance funds and facilities demonstrate that more donor-driven vehicles (e.g. blended finance facilities) show better practice in evaluating impacts than those managed by DFIs or private actors.

In addition, several layers of intermediation may occur in blended finance, which imply a longer delivery mechanism. It also becomes more difficult to reconstruct causal links between inputs and results when conducting impact evaluations. Responses to the 2017 OECD survey of blended finance funds and facilities show that the impact of blending is often assessed based on purely financial indicators, such as return on invested capital and return on equity, or on estimates made by officers and clients, which have not necessarily been updated during the life of the investment.

The entire M&E system for blended finance will need to be strengthened across all actors engaging in the management or implementation of blended vehicles and instruments, where M&E systems may not be as mature as for traditional development co-operation activities. Amongst private sector operations for development finance providers, appraisals do not systematically occur before project approval or renewal, which can raise doubts on the transparency in the investment allocation. Ex post evaluation is seldom applied to the whole portfolio of investments, and its findings need to be better fed back into the decision-making system of the organisation. Multiannual evaluation strategies, which would allow better synchronisation with the decision-making cycle, need to be systematically applied to blended finance (see Chapter 9). If blended finance is to become a tool in its own right within a country's development finance portfolio, all concerned actors will have to meet the same standards in terms of accountability and transparency.

Policy recommendations for moving towards blended finance 2.0

Blended finance is an evolving approach in development finance. The way it is being used suggests opportunities and implications for future efforts. Making progress on blended finance will mean moving from blended finance 1.0, where different forms of development capital are combined to increase efficiency and make projects viable, to blended finance 2.0, where development finance is used much more strategically to mobilise commercial capital at scale and target it towards a range of development issues and contexts. This report and the OECD DAC Blended Finance Principles (OECD DAC, 2017) highlight issues that need to be addressed. Developed concurrently with this report, the Principles present overarching policy guidance to help donor governments improve the effectiveness of future blended finance efforts:

- ***Anchor blended finance use to a development rationale (Principle 1)***

  Donor governments should consider blended finance within a broader financing and development co-operation strategy and support its deployment where it is the most useful tool for particular development outcomes and results. The objective of using blended finance and the results it supports should be well defined for each transaction and blended vehicle. This is particularly important considering the levels of intermediation prevalent in blended finance. Ideally, partners engaged in blending should be aligned with internationally recognised, responsible business conduct standards.

- ***Design blended finance to increase the mobilisation of commercial finance (Principle 2)***

  Donor governments should increase efforts to mobilise finance that does not currently support development outcomes, i.e. commercial finance. This includes supporting the direction of finance towards development outcomes in developing countries. Blended finance should be deployed where financial additionality is clearly demonstrated. Leverage ratios can be a useful indicator for increasing the scope of development finance to achieve high volumes of finance mobilised from commercial actors. However, not all environments will allow for large amounts of commercial finance to be leveraged for every dollar of development finance deployed. Assessments of desired leverage should take into account the geographic context and development issue to be targeted.

  While concessional finance is useful to bridge the viability gap for certain investments, donor governments should seek to minimise concessionality in their blended finance applications. Similarly, providers should aim to deploy concessional finance only to the extent required to crowd in commercial finance. Chapters 6 and 7 illustrate that official investors catalyse commercial capital not only through the terms of their financial contribution but also as a result of their reputations, experience in development and links with developing countries, among other aspects. When concessional finance is deployed, donor governments should ensure that there are clear exit strategies in place.

- *Tailor blended finance to local context (Principle 3)*

  As highlighted in this report, the long term sustainability and impact of solutions supported by blended finance depend on responding to local development priorities and needs. Blended finance should be deployed so as to align with strategic priorities of developing countries, attentive to national and local strategies and plans. If blended finance is going to increasingly feature in a donor's portfolio of approaches, its deployment should be discussed with public and private stakeholders in partner countries at a strategic level. Donor governments should also make efforts to scale up local currency financing so as to support the development of local financial markets and systems.

  In addition, in the long term, a sound enabling environments for investment is essential for the effective and efficient use of blended finance, as it is for the mobilisation of private investment more generally. Donor governments should continue to support policies, regulations, institutions and capacity in support of this, and situate blended approaches alongside support for the enabling environment.

- *Focus on effective partnering for blended finance (Principle 4)*

  In using blended finance to address the risk-return profile of transactions so as to mobilise commercial investors, donors should ensure that risks are allocated in a sustainable and balanced manner between development finance providers and commercial partners. In addition, governments should promote standardisation of approaches to promote scaling up and avoid further fragmentation in blended finance approaches.

- *Monitor blended finance for transparency and results (Principle 5)*

  Gaps in the information and evidence base for blended finance constrain the efficient pricing of capital by potential commercial sources of finance, likely holding back the deployment of their resources towards development uses. Moreover, limited evidence continues to fuel concerns about the effective deployment of blended finance to support the SDGs. Governments should strengthen monitoring and evaluation for blended finance, ensuring that blended finance is considered in M&E strategies for development co-operation. In addition, clear metrics should be defined for blended finance approaches and adequate resources allocated to support M&E activities. Efforts to track and finance flows towards blended finance should also be encouraged and information on these flows should be made publicly available and easily accessible.

Further work needed to address evidence and policy gaps

This report provides a comprehensive overview of the state of blended finance as it currently is being implemented. Research conducted for this report points to areas where further work would be useful in supporting donor governments and development finance providers to move towards the next generation of blended finance.

Improved estimates of the size and scope of the blended finance market. At the time this report has been prepared, no single, consistent and comparable estimate was available of donor government support for blended finance and the commercial finance mobilised as a result. Integration of reporting on amounts mobilised from the private sector into the OECD DAC statistical system and further OECD work on blended finance funds and facilities will allow for initial estimates in this area. This work will be important to better analyse the emerging architecture around blended finance and how it is governed. This, in turn, can help to improve the effectiveness of blending, by ensuring first that the institutional architecture for disbursement is effective and second that the right sectors and countries are targeted. A better understanding of the private sector perspective in terms of risk return and capital allocation also would provide donor governments further policy guidance for blended finance approaches.

Dedicated research on instruments, structure and contexts. Standalone research exercises on specific instruments and structures to inform donor governments about different aspects of the market would be useful to help calibrate policy frameworks and identify gaps. Of particular relevance in this regard is analysis of the comparative impact of concessionality provided through different approaches on the distribution of risks. Dedicated work also is required on a more granular level that looks at different income groups, specific contexts (such as fragility), geographies, national and subnational settings, and development objectives. This would help discern where blended finance could help to make the potential business case and how to calibrate the risk-return balance in these contexts. Furthermore, work could focus on those structures with which the private sector can easily engage and which would have the most potential in terms of replication and scaling up. In this respect, further work should be undertaken on identifying structures that would lend themselves to receiving more patient capital from both local and international institutional investors.

Cross-cutting policy guidance and good practice on blended finance. The OECD DAC Blended Finance Principles provide a good first step towards a cross-cutting standard for blended finance. However, more in-depth policy guidance and identification of good practice under the different principles will be important to help ensure the effectiveness of blended finance. Additional data and statistics are both important for providing actionable data on each of the principles, their implementation over time and progress by development finance actors.

Guidelines to support the measurement of the impact of blended finance. A broad evidence base, global standards and rigorous measurement guidelines on the development impact of blended finance remain to be developed. Linking blended finance to social, environmental and development outcomes, beyond the mobilisation of additional finance will be important going forward. Lessons learned can be exploited from specific communities, such as impact investment groups and the international climate finance community, where the measurement of impact and outcomes are quite advanced.

Notes

1. By definition, development finance is deployed for development uses in developing countries.
2. These include macroeconomic and business risks and/ or regulatory and political risks
3. Currently, the methodologies include only official development investors, and not philanthropic finance. The boundaries applied are stricter than what would be useful for blended finance.

References

AfDB et al. (2017), "Mobilization of private finance by multilateral development banks: 2016", joint report of the African Development Bank, Asian Development Bank, Asian Infrastructure Investment Bank, European Bank for Reconstruction and Development, European Investment Bank, Inter-American Development Bank, Inter-American Investment Corporation, Islamic Corporation for the Development of the Private Sector, Islamic Development Bank, International Finance Corporation, Multilateral Investment Guarantee Agency, New Development Bank and World Bank, www.eib.org/attachments/mdb_joint_report_mobilization_2016_en.pdf.

Benn, J., C. Sangaré and T. Hos (2017), "Amounts mobilised from the private sector by Official Development Finance interventions: Guarantees, syndicated loans, shares in collective investment vehicles, direct investment in companies, credit lines", *OECD Development Co-operation Working Papers*, No. 36, OECD Publishing, Paris, http://dx.doi.org/10.1787/8135abde-en.

Convergence (2017), "The state of blended finance", *Working Paper,* for the Blended Finance Breakthrough Taskforce, Convergence, Toronto, https://convergence.finance/knowledge-detail/1qdtFkf5Fq86S4u8U4G8YU.

Carter, P. (2015), *Why Subsidise the Private Sector? What Donors are Trying to Achieve, and What Success Looks Like,* Overseas Development Institute, London, www.odi.org/sites/odi.org.uk/files/odi-assets/publications-opinion-files/9948.pdf.

Development Initiatives (2016), "*The role of blended finance in the 2030 Agenda: Setting out an analytical approach*", Discussion paper, Development Initiatives, Bristol, UK, http://devinit.org/wp-content/uploads/2016/07/The-role-of-blended-finance-in-the-2030-Agenda-Discussion-paper-July-2016.pdf.

Eurodad (2013), *A Dangerous Blend? The EU's Agenda to 'Blend' Public Development Finance with Private Finance,* European Network on Debt and Development (Eurodad), Brussels, http://eurodad.org/Entries/view/1546054/2013/11/07/A-dangerous-blend-The-EU-s-agenda-to-blend-public-development-finance-with-private-finance.

GEEREF (2017), "What GEEREF is", Global Energy Efficiency and Renewable Energy Fund website, http://geeref.com/about/what-geeref-is.html (accessed 11 September 2017).

OECD/World Economic Forum (2016), *Insights from Blended Finance Investment Vehicles & Facilities,* OECD/World Economic Forum, Paris/Cologny, Switzerland, www3.weforum.org/docs/WEF_Blended_Finance_Insights_Investments_Vehicles_Facilities_report_2016.pdf.

OECD/World Economic Forum (2015), *Blended Finance Vol. 1, A Primer for Development Finance and Philanthropic Funders,* OECD/World Economic Forum, Paris/Cologny, Switzerland, www3.weforum.org/docs/WEF_Blended_Finance_A_Primer_Development_Finance_Philanthropic_Funders_report_2015.pdf.

OECD DAC (2017), "Blended Finance Principles for Unlocking Commercial Finance for the SDGs", *Annex to the DAC High Level Communiqué of 31 October 2017,* www.oecd.org/dac/DAC-HLM-2017-Communique.pdf.

Savoy, C.M., P. Carter and A. Lemma (2016), Development Finance Institutions Come of Age: Policy Engagement, Impact and New Directions, Center for Strategic & International Studies, Washington, DC, https://csis-prod.s3.amazonaws.com/s3fs-public/publication/161005_Savoy_DFI_Web.pdf.

UNCTAD (2014), *World Investment Report 2014, Investing in the SDGs: An Action Plan,* United Nations Conference on Trade and Development (UNCTAD), Geneva, http://unctad.org/en/PublicationsLibrary/wir2014_en.pdf.

PART I
Understanding blended finance

Chapter 2

The imperative of blended finance

Meeting the objectives of the 2030 Agenda for Sustainable Development and the Paris Agreement will require significant investment. This chapter examines recent changes in the landscape of financing for development and recent estimates of the financing needs for the SDGs, which point to the need to mobilise additional investment. It reviews the main barriers to external private investment in developing countries, outlines the potential to scale up private investment for development and explores the role of blended finance in closing the gap.

HIGHLIGHTS

Capital for investments in developing countries has increased over recent years. However, this growth is yet to be consistent with a pathway to meet the SDGs, with recent reports projecting an annual investment gap in the trillions of US dollars.

The relative importance of aid as a source of external finance to developing countries has declined over time, with foreign direct investment and remittances playing a more prominent role in the last decade. Within this context, development finance needs to be used catalytically to mobilise private commercial actors and other sources of financing for development and to target these towards the SDGs.

There is potential for commercial finance to fill the investment gap for the SDGs in developing countries but barriers to investment persist. These include high real and perceived risks associated with these investments, the lack of a pipeline of bankable projects, and weaknesses in the enabling environments for investment.

Blended finance offers an opportunity to use development finance in an innovative way to mobilise commercial investment by improving the risk-return profile of investments and helping un-bankable projects become economically viable.

Key facts

- Annual investment gap for delivering the SDGs in developing countries is estimated at USD 2.5 trillion
- Official development assistance totalled USD 142.6 in 2016; remittance flows to developing countries amounted to roughly three times as much, or USD 429 billion, in the same year
- Institutional investors (i.e. pension funds, insurance companies and mutual funds) in OECD countries alone held USD 90 trillion in assets in 2014
- Blended finance can help mobilise additional finance, including from commercial actors, towards the SDGs.

Introduction

The 2030 Agenda for Sustainable Development and the Paris Agreement establish a comprehensive and ambitious set of development goals for all countries. Underpinning these is the Addis Ababa Action Agenda (AAAA). Agreed by United Nations member countries in July 2015, it provides a global framework for addressing the challenges associated with financing sustainable development. The UN Inter-agency Task Force on Financing for Development found a mixed picture in a stocktaking report in 2017.[1] While initial efforts in multilateral co-operation and policy actions have shown promise, significantly increased investment in the Sustainable Development Goals (SDGs) has yet to materialize and is not on a trajectory to meet the 2030 goals. Against the backdrop of a more challenging global environment and lower-than-anticipated economic growth in many developing countries, implementation gaps remain in implementation of the AAAA. This chapter outlines the scale of the challenge and highlights the need to mobilise additional investment for sustainable development in developing countries through approaches such as blended finance. It reviews the development financing landscape, sets out a role for private investment and summarises the main challenges in scaling up private finance for investments in developing countries.

Financing the Sustainable Development Goals

Increased investment is needed to deliver the global agenda for development

In the aggregate, substantial investments already go in areas critical to achieving development outcomes. Nevertheless, it is widely recognised that current investment levels will not be sufficient to achieve the goals established in the development agenda. Global infrastructure needs alone amount to USD 6 trillion each year for the next 15 years; the current annual investment is estimated at around USD 2.5 trillion to USD 3 trillion (Bielenberg et al., 2016). Annual investment needs increase to nearly USD 7 trillion when costs of ensuring that infrastructure is compatible with low-carbon, climate resilient development pathways are taken into consideration (OECD, 2017a). In developing countries, the annual infrastructure investment gap is estimated at USD 2.5 trillion, the difference between current levels of around USD 1.4 trillion and a need of USD 3.9 trillion (UNCTAD, 2014). In developing Asian economies, excluding the People's Republic of China (hereafter "China"), the climate-adjusted annual infrastructure gap is estimated at 5% of overall gross domestic product (ADB, 2017). The challenge, as the development community has framed it, is to go from "billions to trillions" (AfDB et al., 2015). To achieve the ambitious vision of the development agenda, all available tools must be deployed, and amplified. In recognition of this, increased attention is focusing on how to effectively finance sustainable development, with blended finance emerging as one pillar.

The changing landscape of financing for development

Financing for development comprises all investments that power economic growth and build the capacity of countries and their citizens. It includes external finance and domestic sources, drawing private, public, multilateral, non-governmental and people-to-people investment that represents building blocks to achieve sustainable development.

Among sources of external finance, official development assistance (ODA) is widely considered an important measure of development finance from developed countries. ODA reached record levels in 2016, totalling USD 142.6 billion (OECD, 2017b). However, the relative importance of development aid within total finance flows for development has declined over time. In 2016, for instance, remittance flows to developing countries amounted to three times the total ODA that year, or USD 429 billion (World Bank Group/KNOMAD, 2017). Foreign direct investment (FDI) in 2016 provides another illustration: FDI inflows to just Brazil and India amounted to USD 58.7 billion and USD 44.5 billion, respectively (OECD, 2017c). Private philanthropy also has become a significant contributor to development finance, responsible for USD 7.8 billion per year on average between 2013-15 (OECD, 2017d). Development assistance also comes from countries that are not members of the OECD Development Assistance Committee (DAC), and in 2014 amounted to an estimated USD 32 billion. Figure 2.1 breaks down external financial inflows to developing countries from 2000 to 2015 and shows that total external financing flows more than tripled in the period, with the private sources responsible for the majority of this growth.

Figure 2.1 **External finance to developing countries, current prices, 2000 - 15**

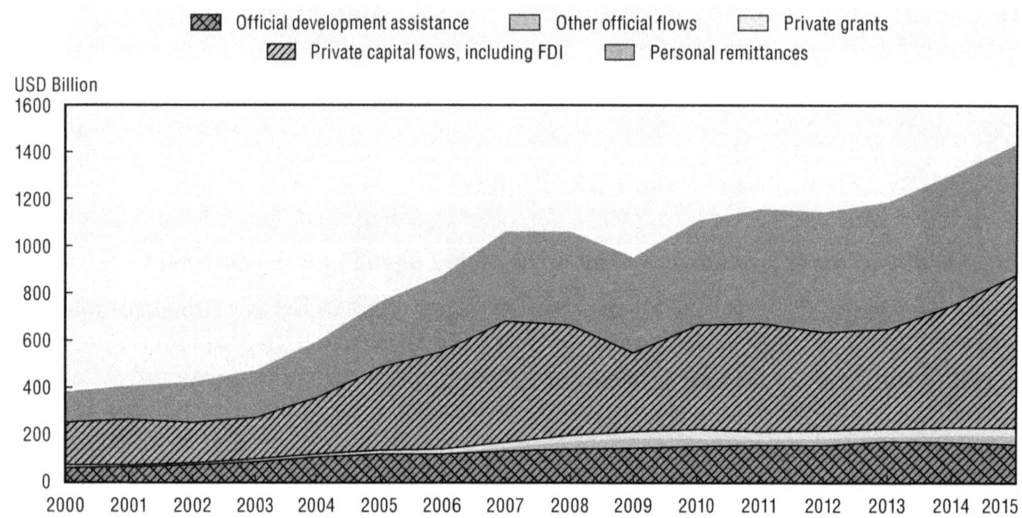

Source: Estimates based on OECD statistics and World Bank data on remittances and private capital flows.

Note: The figures shown are in net disbursements. Figures for official development assistance (ODA), Other Official Flows (OOF) and private grants are based on OECD statistics and are net disbursements. ODA and OOF include outflows from bilateral and multilateral institutions; capital subscriptions are included in private grants. OOF flows were negative in 2000, 2001, 2004 and 2006, and are given a null value in the graph. Private grants cover gross outflows from NGOs and civil society minus support received from the official sector. Remittances are in gross disbursements. Private capital flows include net FDI and portfolio investments.

StatLink http://dx.doi.org/10.1787/888933648233

External sources make up only part of the picture of today's financing for development. A substantial amount of financing is mobilised domestically through government expenditure, private enterprise and/or investment. For example, developing countries in Asia[2] invested USD 881 billion in infrastructure in 2015 alone (ADB, 2017). This is nearly equivalent to the total amount of all external financing sent from DAC countries to all developing countries combined.

Given these trends, there is increasing emphasis on the need for development finance flows to be used as a way to catalyse and mobilise other sources of financing for development through approaches such as blended finance. At the same time, ODA must continue to be used to "leave no one behind", as called for in the 2030 Agenda, and explicitly target the delivery of development outcomes to the poorest and most vulnerable. This is especially the case for the least developed countries, where ODA represents over 70% of total external finance (OECD, 2015).

Mobilising private capital to fill the investment gap

Great potential exists to further mobilise private capital for development

Commercial and private capital has the capacity to fill a significant portion of the investment gap. For instance, it is estimated that institutional investors could provide half the estimated annual global infrastructure investment gap (Bielenberg et al., 2016). Institutional investors (i.e. pension funds, insurance companies and mutual funds) in OECD countries alone held USD 90 trillion in assets in 2014, an amount expected to grow to USD 120 trillion in 2019 (OECD, 2015a). These investors could potentially support development outcomes. Evidence suggests institutional investor interest is growing in the area of infrastructure, however, it should be noted that pension funds currently invest only a tiny percentage (1.1%) of their assets in this area. Institutional investors outside the OECD also may be a promising source of development finance. In addition, sovereign wealth funds hold in excess of USD 7 trillion in assets, most of which are managed in non-OECD countries (Sovereign Wealth Fund Institute, 2017).

Barriers to external private investment in developing countries persist

The demand for investment in the developing world should warrant increased investor attention, especially given the high level of global savings and the relatively small returns many investors are accepting in advanced economies. Gross global savings now stand at 25% of GDP (World Bank, 2017). Looked regionally, the amount of savings is more striking: combined savings of China, Hong Kong, China; Japan, Korea, Singapore and Chinese Taipei are equivalent to about 40% of their combined GDP, representing a 35-year high (Setser, 2016). Meanwhile, returns on investment in advanced economies are unattractive. The yield on ten-year U.S. Treasury bonds has averaged a meagre 2.2% (Wall Street Journal, 2017). Equivalent government bonds issued by Germany or France have yields below 1% (Wall Street Journal, 2017). Similarly, U.S. investment-grade corporate bonds with ten-year yields are trading below 4% (The New York Times, 2017).

While developing countries may offer better returns, there are barriers to unlocking private finance for development purposes. For example, infrastructure suffers from the lack of transparent and bankable pipelines, high development and transaction costs, lack of viable funding models, inadequate risk-adjusted returns, and unfavourable and uncertain regulations and policies (Bielenberg et al., 2016). Regulatory and institutional reforms are needed to make infrastructure more attractive to private investors, generate a pipeline of bankable projects and help spur public-private partnerships (PPPs), and deepen capital markets to help channel savings into infrastructure investments (ADB, 2017). Other impediments to private investment include inadequate public budgets and tax bases, investor protection concerns, uncertain commercial viability of projects, political risk, and foreign exchange volatility. Global financial regulatory issues have emerged as yet another challenge to catalysing investment. Reforms over the last decade have heightened capital requirements for insurance companies and required investment limits on certain asset classes for some pension funds (OECD, 2015c). Banks also have been more risk-constrained as they implement Basel III guidelines. Further, the global environment has become less favourable in recent years for many developing countries as the result of slower global economic growth, challenging macroeconomic conditions, low commodity prices, slowing growth in trade, capital flow volatility and humanitarian crises (Inter-agency Task Force on Financing for Development, 2017).

Balancing risks and returns from investments in sustainable development

A particular challenge is inadequate risk-adjusted returns for many investment opportunities designed to accelerate the pace of sustainable development. This rests squarely on the risk-return trade-off investors must consider before allocating assets (Box 2.1). For example, an investor may be enticed by the prospect of a 12% return on an investment in a developed country, but will also consider the risks associated with the investment in calculating whether to allocate the funds. What is an acceptable level of risk typically depends on the investor's risk capacity and risk appetite. Risk capacity, in essence, is the amount the investor can lose without having a significant impact on the portfolio or fund. Even when risk capacity is present, an investor's risk appetite may lag behind.

Risks related with a project in a developing country may include the regulatory environment, currency volatility, political stability or the economic fundamentals of the project, among others. As the risk grows, so too will investor demands for higher yields or returns and/or shorter maturities for debt instruments. This pressure makes the financing either so expensive or so uncertain in the future that the project likely becomes unviable and never gets off the ground. As a result, private investors will continue to seek other alternatives that better balance returns with risks associated to the investment, even if it means keeping their assets in developed countries with far lower yields. Blended finance, as discussed below, can play a considerable role in addressing the risks that affect risk appetite.

In addition to project-level barriers, a broader range of regulatory and other barriers also affect investor risk appetite and capacity. For example, in the case of infrastructure projects, the lack of recognition of infrastructure as an asset class hinders investors, especially institutional investors, from properly understanding its role within the portfolio, even if on an individual investment basis risks have been managed down to acceptable parameters.

Box 2.1 **The risk-return relationship and private investment**

Data extracted from capital markets illustrate the trade-off that exists between risk and return for both equity and debt instruments. As risk increases, investors will demand higher returns. As risk falls, returns follow suit. Examples below, and Figures 2.2 and 2.3, illustrate the relationship in both advanced and developing economies.

The U.S. market offers robust data over a long time horizon to illustrate the relationship. Short-term U.S. Treasury bills, long-term U.S. government bonds, large cap (market capitalisation) stocks and small cap stocks from 1926 through 2015 earned annual average returns, respectively, of 3.4%, 5.6%, 10% and 12% (Morningstar, 2016). When risks to investors increased in the form of higher probability of default, an unproven business or higher price volatility, so too did the average returns.

This phenomenon is not limited to advanced markets. Figure 2.2 charts sovereign yields of bonds issued in United States dollars and with similar maturities against countries' foreign currency credit ratings published by Standard & Poors (S&P). Credit rating agencies are especially relevant to understanding the risk of a fixed income security as their methodologies generate a rating based on the country's probability of default.

The data illustrate how investors will demand higher yields when presented with a security that has a higher risk of default. The same dynamic occurs when evaluating financing in a local currency.

Box 2.1 The risk-return relationship and private investment *(cont.)*

Figure 2.2 **Yield on sovereign bonds issued in USD**

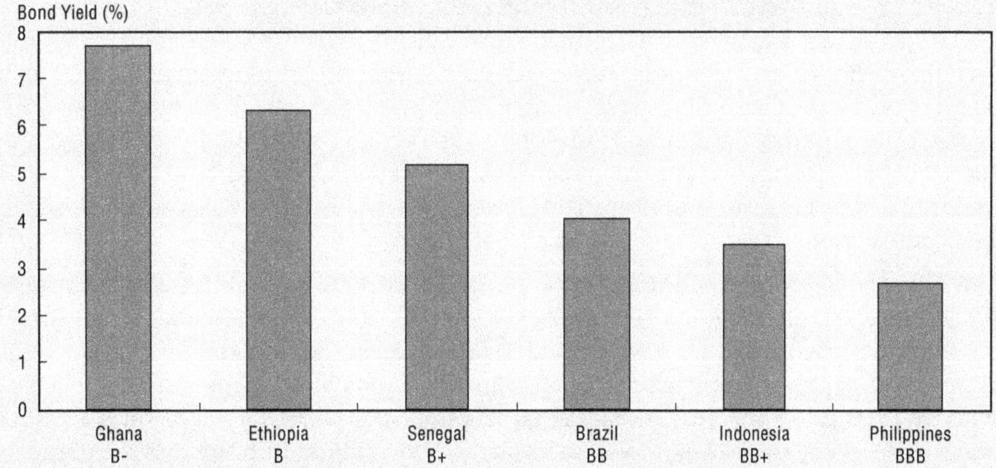

Source: Bloomberg Professional Services (2017), Terminal website, www.bloomberg.com/professional/solution/bloomberg-terminal/ (accessed 17 May 2017).

Note: The figure captures ask yield on sovereign bonds that mature in either 2023 or 2024 and the foreign currency credit rating issued by S&P.

StatLink http://dx.doi.org/10.1787/888933648252

Figure 2.3 compares nine countries with different country risk ratings identified by the Economist Intelligence Unit (EIU) against ten-year bond yields in local currency and illustrates a strong correlation between increasing country risk and higher borrowing costs demanded in the marketplace.

Figure 2.3 **Ten-year local currency bond vs. Economist Intelligence Unit country risk rating**

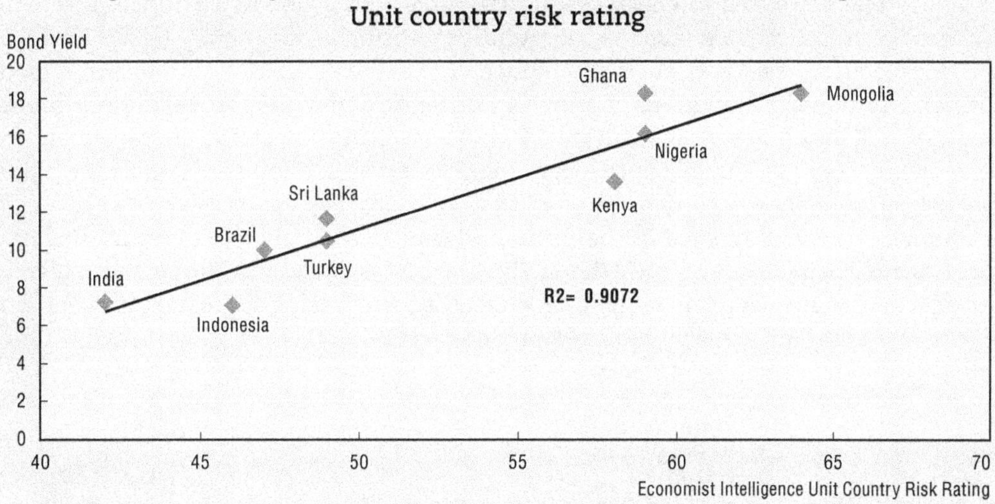

Source: Bloomberg Professional Services (2017), Terminal website, www.bloomberg.com/professional/solution/bloomberg-terminal/ (accessed 17 May 2017). Note: Figure captures closing BVAL or generic ten-year Yield on 16 May 2017.

StatLink http://dx.doi.org/10.1787/888933648271

The role of blended finance in closing the gap

As this report argues, blended finance offers an opportunity to use development aid in an innovative way to mobilise investment and narrow the investment gap. It can help alter the risk-return trade-off that affects the ability of development projects in developed countries to attract the private investment that otherwise would be deployed elsewhere. It can also help projects that may never get off the ground become economically viable projects that have measurable development benefits. Moreover, it allows development assistance, capital from multilateral development banks and other public funds to go much further. For example, an investment in technical assistance, a concessional loan or a partial commercial guarantee can lead to a private investment many times the size of the original public contribution.

While more research and evaluation are urgently needed, early evidence has suggested blended finance can magnify the impact of funds with a development mandate to attract private investment for development goals. A recent survey found that public and philanthropic capital committed to blended finance funds and facilities has been able to attract up to 20 times the amount of capital from private sources (OECD/World Economic Forum, 2016). A separate 2016 survey identified USD 81 billion in private investment that was mobilised by official development finance from 2012 to 2015 through blended finance (Benn, Sangaré and Hos, 2017). This survey data also showed the amount mobilised in 2015 was nearly double the amount in 2012. In addition to mobilising commercial capital at a transaction level, the use of blended finance is a way to spur additional investment by helping to create markets and demonstrate the viability of solutions and technologies.

It is important to highlight that blended finance is not a silver bullet or even a watershed for solving all the challenges associated with mobilising investment to realise the goals of the development agenda. Ultimately, it is only one pillar in an array of development mechanisms working to drive sustainable development. It complements other proven techniques and strategies to engage with and build up the private sector in developing countries such as sharing knowledge, funding research, advancing policy dialogue, providing technical assistance and building local capacity (OECD, 2016). Moreover, it remains important for donor countries to continue to encourage and support regulatory reform, rule of law and best practices in good governance as well as international engagement that fosters peace, stability and global co-operation to address common threats to the planet. Development outcomes also depend on traditional forms of development assistance outside the context of blended finance in the form of grants, debt forgiveness, export and trade finance, concessional lending, and others. These activities are not in conflict with blended finance, but work as a complement to it. Only an all-encompassing approach can muster the resources necessary to achieve the development agenda.

Notes

1. See the Task Force report, *Financing for Development: Progress and Prospects*, https://developmentfinance.un.org/sites/developmentfinance.un.org/files/Report_IATF-2017.pdf.
2. The ADB (2017) figures cover 25 Asian economies that represent 96% of the region's population. See www.adb.org/publications/asia-infrastructure-needs.

References

ADB (2017), *Meeting Asia's Infrastructure Needs*, Asian Development Bank, Manila, www.adb.org/publications/asia-infrastructure-needs.

AfDB et al. (2015), "From billions to trillions: Transforming development finance", Discussion Note, DC2015-002, prepared jointly for the Development Committee meeting of 18 April 2015 by the African Development Bank, the Asian Development Bank, the European Bank for Reconstruction and Development, the European Investment Bank, the Inter-American Development Bank, the International Monetary Fund, and the World Bank Group, http://siteresources.worldbank.org/DEVCOMMINT/Documentation/23659446/DC2015-0002(E)FinancingforDevelopment.pdf.

Benn, J., C. Sangaré and T. Hos (2017), "Amounts mobilised from the private sector by Official Development Finance interventions: Guarantees, syndicated loans, shares in collective investment vehicles, direct investment in companies, credit lines", *OECD Development Co-operation Working Papers*, No. 36, OECD Publishing, Paris, http://dx.doi.org/10.1787/8135abde-en.

Bielenberg, A. et al. (2016), *Financing Change: How to Mobilize Private-Sector Financing for Sustainable Infrastructure*, McKinsey Centre for Business and Environment, http://newclimateeconomy.report/workingpapers/wp- content/uploads/sites/5/2016/04/Financing_change_How_to_mobilize_private-sector_financing_for_sustainable-_infrastructure.pdf.

Bloomberg Professional Services (2017), the Terminal website, www.bloomberg.com/professional/solution/bloomberg-terminal/ (accessed 17 May 2017).

Inter-agency Task Force on Financing for Development (2017), *Financing for Development: Progress and Prospects*, United Nations, New York, https://developmentfinance.un.org/financing-development-progress-and-prospects-2017.

Morningstar Investment Services (2016), "Fundamentals for investors", Morningstar Inc., http://home.mp.morningstar.com/elabsLinks/FundamentalsForInvestors_2016.pdf.

New York Times (2017), Business Day: Markets website, http://markets.on.nytimes.com/research/markets/bonds/bonds.asp (accessed 18 September 2017).

OECD (2017a), *Investing in Climate, Investing in Growth*, OECD Publishing, Paris, http://dx.doi.org/10.1787/9789264273528-en.

OECD (2017b), "Development aid rises again in 2016 but flows to poorest countries dip", online press release, www.oecd.org/dac/development-aid-rises-again-in-2016-but-flows-to-poorest-countries-dip.htm (accessed 10 September 2017).

OECD (2017c), *FDI in Figures*, OECD Publishing, Paris, www.oecd.org/daf/inv/investment-policy/FDI-in-Figures-April-2017.pdf.

OECD (2017d), "Global Private Philanthropy for Development", Results of the OECD Data Survey as of 3 October 2017, OECD, Paris, www.oecd.org/dac/financing-sustainable-development/development-finance-standards/Philanthropy-Development-Survey.pdf

OECD (2016), *Private Sector Engagement for Sustainable Development: Lessons from the DAC*, OECD Publishing, Paris, http://dx.doi.org/10.1787/9789264266889-en.

OECD (2015a), *OECD Business and Finance Outlook 2015*, OECD Publishing, Paris, http://dx.doi.org/10.1787/9789264234291-en.

OECD (2015b), *Annual Survey of Large Pension Funds and Public Pension Reserve Funds: Report on Pension Funds' Long-term Investments*, OECD Publishing, Paris, www.oecd.org/daf/fin/private-pensions/2015-Large-Pension-Funds-Survey.pdf.

OECD (2015c), *Regulation of Insurance Company and Pension Fund Investment*, OECD Publishing, Paris, www.oecd.org/finance/insurance/Regulation-of-Insurance-Company-and-Pension-Fund-Investment.pdf.

OECD/World Economic Forum (2016), *Insights from Blended Finance Investment Vehicles & Facilities*, ReDesigning Development Finance Initiative, OECD/World Economic Forum, Paris/Cologny, Switzerland, www3.weforum.org/docs/WEF_Blended_Finance_Insights_Investments_Vehicles_Facilities_report_2016.pdf.Setser, B. (2016), "The return of the East Asian savings glut", *Discussion Paper*, Council on Foreign Relations, New York, www.cfr.org/sites/default/files/pdf/2016/10/Discussion_Paper_Setser_Asia_Glut_OR.pdf.

Sovereign Wealth Fund Institute (2017), Sovereign wealth fund rankings website, www.swfinstitute.org/sovereign-wealth-fund-rankings/ (accessed 10 September 2017).

U.S. Department of the Treasury (2017), Resource Center: Daily Treasury yield curve rates website, www.treasury.gov/resource-center/data-chart-center/interest-rates/Pages/TextView.aspx?data=yield(accessed 13 September 2017).

UNCTAD (2014), *World Investment Report 2014, Investing in the SDGs: An Action Plan*, United Nations Conference on Trade and Development (UNCTAD), Geneva, http://unctad.org/en/PublicationsLibrary/wir2014_en.pdf.

Wall Street Journal (2017), Market data centerwebsite, http://online.wsj.com/mdc/public/page/mdc_bonds.html (accessed 10 September 2017).

World Bank Group (2016), *The World Bank Annual Report 2016*, World Bank Group, Washington, DC, https://openknowledge.worldbank.org/handle/10986/24985.

World Bank Group (2017), World Bank data - Gross Domestic Product (% GDP), World Bank Group, Washington, DC, https://data.worldbank.org/indicator/NY.GDS.TOTL.ZS (accessed 15 December 2017).

World Bank Group/KNOMAD (2017), "Migration and remittances: Recent developments and outlook", *Migration and Development Brief, No. 27*, World Bank Group/ Global Knowledge Partnership on Migration and Development (KNOMAD), Washington, DC, http://pubdocs.worldbank.org/en/992371492706371662/MigrationandDevelopmentBrief27.pdf.

Chapter 3

Blended finance definitions and concepts

Blended finance has played a role in development financing for some time and is gaining greater attention among donor governments. However, its potential for generating needed investment for the 2030 Agenda for Sustainable Development and the Paris Agreement is constrained by the absence of a mutually agreed understanding of blending even within the development co-operation community. This chapter presents the range of definitions in use, the characteristics and boundaries of blended finance, and efforts to build a framework that addresses concerns about blending while allowing it to achieve its potential. It also highlights key concepts associated with blending such as concessionality, additionality, mobilisation and catalysation.

While blended finance is not a new concept, it has multiple definitions and uses. Most organisations agree that the aim of blending should be to mobilise private or commercial actors but they differ as to what blending entails. The main differences relate to the degree of concessionality of finance that is blended and the combination of participating actors, e.g. public-public, public-private or private-private co-operation.

This report and the OECD DAC Blended Finance Principles define blended finance as the strategic use of development finance for the mobilisation of additional finance towards sustainable development in developing countries. Development finance is official development finance and private philanthropic funds. Additional finance refers to commercial finance, including public and private sources, whose principal purpose is commercial rather than developmental (e. g. investment by public or privately owned pension funds or insurance companies, banks, businesses, etc.).

Blending is time-bound and specific to a transaction. It often involves the use of development finance on concessional terms, but concessionality is not a prerequisite for blending.

Beyond the direct mobilisation of commercial capital in a transaction, the ambition of blended finance is to be catalytic, i.e. to spur the replication of similar projects via demonstration and build functioning markets that can result in larger volumes of commercial capital for development.

Introduction

The term "blended finance" has been used for more than a decade in international development and wider practice (World Bank/IMF, 2005). Different uses of the term reflect different and valid rationales, usually conditioned by the context in which they are applied. In current, broad discussions on financing for development, blended finance is understood as a way of combining public development finance and private investment in support of investments in developing countries (Inter-agency Task Force on Financing for Development, 2017). Yet the term is used in a variety of ways even among development finance providers (see Chapter 4). A common framework is indispensable to the development of priorities, good practice and co-ordinated policy approaches for blending, and thus to the effective application of blended finance at scale. This chapter lays a foundation by examining existing frameworks, sets out a definition for blended finance, and discusses the implications and rationale for this definition.

Defining blended finance is a first step towards a common framework

The motivation for blending is its potential to help increase the financing needed to achieve the Sustainable Development Goals (SDGs) by attracting private and commercial investors to development finance (see Chapter 2). Its chief focus, then, is to mobilise and channel private finance and other flows that currently do not target development towards development objectives and outcomes (OECD DAC, 2017). Most organisations engaging in blended finance share the objective of using financial mechanisms to shift the risk-return profile of projects in developing countries and thus attract and mobilise commercial capital. A further aim is to demonstrate through such projects that similar investments are also viable and thereby create a market that can result in larger volumes of commercial capital (Klein, 2016; European Commission, 2015). In addition to mobilising private investment and making projects viable, blended finance approaches also help to direct private and commercial investment towards underserved areas and aim to deliver development impact as well as financial returns (AfDB et al., 2017; OECD/World Economic Forum, 2015a; Development Initiatives, 2016).

While there is broad agreement on the main objective of blended finance, there is a wide variation in how organisations and actors define it (Box 3.1). Generally, blending is analysed across two dimensions: the degree of concessionality of finance that is blended and the combination of participating actors, e.g. public-public, public-private or private-private co-operation. In all cases, including public-public blending, the rationale for blending is based on mobilising private or additional investment.

Box 3.1 **Definitions of blended finance**

Many institutions, development actors and researchers have developed definitions of blended finance that may differ in approach and emphasis. Following is a sampling of these definitions (italics added).

"In general, blended finance *connotes a combination of public and private finance*, which may or may not involve a form of subsidy" (Klein, 2016).

Blended finance refers to "the strategic use of development finance and philanthropic funds to *mobilise private capital* flows to emerging and frontier markets" (OECD/World Economic Forum, 2015a).

"Blended finance is an approach that can be used to enable the private sector to invest where it would not otherwise be possible. The idea is to mix *concessional funds typically from donor partners with those of commercial development institutions and private investors* in a risk-sharing

Box 3.1 **Definitions of blended finance** *(cont.)*

arrangement, with aligned incentives to make sure official assistance can be leveraged as much as possible with private capital" (IFC, 2016).

"Blending is an instrument for achieving [European Union] external policy objectives, complementary to other aid modalities and pursuing the relevant regional national and overarching policy priorities. The principle of the mechanism is to combine EU grants with loans or equity from public and private financiers." (European Commission, 2015)

"Blended finance is defined as the *complementary use of grants (or grant-equivalent instruments) and non-grant financing from private and/or public sources* to provide financing on terms that would make projects financially viable and/or financially sustainable" (Mustapha, Prizzon and Gavas, 2014).

"Blending as carried out by the EU facilities mixes loans and grants. It entails a *combination of market (or concessional) loans with grant (or grant equivalent) components which may be in various forms*" (European ThinkTanks Group, 2011)

"'Blending' is a mechanism that *links a grant element, provided by official development assistance (ODA), with loans from publicly owned institutions* or commercial lenders" (Eurodad, 2013)

Blended finance "*combines concessional public finance with non-concessional private finance* and expertise from the public and private sector"(UN, 2015).

In blended finance, "*the public aid agencies invest alongside private institutional investors* in commercially sustainable private sector projects in developing countries" (Commons Consultants, 2015).

Blended finance "refers to a *combination of resources*, either from official public sources (governments and/or DFIs) or philanthropic actors with capital from other sources (either official public or private actors)" (Development Initiatives, 2016).

Building on previous definitions and with a focus on the central rationale for blending, the OECD Development Assistance Committee (DAC) defines blended finance as the **strategic use of development finance for the mobilisation of additional finance towards sustainable development in developing countries** (OECD DAC, 2017). Development finance, in the context of this definition, includes official development finance (i.e. both concessional and non-concessional development finance from official sources) and private funds that are governed by a development mandate (e.g. financing provided by philanthropic organisations). Additional finance refers to commercial finance such as public and private sources of finance whose principal purpose is commercial rather than developmental (e. g. investment by public or privately owned pension funds or insurance companies, banks, businesses, etc.).

The OECD DAC definition takes a broader policy perspective to blending compared to the more operationally focused approach taken by multilateral development banks (MDBs) and development finance institutions (DFIs) (Box 3.2). Its focus is to help donor governments and other development finance providers address some of the concerns about how blending has been applied and move towards what is referred to as "blended finance 2.0" in this report — using development finance to attract investors who would not have otherwise financed transactions in developing countries and targeting this finance towards development outcomes. The OECD's approach reflects the shift in priorities already evident among development finance providers. The European Commission, for instance, has adopted an External Investment Plan (EIP, see Box 7.1) that moves from blending public development finance to a stronger focus on mobilising private finance, including through the use of guarantees (Chapter 7). The guidelines developed by MDBs and DFIs also aim to address some of the issues that could be associated with blended finance, but the focus is narrower than the OECD's in that it only considers blended finance operations which involve concessional finance in private sector operations and are carried through MDBs and DFIs (AfDB et al., 2017).

Box 3.2 OECD and development finance institutions, approaches on blended finance

The OECD definition of blended finance reflects an overarching policy perspective that derives from the importance of enhanced mobilisation of financing for development. The OECD approach supports the use of development finance to increase the mobilisation of additional financing for development, in particular from commercial sources. Under this broad approach, finance providers may be governments, foundations, development finance institutions (DFIs), etc.; resources may be concessional or non-concessional; and the investee may be public or private. The OECD framework for blended finance thus considers development finance as only one part of the total financing for a project, but one which is deployed in such a way that it enables overall financing needs to be met to the greatest extent possible by non-development finance. The funding and financing can be within the financing structure of a transaction (blending of development and commercial finance at the debt or equity level); outside the financial transaction (risk mitigation instruments such as foreign exchange risk, political risk insurance or performance-based payments); or a combination of both.

The DFI approach to blended concessional finance for private sector operations is outlined in the DFI Working Group's enhanced guidelines (AfDB et al., 2017). The approach reflects their role as financial institutions with an operational mandate in financing private investment projects. The specific focus of the guidelines is on blending concessional funds with non-concessional resources deployed by DFIs and multilateral development banks (MDBs) to support private sector operations. MDBs and DFIs have developed specific systems, processes and principles for deploying concessional finance in private sector projects that aim to minimise the potential risk of competitive distortion that might hinder rather than reinforce market solutions. Table 3.1 highlights the common areas and differences between the two frameworks for blended finance.

Table 3.1 **Comparing definitions of blended finance (BF)**

		OECD DAC Blended Finance Principles		DFI Working Group Guidelines	
		Development finance used in BF	**Finance mobilised in BF**	**Development finance used in BF**	**Finance mobilised in BF**
Source of finance	Motivation / mandate	Developmental only	Commercial only	Developmental only	Developmental and / or commercial
	Ownership	Public and private	Public and private	Public and private	Public and private
	Terms of finance	Concessional and non-concessional	Non-concessional only	Concessional only	Non-concessional only
Use of finance	Investee	Public and private		Private only	

Note: shaded cells highlight the main differences
Source: Adapted from AfDB et al. (2017) and OECD DAC (2017)

Sources: AfDb et al., 2017, Blended Concessional Finance for Private Sector Projects, www.eib.org/attachments/mdb_dfi_working_group_blended_concessional_finance_private_sector_summary_2017.pdf; OECD DAC (2017), "Blended Finance Principles for Unlocking Commercial Finance for the SDGs", Annex to the DAC High Level Communiqué, 31 October 2017, www.oecd.org/dac/DAC-HLM-2017-Communique.pdf.

Blended finance transactions have specific boundaries

Blending is time-bound and specific to a transaction

Blended finance applies to individual transactions where there is clear mobilisation of commercial finance[1] (Figure 3.1). The blending element, i.e. the development contribution, should be identifiable and reflected in the individual financial arrangements for an investment. Its nature or position in a financing structure, however, can take diverse forms – debt, equity, guarantees, grants, technical assistance, etc. — and the element could be channelled directly to a project or via an intermediary.[2] The development finance element in blending can be placed on the financing side (e.g. concessional debt) or on the revenue generation side (e.g. subsidised tariffs), as long as it meets the basic condition of being instrumental in attracting commercial finance towards projects with clear development objectives and intended outcomes. This condition should determine the choice of development contribution in a given context (see, for example, Barder and Talbot, 2015). The temporal aspects of a blending transaction also require attention, for example related to the mechanisms for accelerated on-selling of assets developed or held by DFIs to private investors. In such cases, there would be no concurrent blending, although the deliberate early exit from assets by DFIs and their transformation into financial products for private market actors may be considered inter-temporary blending.

Figure 3.1 **What is blended finance?**

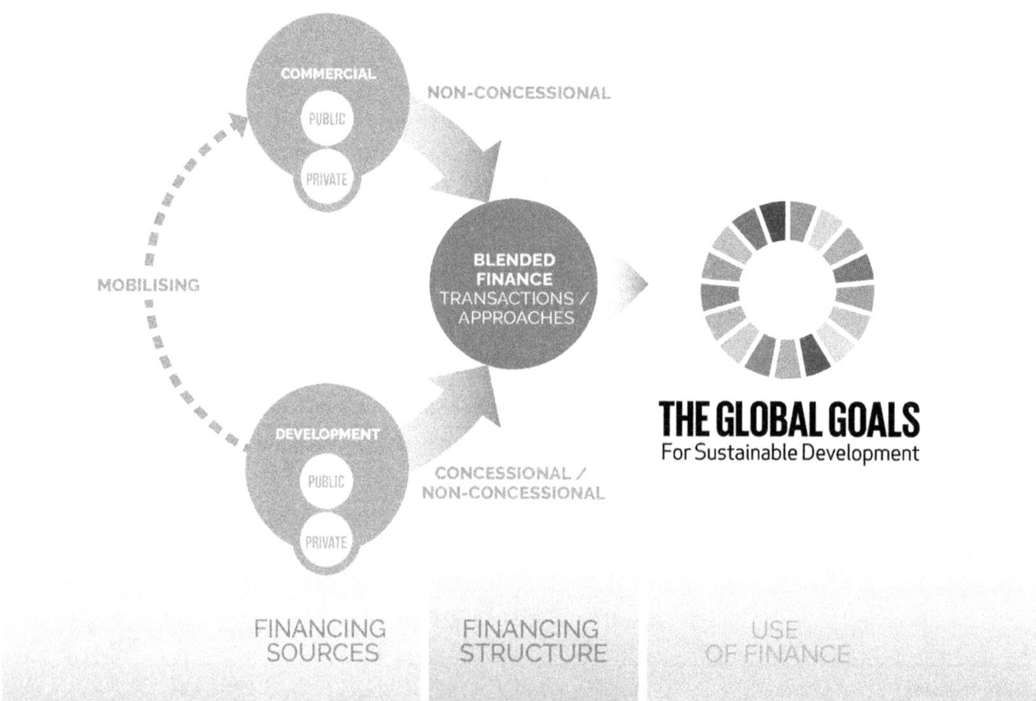

Source: Authors' compilation

Concessionality is a regular feature but not a prerequisite for blending

Concessionality is a regular feature in blended finance transactions, although it is not a defining criterion of blended finance. The Addis Ababa Action Agenda, for instance, refers to blending as the use of grant and non-grant elements for development projects (UN, 2015). In many blended finance transactions, concessional contributions help to make projects with high development returns viable, which would not be the case if they were financed at market-based terms. Some research argues that blended finance needs to involve a concessional element (Larrea, 2016).

However, the development contribution may not require concessionality to unlock private financing. Klein (2016), in his discussion of lessons learned from the International Finance Corporation (IFC) experience of blending, notes that the public finance used in blended finance "may or may not involve a form of subsidy".

While many organisations see concessionality as a basic feature of blended finance, restricting blended finance to the use of concessional resources could limit its role in mobilisation and reduce its effectiveness over time. This would also limit the ability of donors to use blending at scale to engage with the private sector. The example of the Elazig project in Box 3.3 demonstrates the use of innovative structures and mechanisms that have mobilised commercial finance without the use of concessionality. Another example is the new IFC Green Cornerstone Bond Fund, which is using non-concessional development finance to mobilise several times its volume from institutional investors with the aim of stimulating local markets and encouraging local financial institutions in developing countries to issue green bonds by increasing global demand (IFC, 2017). The fund has a simple, two-tier structure, reflecting different risk tolerance and preferences, and does not involve any concessional resources apart from an associated technical assistance facility (ibid.).

Box 3.3 **The Elazig Integrated Health Campus project**

Turkey has made great strides in healthcare in the 21st century as evidenced in universal coverage, declining infant mortality and longer life expectancy. However, health outcomes remain worse than the OECD average due to under-investment. To help address this, the Turkish Ministry of Health launched a programme to build 29 hospital facilities through public-private partnerships. One of these is the Elazig Integrated Health Campus, a EUR 360 million greenfield project for a 1 038-bed integrated healthcare campus in Elazig.

The project deployed innovative financing structures and credit enhancements, resulting in the issuance of bonds with an investment rating two notches above Turkey's sovereign rating. This was achieved thanks to the combination of MIGA political risk insurance and EBRD's unfunded liquidity facilities. The financing comprised senior debt of EUR 288 million, issued in the form of bonds by ELZ finance, a structure backed by infrastructure developers Meridiam and Ronesans; and equity of EUR 72 million. The project's bonds consisted of EUR 83, EUR 125, and EUR 80 million in senior secured A1A, A1B and A2 bonds (underwritten by IFC), respectively, with varying maturity. The issuer could draw bonds gradually according to its needs to lower financing costs. Bond investors include Mitsubishi UFJ Financial Group (MUFG), Intesa Sanpaolo, Siemens Financial Services, Proparco, FMO, and the Industrial and Commercial Bank of China.

The Elazig health project is described in greater detail in Chapter 7 and Annex C.

Source: Moody's (2016)

The need for minimum concessionality is an accepted principle in blended finance, and is central to reducing the risk of distorting markets (OECD DAC, 2017; AfDB et al., 2017). It is also important to ensure the most financially efficient use of development capital. The financially efficient option for development finance providers is to use non-concessional resources, whenever this is consistent with meeting the underlying development objectives – in their specific context, including e.g. country and income level – in a sustainable way.

Blended finance is defined by key features and characteristics

Blended finance is a way of raising resources to achieve development outcomes and impact

As discussed above, the basic rationale for deploying development finance in blended finance transactions and models is to achieve development outcomes. This is reflected in the first principle of the OECD DAC Blended Finance Principles, that is, "anchor blended finance use to a development rationale" (OECD DAC, 2017). The distinctive nature of blending in this context, when compared to other ways of using development finance, is that development outcomes and impact are financed to the largest extent possible by commercial sources of finance, rather than exclusively by development finance.[3]

Blended finance is about attracting additional non-development financing

Development finance resources are deployed on the basis of a development mandate, and are by definition already part of the financing base for sustainable development. To grow this base, and to mobilise finance at the scale that is required to meet development needs, the focus must be on finance that is not already deployed to development priorities, i.e. commercial resources that do not primarily have a development purpose.[4]

In early iterations of blended finance, some development finance providers have looked to public-public blending that uses concessional finance to unlock non-concessional finance within the development finance system.[5] In most cases, such blending has been associated with a private sector focus. For example, grants provided through European Union blending facilities have helped overcome the viability gap for projects that would have otherwise not been bankable for many European development finance institutions based on their financing terms (ADE, 2016). Such blending has enabled important investments by bringing financing to countries and sectors that have not had access to private finance due to the high cost of capital associated with investing in these areas. However, such blending takes place essentially among different types of development finance, and as such is less focused on growing the finance base for development by mobilising additional sources of financing that do not have a specific development mandate.

Blended finance implies a shift from financing the private sector to mobilising private finance

Blended finance is a step change from financing private sector projects in support of development, which is an established area of activity for most OECD DAC members. The objective of these private sector operations has been to support growth of the private sector in developing countries as a way of delivering economic growth and development. Development finance institutions and development banks that are oriented to the private sector thus have functioned, for the most part, as surrogates for private financing of development priorities since such private financing has been and continues to be scarce or non-existent in many developing countries. This activity remains an important dimension in the private sector agenda for development, especially in very immature sectors or markets. In contrast to blended finance, this approach covers financing demand directly and fully through official sources – both individual and multiple institutions – rather than focusing on ways to unlock supply of financing.

Another basic difference is that private-sector operations can channel resources to private sector-led projects, while blended finance focuses on mobilising financing from commercial sources (essentially the private sector) to projects that may be led by either by the public or the private sector. Indeed, in practice, much of the finance mobilised through blended finance is deployed in transactions that involve private sector counterparts on the project implementation side, although this is not a defining feature or condition of blended finance per se. Figure 3.2 illustrates the difference in this regard between a public financing of a private sector investment project versus blended financing for such a project. Both of these aspects appear together in social impact investment, where development finance institutions invest at market terms alongside private partners to generate financial returns and support development impact (Box 3.4).

Figure 3.2 **Financing private sector-led projects vs. mobilising private finance for development**

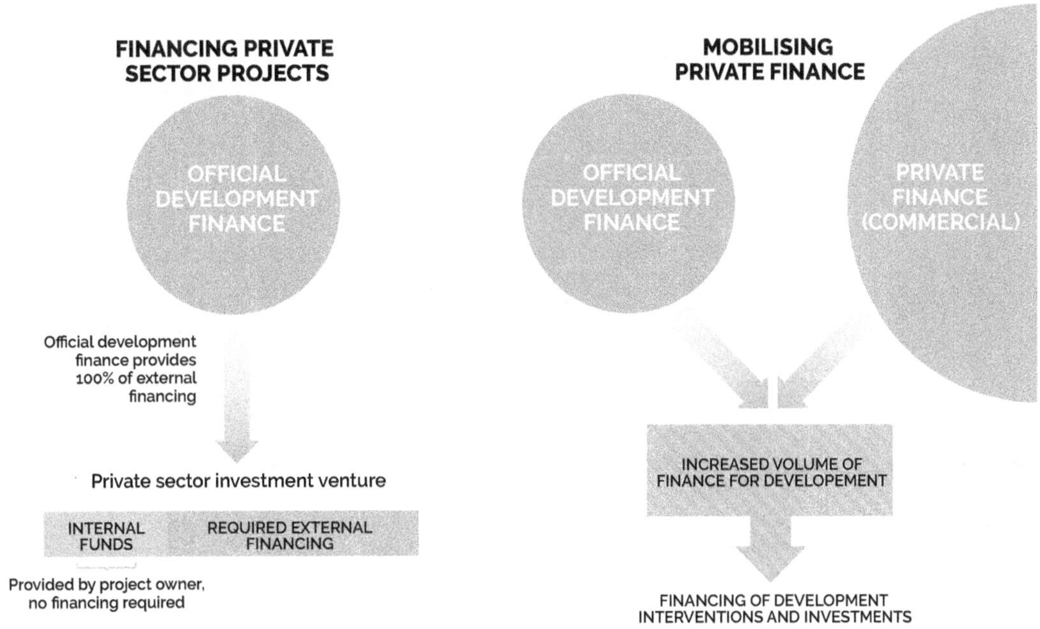

Box 3.4 **Mobilising finance for impact: blended finance and social impact investment**

To deliver the goals set out in the 2030 Agenda for Sustainable Development, investment must be scaled up significantly and used to make a real difference in people's lives. Blended finance can mobilise additional commercial finance towards development uses. Social impact investment ensures that investments are linked to measurable outcomes. When jointly and strategically deployed, these approaches can facilitate the mobilisation of finance for impact to achieve the Sustainable Development Goals (SDGs).

Blended finance is the mobilisation and scaling up of commercial finance for development priorities and projects. Social impact investment, on the other hand, is the provision of finance in order to address social needs with the explicit expectation of a measurable social, as well as financial return (OECD, 2015). As such, social impact investment aims at developing better ways to achieve the SDGs by financing innovative approaches to address social, developmental and environmental challenges. There are many examples

Box 3.4 Mobilising finance for impact: blended finance and social impact investment *(cont.)*

of social impact investment funded business models that demonstrate significant and measurable development impact, ranging from investments in social enterprises to pay-for-success contracts. M-Kopa is one such example of an organisation supported by social impact investment (Wilson, 2016). To date, M-Kopa has supplied over 500,000 homes with affordable solar power in Kenya, Tanzania and Uganda and is continuing to grow and scale the business. Investors in M-Kopa include the Commercial Bank of Africa, Gray Ghost Ventures, Bill & Melinda Gates Foundation, LGT Venture Philanthropy and the UK Department for International Development. This mix of commercial, developmental and impact investors provided different forms of financing including equity, debt or grants over time, which enabled the firm to grow and scale across countries.

Social impact investment and blended finance can come together e.g. in impact funds (see Chapter 6) with an explicit focus on mobilising private finance to be invested in impact-relevant projects. IPDEV 2 is an example of a blended finance fund that is investing in impact funds in Africa with a focus on funding early stage entrepreneurs in a variety of sectors (see Box 6.2). This collaboration aims to attract private capital into and build up the local impact investment sector.

Sources: OECD (2015), *Social Impact Investment: Building the Evidence Base*, OECD Publishing, Paris. http://dx.doi.org/10.1787/9789264233430-en; Wilson, K. (2016), "Investing for social impact in developing countries", in *Development Co-operation Report 2016: The Sustainable Development Goals as Business Opportunities*, OECD Publishing, Paris, http://dx.doi.org/10.1787/dcr-2016-11-en; OECD (forthcoming), *Taking Social Impact Investment to the next level*, OECD Publishing.

Blended finance combines mobilisation at the transaction level with a catalytic ambition over time

The concepts of mobilisation and catalysation are central to blended finance. Catalysation encompasses all activities, whether through public or private institutions, that help to create a more conducive environment for private sector investment. It comprises enhancement of resources through direct means such as mobilisation and indirect means such as policy or regulatory support for developing countries to further enable private sector investment (Chelsky and Gregory, 2016; Benn et al., 2016).

Mobilisation is a subset of catalysation. In blended finance transactions, one form of financing unlocks another that otherwise would not have been available. As a result, blended finance implies direct causality between development finance and additional commercial finance in a given transaction.[6] This makes mobilisation a basic, defining feature of blended finance that should be clearly identifiable in blended finance transactions.

At the same time, mobilisation is specific to the context of individual transactions, and maximising mobilisation is not as a goal in itself, but in relation to the underlying development objective (OECD DAC, 2017). It is therefore important to take into account the efficiency of development finance deployed towards mobilising additional finance. Blended finance is financially efficient if, for a given development objective and at comparable financing cost to the investee, it requires less development finance effort, than if a transaction were fully financed from development finance sources. Effort in this case represents budgetary cost that could also be used as capital to leverage the balance sheets of development institutions. Comparative assessment of financial efficiency will invariably remain hypothetical to a certain degree, given, *inter alia*, limited comparability and fungibility of different resources and associated approaches, instruments, and channels, as well as overall balance sheet constraints of development institutions. They are essential, however, to provide reference points for the appropriate deployment of blended finance.

Crowding in commercial finance is core to blended finance approaches, although in some cases, and especially in very immature markets and high-risk contexts, the scope for mobilisation could be limited. In these and other situations, blending is often deployed because of its expected catalytic effect — including by demonstrating project viability and accelerating market evolution.

Whereas mobilisation happens at discrete points in time through concrete transactions, catalysation takes effect over time. Strictly speaking, an explicit focus on crowding-in commercial finance implies that a catalytic intention is inherent to blending, through stronger demonstration effects and accelerated market evolution. The above example of the Green Cornerstone Bond Fund is a case in point, as its explicit aim is not only transaction-level mobilisation, but the creation of markets for green bonds in developing countries (IFC, 2017).

Rather than through individual transactions or financial structures, a more appropriate way to assess catalysation in blended finance is to track the evolution of mobilisation over successive transactions of a comparable or similar nature (e.g. similar sectors and geographies). Effective catalysation would be consistent with a pattern of increasing mobilisation of commercial finance and decreasing use of development finance efforts over time (Figure 3.3).

Figure 3.3 **Stylised representation of transaction-level mobilisation and catalysation over time**

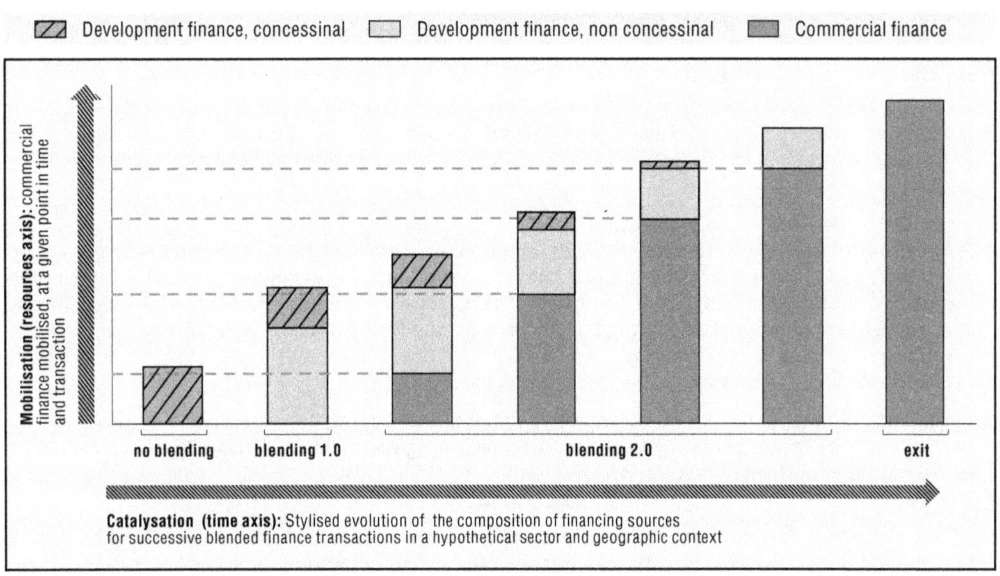

Individual development finance providers commonly prioritise different profiles for their blended finance interventions according to their development objectives and comparative advantages (Chapter 4). To the extent that the catalytic effect is an explicit part of the rationale for blended finance, a strategic or programmatic approach to blending would comprise an expectation of the evolution of blended structures over time in a given context. Increasing leverage over time may not be an indicator of increasing development impact in and of itself; however, it is an indication of increasing efficiency of development finance for achieving a given objective. It is, moreover, a sign of increasing market maturity and successful mobilisation. These eventually should signal that development finance is no longer required and should exit (see Principle 2b in OECD DAC, 2017).

Notes

1. The OECD methodologies for measuring private finance mobilised as a result of official interventions refer to the first level of mobilisation, i.e. the direct impact of the instruments. For example, direct mobilisation could refer to an official investor investing in the equity of company and mobilising additional commercial debt in the same financing round. This is based on based on the principles of avoiding double counting and feasibility as applied to these methodologies (Benn et al, 2017). The use of budgetary resources as capital for official development institutions does not fall within the scope of mobilisation.
2. An example, discussed further in Chapter 7, is the KfW project in Tamil Nadu, India, which successfully mobilised private finance via the government of India.
3. It should be noted that this relates to the financing of development transactions. It does relate to the implementation or to the delivery channel used, e.g. whether through a public or private counterpart and in the case of private channels, whether commercial, non-profit or civil society organisation. These would usually constitute key considerations for achieving the development objective in their own right.
4. Official development finance volumes also need to continue to increase. However, the financing needs to achieve the development agenda exceed the potential of internal growth of this finance.
5. A basic form of such blending with sovereign counterparts has existed in an institutionalised form through the soft windows of multilateral development banks.
6. In this regard, co-financed investments are considered blending if co-financing comprises both finance from development and commercial financial institutions and the deployment of the latter is conditional on the presence of the former. Put another way, commercial finance comes into the co-financing because of the co-finance with development finance, even if at *pari passu* terms. Co-financing where the development finance contribution is not required to enable the private finance would not be considered blended finance, and the deployment of development finance would not generate financial additionality.

References

ADE (2016), *Evaluation of Blending: Final Report, Volume I – Main Report*, commissioned by the European Commission, Analysis for Economic Decisions (ADE), Louvain-la-Neuve, Belgium, https://ec.europa.eu/europeaid/evaluation-blending_en.

AfDB et al. (2017), *Blended Concessional Finance for Private Sector Projects*, a joint summary report prepared by a DFI working group composed of the African Development Bank (AfDB), the Asian Development Bank, the Asia Infrastructure Investment Bank, the European Bank for Reconstruction and Development, European Development Finance Institutions, the European Investment Bank, the Inter-American Development Bank Group, the Islamic Corporation for the Development of the Private Sector, and the International Finance Corporation, www.eib.org/attachments/mdb_dfi_working_group_blended_concessional_finance_private_sector_summary_2017.pdf.

Barder, O. and Talbot, T. (2015), "Guarantees, subsidies, or paying for success? Choosing the right instrument to catalyze private investment in developing countries", *Working Paper*, No. 402, Center for Global Development, Washington, DC, https://www.cgdev.org/sites/default/files/CGD-Working-Paper-402-Barder-Talbot-Supporting-Private-Sector-0.pdf.

Benn, J. et al. (2016), "Amounts mobilised from the private sector by Official Development Finance interventions: Guarantees, syndicated loans, shares in collective investment vehicles, direct investment in companies, credit lines", *OECD Development Co-operation Working Papers*, No. 26, OECD Publishing, Paris, http://dx.doi.org/10.1787/5jm3xh459n37-en.

Chelsky, J. and Gregory, N. (2016), "Concepts of mobilization, cofinancing and catalysation used by World Bank Group" PowerPoint presentation, World Bank, Washington, DC.

Commons Consultants (2015), *The Pitfalls of Innovative Private Sector Financing: Emerging Lessons from Benchmarking of Investment Funds Supported by Aid Agencies*, Summary Report, Commons Consultants, Copenhagen, www.norfund.no/getfile.php/134022/Bilder/Publications/Pitfalls%20of%20Innovative%20Private%20Sector%20Financing_Commons%20Consultants_final_150826.pdf.

Development Initiatives (2016), "The role of blended finance in the 2030 Agenda: Setting out an analytical approach", *Discussion paper*, Development Initiatives, Bristol, UK, http://devinit.org/wp-content/uploads/2016/07/The-role-of-blended-finance-in-the-2030-Agenda-Discussion-paper-July-2016.pdf.

Eurodad (2013), *A Dangerous Blend? The EU's Agenda to 'Blend' Public Development Finance with Private Finance*, European Network on Debt and Development (Eurodad), Brussels, http://eurodad.org/Entries/view/1546054/2013/11/07/A-dangerous-blend-The-EU-s-agenda-to-blend-public-development-finance-with-private-finance

European Commission (2015), "EU blending: European Union aid to catalyse investments", European Commission, Brussels, http://ec.europa.eu/europeaid/eu-blending-european-union-aid-catalyse-investments-0_en.

European Think-Tanks Group (2011), *European Blending Facilities: Implications for Future Governance Options*, Overseas Development Institute, London, https://www.odi.org/sites/odi.org.uk/files/odi-assets/publications-opinion-files/6658.pdf.

IFC (2017), "Amundi to create world's largest green-bond fund dedicated to emerging markets", press release, 21 April 2017, International Finance Corporation, Washington, DC, https://ifcextapps.ifc.org/IFCExt/pressroom/IFCPressRoom.nsf/0/2CC3EDA1AE8B9B558525810900546887.

IFC (2016), *New Horizons in African Finance: Reducing Risk and Mobilizing Financing on a New Scale*, International Finance Corporation, Washington, DC, https://openknowledge.worldbank.org/handle/10986/26432.

Inter-agency Task Force on Financing for Development (2017), *Financing for Development: Progress and Prospects*, United Nations, New York, https://developmentfinance.un.org/financing-development-progress-and-prospects-2017.

Klein, M. (2016) "Blending public and private finance: What lessons can be learned from IFC's experience?", *EMCompass Note*, No. 3, World Bank Group, Washington, DC, http://documents.worldbank.org/curated/en/383411468197952433/Blending-public-and-private-finance-what-lessons-can-be-learned-from-IFC-s-experience.

Larrea, J. (2016), "Sizing up 'Blended Finance': A guide to a new financing approach to fuel sustainable development", ImpactAlpha website, 27 July 2016, http://impactalpha.com/sizing-up-blended-finance-a-guide-to-a-new-financing-approach-to-fuel-sustainable-development/.

Moody's (2016), " ELZ Finance S.A.: Pre-sale report - Elaziğ hospital PPP exceeds Turkey's sovereign rating with strong multilateral support", Report Number 1048045, *Infrastructure and Project finance*, Moody's Investor Services, London, UK.

Mustapha, S., A. Prizzon and M. Gavas (2014), *Topic Guide: Blended Finance for Infrastructure and Low-Carbon Development*, Evidence on Demand, Overseas Development Institute, London, http://dx.doi.org/10.12774/eod_tg9_jan2014.odi.

OECD DAC (2017), "Blended Finance Principles for Unlocking Commercial Finance for the SDGs", Annex to the DAC High Level Communiqué,31 October 2017, www.oecd.org/dac/DAC-HLM-2017-Communique.pdf.

OECD/World Economic Forum (2016), *Insights from Blended Finance Investment Vehicles & Facilities*, ReDesigning Development Finance Initiative, OECD/World Economic Forum, Paris/Cologny, Switzerland, www3.weforum.org/docs/WEF_Blended_Finance_Insights_Investments_Vehicles_Facilities_report_2016.pdf.

OECD/World Economic Forum (2015a), *A How-To Guide for Blended Finance* OECD/World Economic Forum, Paris/Cologny, Switzerland, www3.weforum.org/docs/WEF_Blended_Finance_How_To_Guide.pdf.

OECD/World Economic Forum (2015b), *Blended Finance Vol. 1, A Primer for Development Finance and Philanthropic Funders*, OECD/World Economic Forum, Paris/Cologny, Switzerland, www3.weforum.org/docs/WEF_Blended_Finance_A_Primer_Development_Finance_Philanthropic_Funders_report_2015.pdf.

Romero, M. J. and J. Van de Poel (2014), *Private finance for Development Unravelled: Assessing How Development Finance Institutions Work*, Eurodad, Brussels, www.eurodad.org/files/pdf/53bebdc93dbc6.pdf.

UN (2015), "Addis Ababa Action Agenda", Outcome document adopted at the Third International Conference on Financing for Development, Addis Ababa, Ethiopia, 13-16 July 2015, and endorsed by the UN General Assembly in its resolution 69/313 of 27 July 2015, www.un.org/esa/ffd/wp-content/uploads/2015/08/AAAA_Outcome.pdf.

World Bank/IMF (2005), "Moving forward: Financing modalities toward the MDGs", Background document, DC2005-0008/Add. 1, prepared for the Development Committee meeting of 17 April 2005, World Bank/IMF, Washington, DC, http://siteresources.worldbank.org/DEVCOMMINT/Documentation/20449410/DC2005-0008(E)-FinMod%20Add1.pdf.

Making Blended Finance Work for the Sustainable Development Goals

Chapter 4

The role of development actors in blended finance

Development finance actors play a key role in blended finance, providing the capital that mobilises the commercial sector to engage. This chapter explores the changing role of different development actors involved in blended finance including donor governments and aid agencies, multilateral development banks, and bilateral development finance institutions. It highlights their current engagement in blending, motivations and drivers, and maps challenges faced. While the focus is on public development actors, the chapter also briefly maps the main private actors engaging in blended finance.

The three complementary channels of support for blended finance within development finance are: government ministries and bilateral aid agencies, public sector operations of bilateral and multilateral development banks, and specialised private sector-oriented development finance institutions.

Governments and bilateral aid agencies typically engage in blended finance by providing grants and other forms of concessional financing. Blended finance is gaining importance among donor governments, but is yet to be fully reflected in development co-operation policies and strategies.

Public sector operations of bilateral and multilateral development banks (MDBs) provide finance for, and also manage, blended finance funds and facilities. Increasingly, MDBs are integrating blending into the core of their offering to developing countries.

Specialised, private sector-oriented development finance institutions (DFIs) play a critical role in blending by deploying a range of instruments and structuring mechanisms to mobilise the private sector. DFIs balance risk, returns and development impact in investment decision making.

Philanthropic organisations also are emerging as important actors in blended finance, as reflected in the shift in recent years from a grant-based to an impact investing approach and in the use of a broader range of financial instruments. Many commercial actors are also engaging in blending, among them institutional investors, private equity funds, venture capital, etc.

Key facts

- 17 of 23 DAC members responding to a survey report they are engaging in blended finance; 10 of those report having well-established programmes that have been in operation for a number of years and/or cover a range of instruments.
- MDBs provided 65% and bilateral DFIs provided 35% of development finance for private sector projects in 2014.
- European DFIs committed EUR 6 billion in new investments in 2015, equivalent to roughly one-tenth of official development assistance from EU member states and the EU in the same year.

Introduction

Development finance providers play a key and critical role in blended finance, providing the public or private development finance that mobilises the private sector to engage. There are three main channels of support within development co-operation when working with the private sector: government ministries and bilateral aid agencies, public sector operations of bilateral and multilateral development banks, and specialised private sector operations or development finance institutions (Crishna Morgado and Lasfargues, 2017; IFC, 2011) (Figure 4.1). They have different motivations for engaging in blended finance yet complement one another. Donor governments usually provide financing for and can also directly engage in blending. Multilateral development banks (MDBs) and development finance institutions (DFIs) usually act as intermediaries for blended finance by deploying instruments and structuring mechanisms, but can also utilise their own finance for blending (see Chapters 6 and 7). This chapter explores the role of different development actors and outlines the main drivers and challenges each face in engaging in blending.

Figure 4.1 **Complementary channels of international development finance**

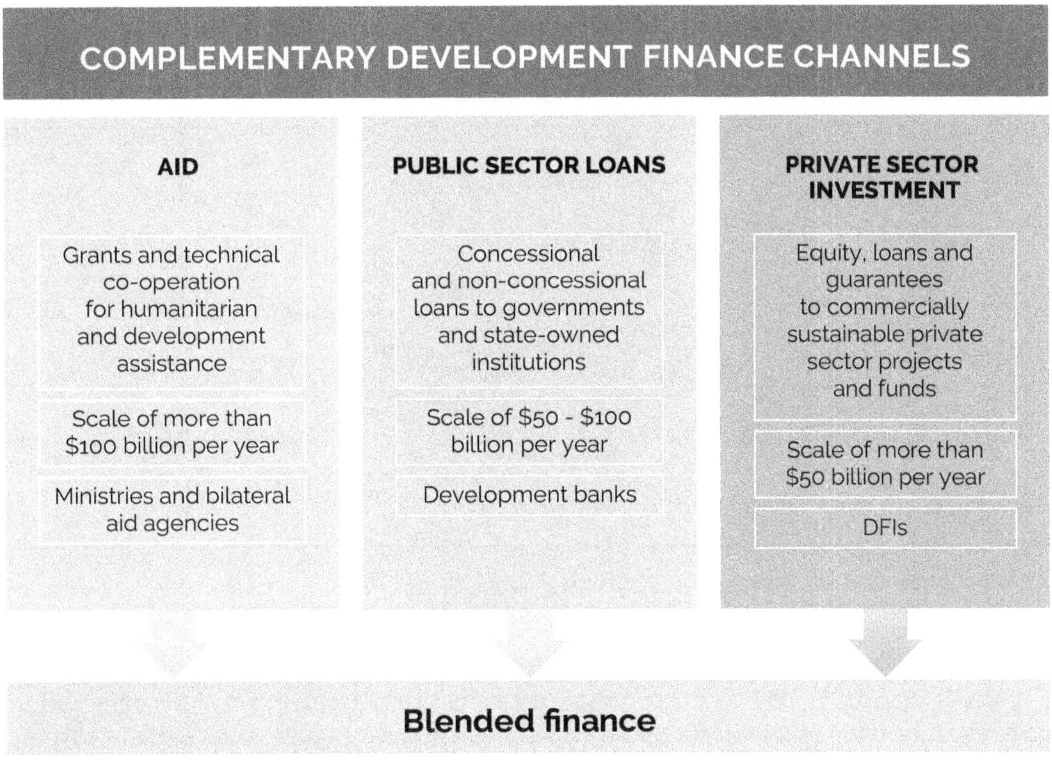

Source: Adapted EDFI (2016), *Flagship Report 2016 - Investing to Create Jobs, Boost Growth and Fight Poverty*, https://www.oe-eb.at/en/news/news/2016/edfi-report-2016.html and IFC (2011), "Development outcome tracking system", www.ifc.org/wps/wcm/connect/5fd0a7004a57bb0bb346bf8969adcc27/DOTS+Handout+2011.pdf?MOD=AJPERES.

Governments, ministries and aid agencies provide finance for blending

In the context of international financing for development, governments, and their ministries of development co-operation and bilateral aid agencies, provide grants and other forms of concessional financing for development including as capital injections to other development agencies. When working directly with partners, they usually work with the public sector and civil society. Members of the OECD Development Assistance Committee

(DAC) are the major government providers of bilateral official development assistance (ODA). As such, they can be considered the source of much of the development finance that has gone towards blending targeting developing countries in recent years.

Blended finance is gaining importance among DAC members

Donor governments are increasingly interested in the opportunities that blended finance provides. The majority of OECD DAC members are already engaging in blended finance, although they are at different stages in terms of the range of instruments used. As shown in Figure 4.2, 17 of 23 DAC members responding to a survey report they are engaging in blended finance; 10 of those reported having well-established programmes that have been in operation for a number of years and/or cover a range of instruments and 7 reported having blended finance programmes at an early stage of development. Nine members also reported they are scaling up their blended finance operations by expanding the range of instruments, issues or geographic regions. Two countries, Finland and Portugal, are initiating new blended finance programmes. Six DAC members did not respond to the survey. Annex A presents DAC members' blended finance engagement in greater detail based on responses to the survey.

Figure 4.2 **OECD DAC members' current engagement in blended finance (BF)**

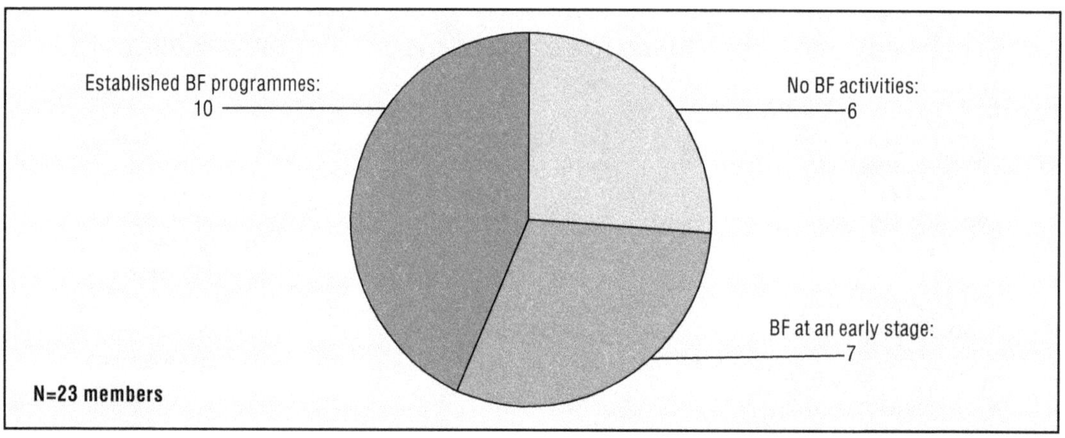

Note: This figure is based on 23 responses to an OECD survey of OECD DAC members. 'Early stage programmes' are those that were described as such in the survey responses or those that have come into being in the three years since 2014.
Source: Based on a survey conducted for this report in 2017

While blended finance is getting more attention, this has yet to be fully reflected in policies and strategies on private sector engagement and development co-operation. Of the 17 DAC members engaging in blended finance, only 6 have a strategy or guidance in place to govern blending and only 4 actively monitor blended finance activities separately. Chapter 9 further discusses constraints and challenges faced by development finance providers engaging in blending. Most members, however, consider a better understanding of blended finance to be important for future activity in the area.

References to blending vary across development co-operation providers

Donor governments are increasingly engaging with the private sector as a way to promote development, deliver poverty reduction and, in particular, mobilise investment for the Sustainable Development Goals.[1] This is happening in the context of a decline in the volume of ODA relative to other finance flows to developing countries (e.g. foreign direct investment, remittances) and awareness that development financing needs to be used in a catalytic way to mobilise and help channel these other resources towards development priorities (Chapter 1).

Most references to blended finance in international discussions on financing for development (IATF, 2017) agree that blended finance is a way to mobilise investment. However, descriptions about what blending actually entails or what its objectives should be are far from consistent across development finance providers. In the past, the most common reference to blending has been the mixing of concessional resources, either loans or grants, with less concessional or non-concessional resources (see Annex A). However, even this varies. Some institutions refer to "public-public blending" — i.e. the use of blending to mobilise public resources provided at near market rates, for example, those provided by bilateral DFIs. Other institutions refer to "public-private" blending as a way of mobilising private investment. As noted by Mustapha, Prizzon and Gavas (2014), the most commonly cited objectives for blending include:

- Enhancing the viability of projects that have positive economic/development benefits but inadequate risk-adjusted financial returns (due to policy frameworks etc.)
- Improving the efficiency of public spending by crowding in private investment
- Reducing the risks of investment and attracting private capital that would not otherwise flow to the project
- Helping demonstrate and spur market development

Donor governments are developing a range of governance systems for private sector operations and particularly for blended finance

Donor governments usually blend with private and commercial actors indirectly, either through bilateral and multilateral development banks, DFIs and other intermediaries or through funds/mechanisms managed by third parties. They also do so directly, although it is less common. The overarching governance of development co-operation in a country influences the governance of blended finance (Figure 4.3). Many donor governments choose to devolve the implementation of their programmes to development banks and aid agencies, and have established DFIs as specialised institutions to work with the private sector. This multi-layered governance has an effect on the management and perceived transparency of blended finance. For example, monitoring the flows of development finance and the results it generates becomes more complicated as the delivery chain grows longer (see Chapter 9). There are three main groups of governance systems in place among DAC members:

- In the majority of DAC member countries, ministries devolve development co-operation to aid agencies, DFIs and export credit agencies (ECAs). One or more ministries may manage these institutions[2] and their working modalities differ greatly due to different institutional arrangements and mandates. For example, the Swedish International Development Cooperation Agency (Sida) carries out the bulk of Sweden's development co-operation portfolio including using blended instruments like guarantees to mobilise private investment; Swedfund, a DFI, works directly with the private sector providing financing at market rates. The Ministry for Foreign Affairs of Sweden governs both Sida and Swedfund. Similarly, the Ministry of Foreign Affairs of Japan governs the Japan International Cooperation Agency (JICA). JICA carries out public sector lending but also engages in blending through its work with publicly owned financial institutions, for example, through credit lines.

- In some DAC member countries, ministries devolve a large part of development co-operation activities to bilateral development banks. In France and Germany, the DFI is embedded within these banks, and the development banks act as an intermediary between the DFI and the government. In both cases, development banks and DFIs engage in blending.
- Some DAC members implement development co-operation only through ministries or dedicated aid agencies and do not have a separate DFI. Among these are Canada, Ireland, New Zealand and Australia. Where blending occurs in such countries, ministries may invest directly alongside private partners through specialised platforms such as Australia's Business Partnerships Platform. However, the emphasis usually is on investing indirectly through MDBs and funds managed by third parties.

Figure 4.3 **Stylised representation of OECD DAC member governance of private sector operations and blended finance**

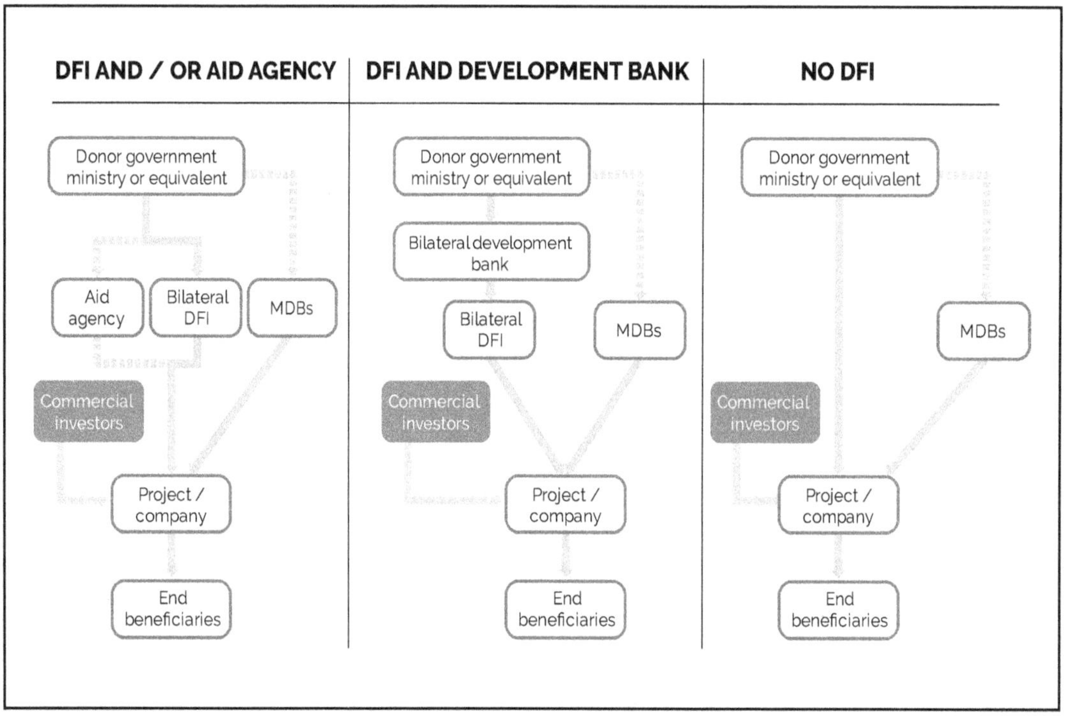

Note: DFI – development finance institution, MDB – multilateral development bank
Source: Authors' compilation

Development banks and development finance institutions are critical players in the blended finance landscape

Development banks and finance institutions play a critical role in blending by deploying instruments and structuring mechanisms to mobilise the private sector (see Chapter 5). Within this broad group of actors, it is useful to distinguish between development banks and DFIs based on their roles in engaging with the private sector. At a very general level, bilateral and multilateral development banks pursue both public and private sector operations. Public sector operations of bilateral and multilateral development banks provide concessional finance and grants and work largely with the public sector, including with state-owned entities, while their private sector operations have a specific mandate to engage with the private sector. In addition to development banks, many DAC member countries also have specialised bilateral DFIs. Among these are the CDC Group plc of the United Kingdom and the Overseas Private Investment Corporation (OPIC) of the United States. DFIs and private sector operations of development banks provide equity, loans, guarantees and insurance to private sector projects and companies, most often at non-concessional terms. Some bilateral support is also channelled through export credit agencies, as is the case with Korea and its Export–Import Bank of Korea.

MDBs are integrating blending into the core of their offering to developing countries

Among development finance providers, MDBs provide the largest share of private sector investments through dedicated private sector operations involving standalone institutions such as the International Finance Corporation (IFC) or embedded with development banks such as the Asian Development Bank's Private Sector Operations Department. In 2014, MDBs provided 65% and bilateral DFIs provided 35% of development finance for private sector projects (EDFI, 2016).

In the context of financing for the Sustainable Development Goals, multilateral development banks increasingly are working together at the international level to address the "billions to trillions" agenda including by taking concerted action on mobilising private resources (World Bank Group, 2015). Many MDBs have initiated efforts to optimise their balance sheets and have been reporting progress on these to G20 governments since 2015 (AFDB et al., 2017). The G20 International Financial Architecture Working Group released principles in 2017 to support MDBs in crowding in private finance, and blending of 'concessional resources and private capital' is one of the six principles put forward. MDBs have also started collectively reporting on the private finance that has been mobilised as a result of their actions.

MDBs are also beginning to situate blending within their overall financing approach.[3] This is best illustrated by the "cascade" approach of the World Bank Group (2017). This approach, taking account of scarce public resources, prioritises commercial sources of investment for a project, enabled by government and MDB efforts to improve the investment environment and correct market failures. Where risks remain high for investors, the second option would be to use public resources from developing countries and development finance providers to mitigate risks and mobilise investment through the use of blending and risk mitigation instruments. If neither of the first two approaches is feasible, public resources from developing countries and development finance providers is used to cover the costs of the project in its entirety. This approach is at the core of the new Private Sector Window set up by the World Bank Group (Box 4.1). MDBs have also assumed a greater role in managing blended finance facilities (AfDB et al., 2015; World Bank Group, 2015; Nelson, 2015; Faure, Prizzon and Rogerson, 2015). The World Bank, for instance, hosts two major environment-focused facilities, the Global Environment Facility (GEF) and the Climate Investment Funds (CIFs), that both provide financing for blended transactions related to climate mitigation and energy initiatives, among other instruments. Chapter 6 provides an overview of such facilities.

Box 4.1 IFC-MIGA-IDA private sector window

Acknowledging the important role of the private sector in development, the World Bank Group — the International Development Association (IDA), the International Bank for Reconstruction and Development (IBRD), the Multilateral Investment Guarantee Agency (MIGA) and IFC — has been supporting the private sector in developing countries for many years. However, the support to the private sector in IDA countries still lacks scale and scope. In recognition of this loophole and in order to harness synergies among different areas of the World Bank Group, MIGA, IFC, and IDA launched a dedicated USD 2.5 billion Private Sector Window focused on IDA countries. The window offers various types of risk management and support to outside investors with projects that would help developing countries achieve the Sustainable Development Goals. The Private Sector Window will provide concessional funds that will go towards blended finance transactions. It will be implemented through four facilities managed by IFC and MIGA: a Risk Mitigation Facility for Infrastructure (USD 800 million to USD 1.2 billion); a MIGA Guarantee Facility (USD 500 million); a Local Currency Facility (USD 300-500 million); and a Blended Finance Facility (USD 400-800 million).

Source: World Bank (2017), "Leveraging the private sector in IDA countries", http://ida.worldbank.org/sites/default/files/pdfs/ida-private-sector-april-2017.pdf.

Bilateral development banks and DFIs play a critical role in blending

Bilateral development banks such as Germany's KfW and the French Development Agency (AFD) have integrated blending approaches into their portfolios, especially through the use of credit lines and guarantees, and also by setting up funds (Chapter 5). In addition, they also provide technical assistance that helps to develop projects, carry out feasibility studies and build capacity in local financial institutions. An increasing number of DAC members have established their own bilateral DFIs over the last decade to engage specifically with investors and businesses. In addition to OPIC in the United States, a number of European DFIs have been established (see Box 4.2). Most of these are independent entities, such as the Netherlands Development Finance Company (FMO). Some are embedded in bilateral development banks such as the German Investment Corporation (DEG) in KfW and Proparco in AFD. Canada is setting up a new DFI under Export Development Canada; it is due to be operational by the start of 2018 and will help to leverage resources and complement Canadian ODA.[4]

Most bilateral DFIs have relatively small operations when compared with bilateral aid agencies and development banks or the multilateral equivalents. Still, they are important players in the blended finance space as they have traditionally taken what is called the most "commercial" approach to development investments of the different development finance actors who engage in blended finance. The shared mandates of DFIs are to generate returns on the capital they were provided by shareholders and support projects with a positive development impact in the private sector in developing and emerging markets (IFC et al., 2011; Romeo and Van de Poel, 2014; te Velde and Warner, 2007; Kingombe, Massa and te Velde, 2011; Dalberg, 2010). The first objective incentivises DFIs to give project proposals the same scrutiny they would get from commercial investors; the second objective obligates them to take greater risks and invest in projects that would otherwise not be funded.

Bilateral DFIs support broader catalysation of finance by taking a pathfinder and market leader role, especially in countries where there are few alternative sources of financing. For example, venture capital investments by DFIs can provide a significant boost to markets in low-income countries that have growing economies but where political risk remains high. While the investment itself may not always immediately crowd in private capital (and thus count as blended finance), it kick-starts a sector. This results in significant development impact and in the long run, as the project or sector grows and becomes less risky to investors, further capital is mobilised. In addition to their traditional role, bilateral DFIs have been involved in blended finance until now mostly through managing and co-investing alongside concessional contributions from ministries and aid agencies. DFIs have also invested in private equity funds that serve developing countries and target developmental sectors such as clean energy or access to finance (see Chapter 6). In many cases, these funds have attracted additional commercial investment. An example is IPDEV 2, which is described in Box 6.2.

Box 4.2 **Overview of European development finance institutions**

European Union (EU) countries have established 15 DFIs that provide financing, largely on commercial terms, to international companies and companies based in developing countries. Operations of European DFIs have been growing rapidly, increasing up to EUR 36.3 billion in commitments at the end of 2015 from a combined portfolio of EUR 10.9 billion in commitments at the end of 2005. In 2015, European DFIs committed EUR 6 billion in new investments, equivalent to roughly one-tenth of official development assistance from EU member states and the EU in the same year. This increase in DFI financing over the last decade has been supported by a doubling in shareholder equity, partially through retained profits and through capital replenishments from shareholder governments. The three largest European DFIs in terms of new commitments per year are FMO (Netherlands), DEG (Germany) and Proparco (France).

Figure 4.4 **New commitments by European DFIs in 2015**

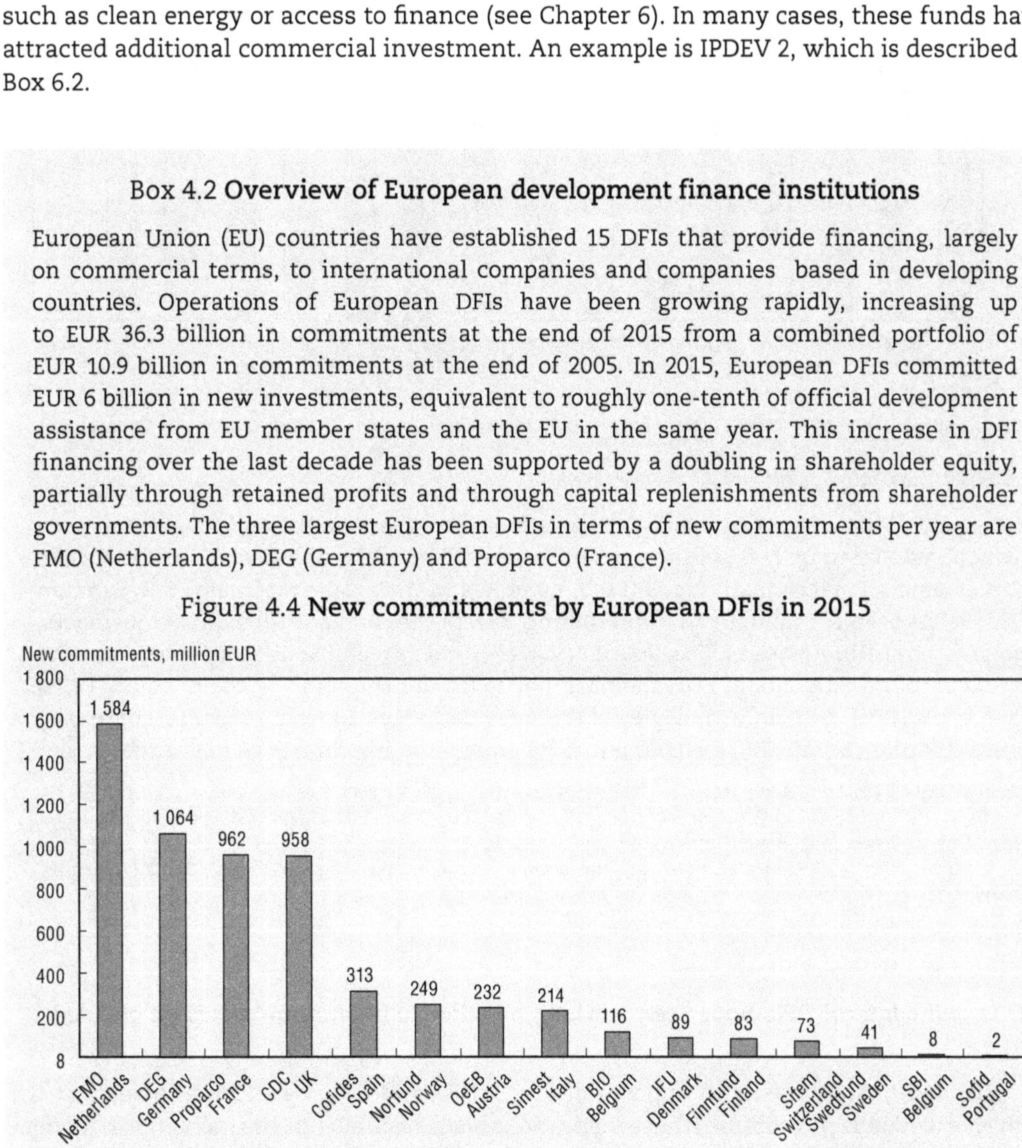

Source: Adapted from EDFI (2016), Flagship Report 2016 - Investing to Create Jobs, Boost Growth and Fight Poverty, https://www.oe-eb.at/en/news/news/2016/edfi-report-2016.html.

StatLink http://dx.doi.org/10.1787/888933648290

Box 4.2 **Overview of European development finance institutions** *(cont.)*

Figure 4.5 **Breakdown of European DFI portfolio, by instrument, 2015**

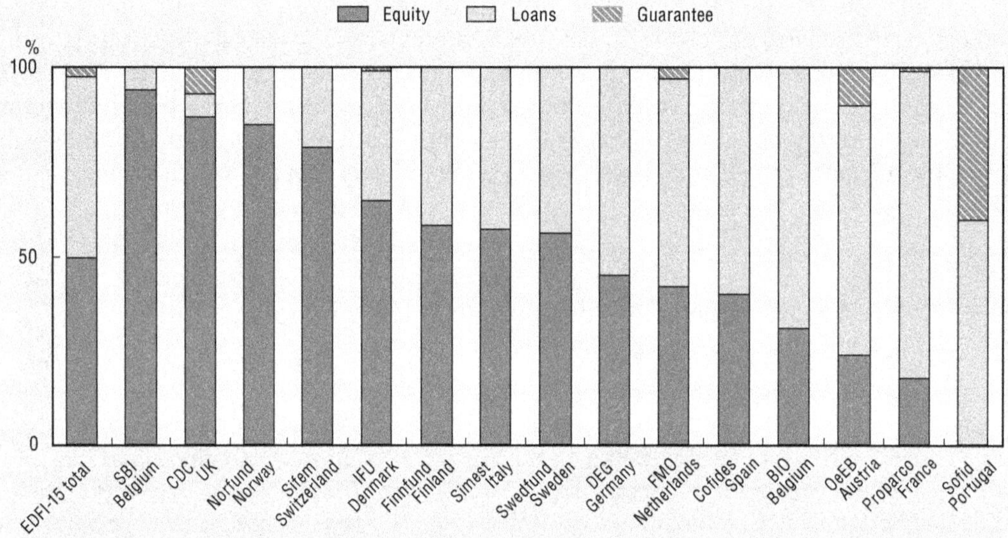

Source: Adapted from EDFI (2016), Flagship Report 2016 - Investing to Create Jobs, Boost Growth and Fight Poverty, https://www.oe-eb.at/en/news/news/2016/edfi-report-2016.html.

StatLink http://dx.doi.org/10.1787/888933648309

The major focus areas of European DFI operations are infrastructure and financial sectors, which make up roughly one-third each of the overall portfolio of Association of European Development Finance Institutions (EDFI) members in 2015. Geographically, Sub-Saharan Africa has been the main focus, representing 31% of the total portfolio of EDFI members, followed by Latin America (20%), South Asia (14%), and East and Southeast Asia (13%). The majority of investments in EDFI member' portfolios are through the use of equity (50%) and loans (48%), with only 2% deployed through guarantees. In terms of addressing cross-cutting issues, 22% of EDFI member portfolios were targeting climate change issues.

Source: EDFI (2011), Annual Report 2011 - Long-term finance for private sector enterprises, www.cofides.es/ficheros/OTRA_DOCUMENTACION/2011_EDFI_Annual_report.pdf; EDFI (2016), Flagship Report 2016 - Investing to Create Jobs, Boost Growth and Fight Poverty, https://www.oe-eb.at/en/news/news/2016/edfi-report-2016.html; and OECD (2017a), "Investing in Climate, Investing in Growth", OECD Publishing, Paris, http://dx.doi.org/10.1787/9789264273528-en.

MDBs and bilateral DFIs have been working together to align approaches on blended finance

Blended finance offers an opportunity for MDBs and DFIs by helping to support the supply of bankable projects, but these institutions also acknowledge the risks and challenges associated with blending and the use of concessional finance in private sector projects. This includes the need to ensure additionality of public sector support, the importance crowding in the private sector, and the challenge of ensuring commercial sustainability. MDBs and DFIs have developed their own principles and guidelines for the use of blended concessional finance in private sector operations (DFI Working Group, 2017). Initially developed in 2013 and updated in 2017, these principles address five aspects: additionality/rationale for using blended finance; crowding in and minimum concessionality; commercial sustainability; reinforcing markets; and promoting high standards.

DFIs balance risk, returns and development impact in investment decision making

Bilateral DFIs typically are at the forefront of managing the interplay between risk, return and development. DFIs resemble commercial operators in the development finance landscape, in that they often are investing in and making a return on investments. However, the development element in the interplay of considerations will impact how DFIs price risks and target returns when using both concessional and non-concessional tools. Typically the number of jobs created as a way of supporting economic growth has been the impact metric. However, blended finance may need to play a more targeted role in the future. If blended finance is to expand and be deployed for a broader range of development issues, more and better impact metrics will be required.

Risk and return are also elements to be weighed. Blended finance addresses risks that other financial partners are unwilling to take or do not possess the instruments to address. Return is important for the private sector, which is looking for profitability among other goals in a project. A blended finance mechanism is one way through which DFIs can engage with the private sector on project risk. If a risk has been addressed, then the returns should be commensurate with the risks of the total project. These include the risk reducted as a result of the public blended finance contribution. However, it is not optimal for a blended finance transaction to result in returns that greatly exceed the private sector's risks as this could have elements of subsidisation. Addressing risk, return and development impact is critical in ensuring crowding in, defining the private sector's role in developing the project, and creating conditions to allow eventual withdrawal of the blended finance instrument (Figure 4.6). The right policy tools must be developed so that decisions address these competing tensions so that actors work effectively together and optimum outcomes are delivered.

Figure 4.6 **Balancing risk, return and development**

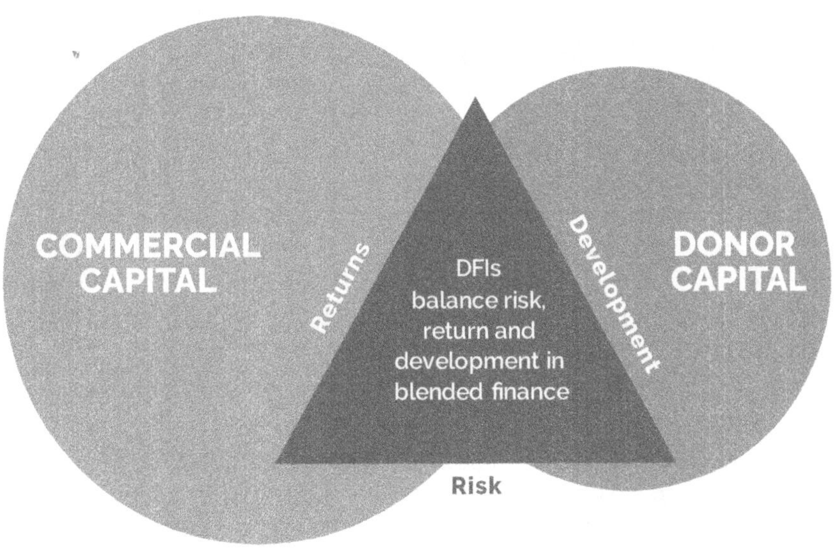

Source: Authors' compilation

A wide range of partners are engaging in blended finance

Philanthropic development finance supports blended finance

Private philanthropy is a growing, and important source of development finance, complementing contributions from donor governments. Philanthropic giving for development objectives from 130 major foundations amounted to USD 7.8 billion per year, on average, between 2013-15 (OECD, 2017b). Philanthropies are important actors in blended finance due to their relatively low levels of risk aversion and their willingness to invest in innovative business concepts and financing models. Many foundations and philanthropic investors are shifting from a grant-based approach to (impact) investing, and are using the entire range of financial instruments including seed funding and mezzanine investment (OECD, 2015a; UN Global Compact, 2015).

Commercial private actors are engaging in blended finance

Many different commercial private actors, ranging from institutional investors to banks and corporations, are engaging in blending. **Institutional investors** such as pension funds, insurance companies, investment funds, endowments or sovereign wealth funds collectively manage a significant amount of capital, which makes them highly influential in decisions around the allocation of capital and investment. Institutional investors also have a long-term outlook due to the nature of their liabilities and make strategic choices about how they allocate funds across assets, usually through a diversified set of financial instruments like bonds (government, corporate or green bonds) and listed equity (infoDev, 2013; UNTT, 2014; UN Global Compact, 2015).

However, they are not monolithic. Differences in the operating environment of individual investors, such as rules that govern investment portfolios, investor circumstance, liquidity, and risk tolerances can all affect an investor's long-term strategic allocation. While institutional investors often invest in developed markets, individual investors have demonstrated a strong appetite for emerging markets (Braham L., 2017). Furthermore, pension funds in search of higher yielding portfolios have been looking beyond traditional products. A recent survey by the OECD (2015b) shows several prominent pensions funds with sizeable allocations in real estate, private equity and hedge funds. Some large sovereign wealth funds and pension funds invest directly into companies, amassing sizeable ownership stakes (The Economist, 2014). OECD research also points to growing interest amongst institutional investors in developing Environmental, Social, and Governance investment strategies for their portfolios, which could offer opportunities to align strategies for blending capital with investors utilising such frameworks (OECD, 2015b; OECD, 2017c).

The institutional investor allocates assets and drives investment choices, but other players in the blended finance space use proprietary investment strategies and attract institutional investors based on their financial performance. While such firms represent a very small part of blending today, they have the potential to play a much bigger role going forward. One example is **private equity** funds, which acquire companies or amass large ownership stakes to accrete value through strategies such as turning around a struggling business or driving growth. They often enhance returns by utilising a high degree of financial leverage. **Venture capital** firms provide equity for early stage companies that demonstrate a potential to grow quickly and generate large returns on investment. **Infrastructure funds** represent a growing share of institutional investment in infrastructure, and are a growing opportunity for developing countries to attract foreign and domestic sources of capital for blending (OECD, 2015b). **Hedge funds** employ highly managed investment strategies to drive returns higher than relevant market benchmarks. These funds can be relatively illiquid, restricting investors to making withdrawals only in certain periods.

Commercial banks contribute to blending by providing debt financing. Operating across the entire range of economic activities from infrastructure to health, banks contribute in terms of financing as well as in regard to standards for sustainable development. Transparency guidelines and investment standards, whether imposed by national banking authorities or self-imposed, facilitate the development impact of banks (UN Global Compact, 2015). Large universal banks go beyond traditional commercial banking. Along with investment banks, they serve a vital interface role in any financial structure, often acting as the facilitators in a financial structure, creating financial security and connecting investors to appropriate investment opportunities. Many other private actors also facilitate blended finance including law firms, consulting firms, ratings agencies and insurance companies.[5]

Corporations contribute to blending through investments. These may take the form of an equity-financed expansion of their services in infrastructure, education or health and the development of innovative products and services that address sustainable development issues. Multinational companies have a direct impact on society and the environment and indirect impacts on small and medium-sized enterprises (SMEs) operating along the supply chain of large corporations. Investments by parent companies in subsidiaries or entities in the supply chain can help the SMEs adapt sustainability practices in their operations (UN Global Compact, 2015). Multinational as well as local companies also are involved in project design, staffing, construction and operation of the subsidiary or legally independent project company. Through these relationships, they may use their assets to raise additional finance via debt markets. Moreover, corporations can take advantage of cheaper sources of capital in domestic markets through guarantees provided by export credit agencies.

SMEs that operate completely separately from multinational corporates represent promising targets for blended finance as a lack of cost-effective finance often constrains their success. Recalibrating their cost of capital through blended finance can be critical to raising sufficient funds to make investments that are essential to their ability to grow and compete. From a development standpoint, SMEs can be an effective catalyst to building capacity or developing a local market. It also is becoming clear that they are essential to development, given that SMEs constitute 60% of total employment and 40% of national income in developing countries (Ayyagari, Demirgüç-Kunt and Maksimovic, 2017).

Notes

1. Private sector engagement also is driven by the need to leverage skills and expertise of private actors, promote innovation and core business to benefit sustainable development, promote a healthy private sector in developing countries, and promote domestic businesses in DAC member countries. See OECD, 2016. *Private Sector Engagement for Sustainable Development: Lessons from the DAC,* http://dx.doi.org/10.1787/9789264266889-en.
2. This is the case for 13 DAC members. Nine of them have an agency and a DFI: Belgium, the EU, Italy, Portugal, Spain, Switzerland and the United States. Four do not have agency, but do have a DFI: Denmark, Finland, Netherlands and the United Kingdom.
3. It should be noted that MDBs use the term "blended finance" to refer specifically to blended concessional finance used for private sector operations only. This differs from the definition used in this report (see Box 3.2).

4. For a description of Canada's Development Finance Institution, see http://international.gc.ca/world-monde/international_relations-relations_internationales/multilateral-multilateraux/dfi-ifd.aspx?lang=eng.
5. Law firms draft and execute legal documents essential to the underlying securities. Consulting and accounting firms provide sector-specific and technical expertise and advice. Rating agencies evaluate fixed-income securities and projects to provide informed analysis on the creditworthiness of the investment. Insurance companies provide products to protect investors from risks associated with their investment.

References

AfDB et al. (2017), "Mobilization of private finance by multilateral development banks: 2016", joint report of the African Development Bank and a group of multilateral development banks (MDBs), www.eib.org/attachments/mdb_joint_report_mobilization_2016_en.pdf.

AfDB et al. (2015), "From billions to trillions: Transforming development finance", *Development Committee Discussion Note*, DC2015-002, prepared jointly for meeting of 18 April 2015 by the African Development Bank, the Asian Development Bank, the European Bank for Reconstruction and Development, the European Investment Bank, the Inter-American Development Bank, the International Monetary Fund, and the World Bank Group, http://siteresources.worldbank.org/DEVCOMMINT/Documentation/23659446/DC2015-0002(E)FinancingforDevelopment.pdf.

Ayyagari, M., A. Demirgüç-Kunt and V. Maksimovic (2017), "SME Finance", World Bank Group, *Policy Research Working Paper*, No. 8241, http://documents.worldbank.org/curated/en/860711510585220714/pdf/WPS8241.pdf.

Braham, L. (2017), "Have you been duped by market diversification dogma?", CNBC.com website, 10 October 2017, www.cnbc.com/2015/09/13/have-you-been-duped-by-diversification-time-to-find-out.html.

Crishna Morgado, N. and B. Lasfargues (2017), "Engaging the private sector for green growth and climate action: An overview of development co-operation efforts", *OECD Development Co-operation Working Papers*, No. 34, OECD Publishing, Paris, http://dx.doi.org/10.1787/85b52daf-en.

Dalberg (2010), *The Growing Role of the Development Finance Institutions in International Development Policy*, Dalberg Global Development Advisors, Copenhagen, www.bio-invest.be/en/component/downloads/downloads/38.html.

DFI Working Group (2017), Blended Concessional Finance for Private Sector Projects, a joint summary report prepared by AfDB, EBRD, EDFI, EIB, IDBG, ICD and IFC, www.eib.org/attachments/mdb_dfi_working_group_blended_concessional_finance_private_sector_summary_2017.pdf.

EDFI (2016), *Flagship Report 2016 - Investing to Create Jobs, Boost Growth and Fight Poverty*, Association of European Development Finance Institutions (EDFI), Brussels, https://www.oe-eb.at/en/news/news/2016/edfi-report-2016.html.

EDFI (2011), *Annual Report 2011 - Long-term finance for private sector enterprises*, Association of European Development Finance Institutions (EDFI), Brussels, www.cofides.es/ficheros/OTRA_DOCUMENTACION/2011_EDFI_Annual_report.pdf.

Faure, R., A. Prizzon and A. Rogerson (2015), *Multilateral development banks: A short guide*, Overseas Development Institute, London, www.odi.org/sites/odi.org.uk/files/odi-assets/publications-opinion-files/10098.pdf.

G20 International Financial Architecture Working Group (2017), *Principles of MDBs' strategy for crowding-in Private Sector Finance for growth and sustainable development*, www.bundesfinanzministerium.de/Content/DE/Downloads/G20-Dokumente/principles-on-crowding-in-private-sector-finance-april-20.pdf?__blob=publicationFile&v=2.

IATF (2017), *Financing for Development: Progress and Prospects: Report of the Inter-agency Task Force on Financing for Development 2017*, United Nations publication, New York, https://developmentfinance.un.org/financing-development-progress-and-prospects-2017.

IFC et al. (2011), *International Finance Institutions and Development Through the Private Sector*, a joint report of 31 multilateral and bilateral development finance institutions, International Finance Corporation, Washington, D.C., www.eib.org/attachments/ifi_report-9-13-11.pdf.

infoDev (2013), *Crowdfunding's Potential for the Developing World*, Information for Development Program (infoDev)/The World Bank - Finance and Private Sector Development Department, Washington, D.C., www.infodev.org/infodev-files/infodev_crowdfunding_study_0.pdf.

Kingombe, C., I. Massa and D.W. te Velde (2011), *Comparing Development Finance Institutions: Literature Review*, Overseas Development Institute, London. www.gov.uk/government/uploads/system/uploads/attachment_data/file/67635/comparing-DFIs.pdf.

Mustapha, S., A. Prizzon and M. Gavas (2014), "Blended finance for infrastructure and low-carbon development", *Topic Guide*, Evidence on Demand, Crown copyright, Overseas Development Institute, London, http://dx.doi.org/10.12774/eod_tg9_jan2014.odi.

Nelson, R.M. (2015), *Multilateral Development Banks: Overview and Issues for Congress*, Congressional Research Service, Washington, DC, www.fas.org/sgp/crs/row/R41170.pdf.

OECD (2017a), "Investing in Climate, Investing in Growth", OECD Publishing, Paris, http://dx.doi.org/10.1787/9789264273528-en.

OECD (2017b), "Global Private Philanthropy for Development", Results of the OECD Data Survey as of 3 October 2017, OECD, Paris, www.oecd.org/dac/financing-sustainable-development/development-finance-standards/Philanthropy-Development-Survey.pdf.

OECD (2017c), "Investment Governance and the Integration of Environmental, Social, and Governance Factors", OECD, Paris, https://www.oecd.org/finance/Investment-Governance-Integration-ESG-Factors.pdf.

OECD (2016), *Private Sector Engagement for Sustainable Development: Lessons from the DAC*, OECD Publishing, Paris, http://dx.doi.org/10.1787/9789264266889-en.

OECD (2015a), *Social Impact Investment: Building the Evidence Base (Preliminary Report)*, OECD Publishing, Paris, http://dx.doi.org/10.1787/9789264233430-en.

OECD (2015b), *Annual Survey of Large Pension Funds and Public Pension Reserve Funds: Report on Pension Funds' Long-term Investments*, OECD Publishing, Paris, www.oecd.org/daf/fin/private-pensions/2015-Large-Pension-Funds-Survey.pdf.

OECD (2014), *OECD Development Co-operation Peer Reviews: Japan 2014*, OECD Publishing, Paris, http://dx.doi.org/10.1787/9789264218161-en.

Romeo, M. J. and J. Van de Poel (2014), *Private finance for Development Unravelled: Assessing how Development Finance Institutions Work*, Eurodad, Brussels, www.eurodad.org/files/pdf/53bebdc93dbc6.pdf.

te Velde, D.W. and M. Warner (2007), "The use of subsidies by Development Finance Institutions in the infrastructure sector", *Working Paper*, No. 283, Overseas Development Institute, London, www.odi.org/sites/odi.org.uk/files/odi-assets/publications-opinion-files/564.pdf.

The Economist (2014), "In-house revolt: Big pension and sovereign-wealth funds are cutting out the middleman", 1 November 2014, www.economist.com/news/finance-and-economics/21629560-big-pension-and-sovereign-wealth-funds-are-cutting-out-middleman-house.

UN Global Compact (2015), *Private Sector Investment and Sustainable Development: The Current and Potential Role of Institutional Investors, Companies, Banks and Foundations in Sustainable Development*, jointly published by United Nations Global Compact, United Nations Conference on Trade and Development (UNCTAD), Principles for Responsible Investment (PRI) Initiative, and United Nations Environment Programme Finance Initiative (UNEP FI), www.unglobalcompact.org/docs/publications/Private_Sector_Investment_and_Sustainable_Development.pdf.

UNTT (2014), "Challenges in raising private sector resources for financing sustainable development", Chapter 3, in *UN System Task Team's Working Group on "Financing for Sustainable Development"*, http://sustainabledevelopment.un.org/content/documents/2106Chapter%203-challenges%20in%20raising%20private%20sector%20resources.pdf.

World Bank (2017), "Leveraging the private sector in IDA countries", World Bank Group, Washington, DC, http://ida.worldbank.org/sites/default/files/pdfs/ida-private-sector-april-2017.pdf.

World Bank Group (2017), "Forward look: A vision for the World Bank Group in 2030 – progress and challenges", report for Development Committee Meeting of 22 April 2017, DC2017-0002, World Bank Group, Washington, DC, http://siteresources.worldbank.org/DEVCOMMINT/Documentation/23745169/DC2017-0002.pdf.

World Bank Group (2015), *Financing for Sustainable Development: From Billions to Trillions - What Will it Take?*, Summary report, Development Finance Forum of the World Bank Group, Rotterdam, http://bit.ly/1HtFFvF.

Making Blended Finance Work for the Sustainable Development Goals

Chapter 5

Blended finance instruments and mechanisms

Blended finance involves the use of different financial instruments that can be used alone or together to address unfavourable risk-return profiles of investment in developing countries. This chapter outlines the main risks facing commercial investors in developing countries. It presents the types of financial instruments that can be used in blended finance and outlines the main mechanisms and structures that blending entails. The chapter presents examples to illustrate how different instruments and approaches come together to crowd in private, commercial investment for development outcomes.

HIGHLIGHTS

Investors often associate investment in developing countries with an unfavourable risk-return relationship. Perceived and real risks associated with investments include macroeconomic and business risks that influence investments in a project or company and regulatory and political risks that are associated with uncertainties in the broader enabling environment in a country.

Several financial instruments can be used in blended finance to address the risk-return profile of investments. These include direct investments (debt, equity and mezzanine investments), credit lines, bonds, currency hedging, political risk insurance, and grants and technical assistance.

Blending also can entail the structuring of one or several instruments together. Approaches like securitisation offer organisations the ability to utilise existing assets on their balance sheets to raise capital. Other approaches include syndicated loans, funds and public-private partnerships.

Initial evidence from OECD analyses of amounts mobilised from the private sector by official development finance shows that instruments can be applied in different contexts and sectors to mobilise commercial capital.

Key facts

- Official development finance mobilised USD 81.1 billion from the private sector in 2012-15 through the use of financial instruments: guarantees, shares in collective investment vehicles, syndicated loans, direct investment in companies (i.e. equity) and credit lines
- Across instruments, guarantees are found to have mobilised the largest share of finance across the four years (USD 35.9 billion)

Introduction

Blended finance is not an asset class but rather it is associated with a mix of different financial instruments. An effective blended finance transaction should structure and/or calibrate traditional financial instruments in such a way as to address investor concerns regarding the risk-return profile of investment opportunities in developing countries in order to mobilise commercial capital while ensuring delivery of the expected development outcomes. Therefore, blended finance can operate on both ends of the risk-return spectrum (Figure 5.1). For instance, blended finance can be applied to de-risk projects by providing guarantees or grant funding. Alternatively, subordination mechanisms and other instruments that enhance the capital structure of a project or portfolio of projects may lead to enhanced returns. These enhanced returns would compensate commercial investors for taking on a high level of risk. This chapter presents the main types of risk facing private investors, outlines instruments that can be used in blended transactions, and describes financial structures. It underscores that the effectiveness of blended finance instruments in de-risking varies by the type of risk and presents examples to illustrate how different approaches come together.

Investments in developing countries and emerging markets are associated with risks

Investors often associate investment in developing countries with an unfavourable risk-return relationship (Chapter 2). This is one reason for under-investment in these countries, while returns in fact may be relatively high compared with many OECD countries, given the current low interest rate environment.[1] Consequently, the perceived as well as the real risks associated with investments in developing countries are driving decisions of commercial investors not to invest. Financial risks stem from a variety of sources that can be grouped in two broad categories: macroeconomic and business risks, and regulatory and political risks (OECD/World Bank Group, 2015). While these risks are associated with any investment, they play out differently in developing countries and emerging markets. This is due in part to the nature of the investment. For example, cross-border investments in either developed or developing countries are inherently associated with currency risk. Some risks associated with investments are attributable to the country itself, for example its poor credit rating. Risks also can vary across regions.

Macroeconomic and business risks are decisive determinants of investors' willingness to invest in a company, project or portfolio of projects. Credit risk, which is associated with the probability of default of the counterparty in a financial transaction, is most pivotal in driving lending decisions. Commercial investors usually manage credit risk by assessing the risk of default internally and/or making use of market intelligence including that provided by rating agencies Moody's and Standard & Poor's, for example. In addition to counterparty inherent risk, liquidity[2] and market risk[3] play important roles in assessment of potential investments. Market risk, particularly in the form of equity risk, influences decisions regarding investment in equity. A lack of relevant information may hamper the assessment of risks such as market risk and credit risk in developing countries, especially at subnational levels. For instance, reporting standards may not meet investor needs. Limited coverage across developing countries may limit the availability of independent external evaluations including by credit rating agencies. Foreign currency risk[4] associated with inflation and fluctuating exchange rates also weigh strongly on investment decisions of commercial investors when regarding developing countries.

Regulatory and political risks are associated with uncertainties related to the enabling environment in a country. In general, investors are attracted by stable conditions that allow them to anticipate risks and price those risks adequately into financing terms and conditions. Political risks, however, are rather subjective and hard to quantify. These include changes in regulations affecting specific sectors, for instance the implementation of feed-in-tariffs in the renewable energy space, and institutional risks related to enforceability of contracts. Government interventions in investors' exposure-related fields affect the investment decision ex post and therefore pose a significant challenge ex ante to investors. Within regulatory and political risks, breach of contract is a major concern for investors in the developing country context (OECD/World Bank Group, 2015). Other examples are currency inconvertibility and transfer restrictions, expropriation, and any default related to war, terrorism and civil disturbance. Political insurers such as the Multilateral Investment Guarantee Agency (MIGA) increasingly are covering such risks.[5]

Technical risk is a third dimension of risk that is associated particularly with infrastructure projects. These risks are decisive in infrastructure investments because the underlying asset is subject to a variety of construction risks in new, greenfield projects and/or operating risks in brownfield investments. Prominent examples of technical risks are construction delays, cost overruns and environmental risks associated with renewable energy investment.

Blended finance transactions can include the use of *financial instruments* to crowd in commercial investments as well as *mechanisms to structure* or *intermediate instruments* with the same purpose (Figure 5.1). Instruments can facilitate private investments in the financing structure of a project, both at concessional terms and market rates. In addition, instruments such as guarantees or insurance can facilitate private investment without the investor bearing some or all of the risk of default.

Figure 5.1 **Blended finance instruments and mechanisms**

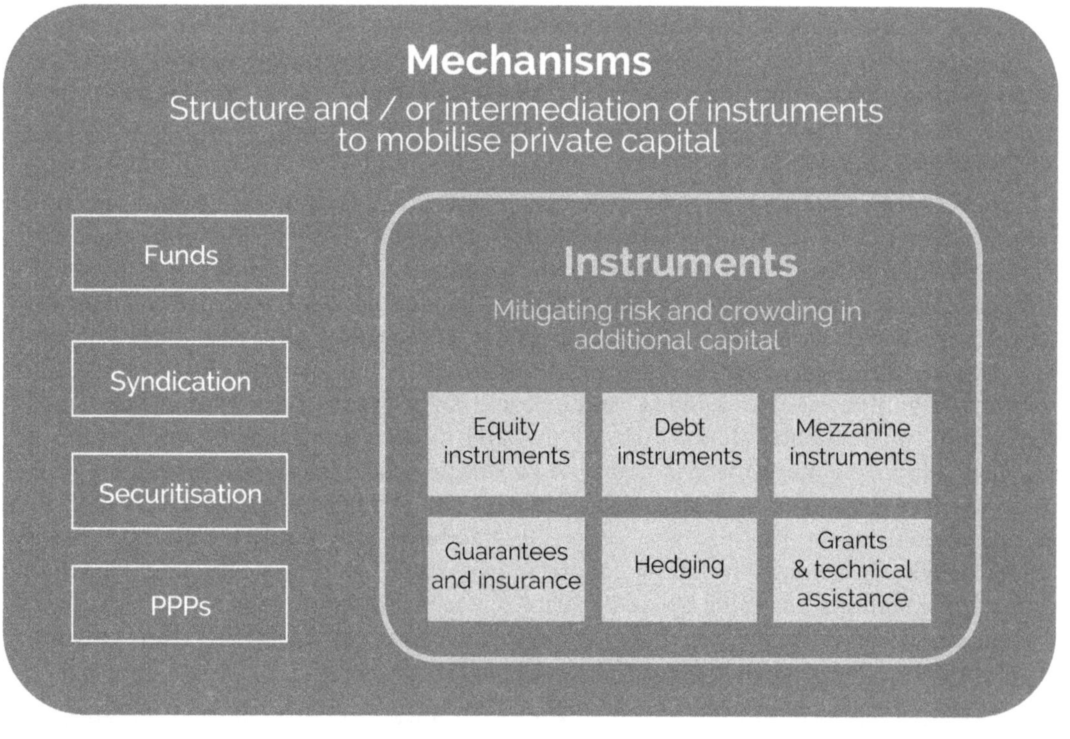

Note: PPPs - Public Private Partnerships
Source: Authors' compilation

A range of blended finance instruments can be used to crowd in commercial capital

Direct investment can incentivise commercial investment

The standard financial instruments in both corporate finance and project finance are debt, equity investments and mezzanine investments that comprise characteristics of both equity and debt (Benn, Sangaré and Hos, 2017).[6] These instruments have the same underlying economics irrespective of the investee or recipient (Box 5.1). Development finance institutions in general routinely use these instruments to finance projects in developing countries, at both market rates and concessional terms, but the instruments also have specific roles in mobilising additional sources of finance (OECD/World Economic Forum, 2015).

When applied at market rates, for example, these instruments can improve the viability of investments and boost investor confidence. Commercial investors then can leverage the due diligence capacity of development finance institutions. The presence of development finance providers also contributes to investor confidence overall, given that they have experience with unexpected events that may affect an investee's ability to adhere to obligations associated with the investment. This benefit is amplified when development finance providers are invested in the riskier parts of the balance sheet — for example, when they are equity shareholders — as this can mobilise commercial mezzanine or debt providers (Benn, Sangaré and Hos, 2017).

The use of direct investment instruments such as equity and debt on concessional terms also can shift the risk-return relationship of a project in order to facilitate commercial investment. By making a project more attractive to commercial investors, concessional finance also can support the investee's financial sustainability. Where the risk-adjusted financing rate is too expensive for companies and projects, concessional finance can bring down the weighted average cost of capital and bridge the gap between demand and supply of capital. An example is the European Commission's concessional equity investment in the Kenyan Lake Turkana Wind Power project via the Africa Infrastructure Trust Fund (EU-AITF to enable financial closure (see case study 2 in Chapter 7). The European Commission engagement re-balanced the risk-return relationship, boosting commercial investor confidence sufficiently to close the project.

Box 5.1 The types of investees that blended finance can target

Companies and financial Institutions. Typically, development finance institutions (DFIs) have invested directly in corporate entities and financial institutions, conducting on-balance-sheet investments without an intermediary. This is an important field of development finance that targets business expansion and social impact. Equity investments and mezzanine or debt funding are the main types of instruments, and provide external capital when no other commercial investor is willing to invest. When these direct investment instruments mobilise additional external commercial finance, they become blended finance instruments.

Projects. Project finance has been used for decades to facilitate investment in large-scale development projects that are complex, time consuming, costly, and often too big for any single sponsor company to finance from its balance sheet. Such projects may have several layers of financing. Sponsors of the project also may establish a legally independent project company that is bankruptcy remote — meaning that investors have limited or no recourse to the project sponsors to recoup their investment in the event of bankruptcy of the project company. Investors base their investment decision on the merits and credit quality of the project and are repaid by cash generated by the project company.

Box 5.1 The types of investees that blended finance can target *(cont.)*

Portfolios of projects. Rather than investing directly in a corporate entity or a project, investors can invest via funds or facilities that pool the resources of different actors. Investors then own equity in or hold notes of the fund or facility. The funds are directed to specific investment segments such as climate finance or small and medium-sized enterprises (SMEs) and may invest in both projects and companies depending on their strategy. Such funds have the flexibility to devise different types of instruments including equity, debt or guarantees, and project support via technical assistance. They may also invest in a portfolio of assets by buying securities backed by a pool of assets; investors are debt holders in such transactions.

Governments. Development mandate investors can work directly with a government to improve its capacity to work with and through the private sector. An example, presented in greater detail in chapter 7, is the KfW intervention to enhance government capacity so that Indian municipalities can access market rate, private investment for local infrastructure projects. However, government lending as such is limited by the debt capacity of developing countries and emerging markets. As noted by the IMF (2016), high levels of debt are associated with lower growth rates.

Sources: Authors' compilation

Credit lines can mobilise commercial finance at multiple levels

Credit lines are a specific form of debt instrument. For example, a credit line can provide a local financial institution (LFI) in a developing country a credit facility that it may draw down (or repay) as needed, with the aim of increasing access to finance for particular borrower segments such as SMEs. A credit line thus facilitates mobilisation of additional commercial capital at the LFI level and at the end-borrower level (Benn, Sangaré and Hos, 2017). An example is a EUR 150 million credit line from the European Investment Bank (EIB) to Banco Santander SA of Mexico, a LFI, in order to address the limited capital and short maturities available for financing local SMEs. This exposure may lead other commercial investors to decide to invest in the LFI; Mexican SMEs and mid-caps also are expected to expand through additional equity sponsoring. Overall the EIB credit line is expected to mobilise more than USD 200 million of commercial finance for development purposes (ibid.).

Bonds enable large-scale commercial investment

Project companies and corporate entities can issue bonds, which are fixed-income securities, to raise long-term debt finance for projects or ongoing operations. Figure 5.2 presents the structure of an infrastructure project bond. Bonds are marketable, liquid assets that address commercial investors' preferences and they are the dominant asset class favoured by pension fund managers in OECD countries (OECD, 2015b). The Elazig Hospital project in Turkey is a recent example of a project bond issuance. In this case, the private project company issued bonds that were backed by credit enhancement from MIGA (from a political risk perspective) and the European Bank for Reconstruction and Development (from a liquidity risk perspective). As a result, the bonds received an investment grade rating that boosted commercial investors' confidence (see case study 8 in Chapter 7).

Figure 5.2 **Visualising project bonds**

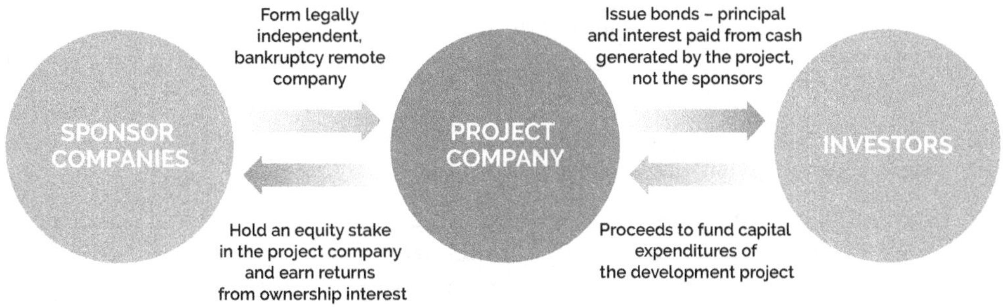

Source: Authors' compilation

Guarantees and insurance provide credit enhancement

Guarantees usually provide protection against either political or commercial risks. A guarantee is an obligation by the guarantor to pay an agreed-upon amount of a loan or other financial instrument in the event that the guaranteed party cannot reimburse the claims or the project otherwise fails (Figure 5.3). When a covered event occurs, the investor has protection from losses as stipulated by the guarantee agreement. Both private and public entities provide guarantees, typically with a premium associated with the investment instrument to which they are attached. Private entities are profit-motivated in their pricing; public entities such as sovereign or multilateral institutions take other objectives into consideration. An example is the commercial risk guarantee provided by the Swedish International Development Cooperation Agency (Sida) for a corporate bond issued by MTN Uganda, a telecom sector company, in order to support the company's plans to expand to rural areas (IMF, 2016b). In addition to supporting an increase in access to telecom services, the guarantee supported the issuance of the first corporate bond in the market, which in turn helped to strengthen the country's financial sector. The guarantee had eight-year tenure and was never claimed. Sida's intervention enabled the company to issue local currency promissory[7] private placements. The bond issuance crowded in mainly institutional investors.

Figure 5.3 **Visualising guarantees**

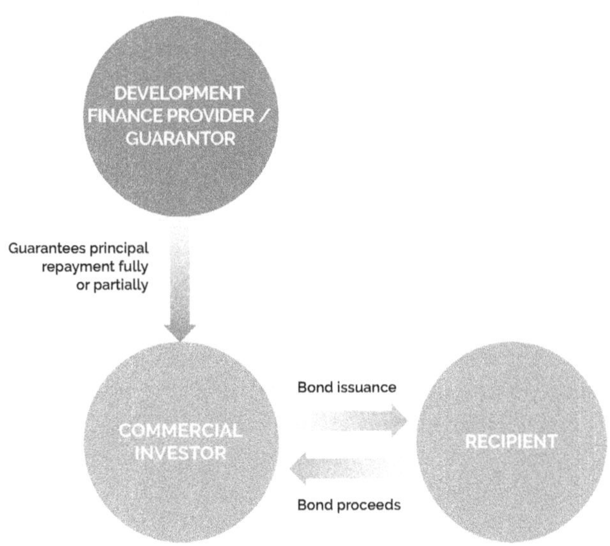

Source: Authors' compilation

Like guarantees, insurance can reduce specific types of risk in transactions by transferring the risk of loss to the provider for a predefined premium. It is available to cover mainly political risks as well as technical/physical risk in the infrastructure landscape (OECD, 2015a; OECD, 2015b). Insurance is seen to be effective for infrastructure overall and has been applied to mitigate climate risk.

Grants and technical assistance strengthen project capacity

Grants and technical assistance are deployed when development impact needs to be supported by specific project capacity. Grants are a direct monetary contribution to a project or fund without the expectation of a repayment in the future. Grants and technical assistance have the capacity to mobilise commercial investment. Technical assistance can constitute a broad range of activities. Within blended finance, development finance providers usually contribute technical assistance in the project preparation phase to support activities such as feasibility studies, policy advice, capacity building and awareness raising that contribute to the overall success of a project and so boost investor confidence. Technical assistance also can take the form of monetary contributions, when multilateral development banks, other development banks or development finance institutions provide the financing for technical assistance.

Facilitating commercial, local currency investment

Development projects often generate cash flow and returns in local currency, for example in the context of infrastructure investment (OECD, 2015a; OECD, 2015b). It may be appealing to issue a bond or receive a loan to fund a development project or local enterprise in a major currency like the US dollar, euro or Japanese yen, given that they have lower yields and longer terms than instruments in local currency. However, this can place too much foreign exchange risk on the project or entity because the potential depreciation of the local currency can increase financing costs, when the revenue is generated in local currency.

Local currency financing also often requires hedging against foreign exchange risk to attract adequate investment. For example, a bank might lend funds to a project in local currency and then enter into a cross-currency swap to protect against changes in currency exchange rates. The premium attached to the instrument (or derivative) frequently is quite expensive since many emerging market currencies are so vulnerable to exchange rate volatility. Moreover not all currencies can be hedged on private markets. Therefore, multilateral organisations and currency exchange funds capitalised by donor countries offer more cost-effective options to reduce the cost of capital for the intended development purpose. One example is The Currency Exchange Fund (TCX), which is funded by governments and private investors. It has hedged more than USD 4 billion in 54 currencies, thereby providing long-term local currency in emerging countries without alternative hedging mechanisms and without access to hard currencies such as US dollars and euros (TCX, 2017a).

How TCX works can be seen in the case of M-Kopa, a Kenya-based company that provides decentralised solar solutions in Kenya, Tanzania and Uganda (OECD, 2017). A private fund manager, ResponsAbility Investments, disbursed a local currency-indexed loan to M-Kopa. The company, using local banks, immediately transferred this USD loan into local currency. When the loan repayment is due, the borrower exchanges the same amount it initially received in local currency and repays in US dollars. As the USD amount will not be the same as the initial loan payment due to exchange rate volatility, the hedging partner TCX steps in and provides the differential to the lender (see Figure 5.4).

Figure 5.4 **How a local currency-indexed loan works**

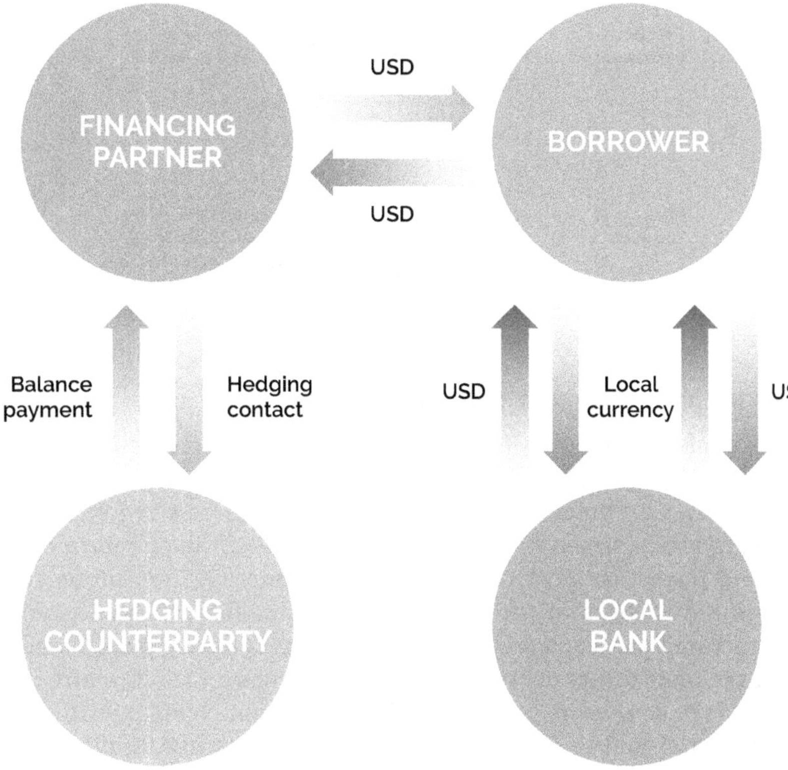

Source: TCX (2017b), «*M-Kopa connects low income homes to affordable solar energy – fast*», http://climatefinancelab.org/wp-content/uploads/2017/03/M-Kopa-Description.pdf (accessed 13 December 2017).

Blended finance mechanisms are used to structure instruments and unlock commercial capital

Securitisation can connect institutional investors with a portfolio of developmental projects

Securitisation offers corporations, banks, state-owned enterprises and governments the ability to utilise existing assets on their balance sheets to raise capital and free their balance sheets. Assets that are ideal for securitisation provide a stable and predictable future cash flow and commonly include mortgages, loans, accounts receivables and leases, among others. This approach has constraints in lower income countries that can include the need to establish a legal/regulatory framework, upfront costs, shallow local capital markets and small portfolio sizes. Figure 5.5 illustrates the general mechanics of securitisation by which an originator transfers ownership of assets on its balance sheet to raise capital. In the development finance context, the securitisation of loans provided by financial institutions can enable an influx of funds that provide necessary capital to finance new loans for entrepreneurs (see case study 8 in Chapter 7).

Figure 5.5 **Visualising securitisation**

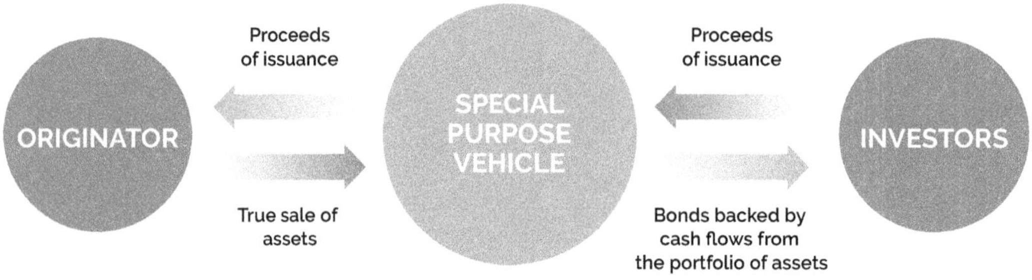

Source: Authors' compilation

Funds and facilities pool development and commercial finance

Collective investment vehicles (CIVs) or funds are legal entities in which different actors pool their resources to subsequently own equity. The funds are directed to specific investment segments, e.g. climate finance or small and medium-sized enterprises, and so use different types of instruments. These include investment in the form of equity, debt or guarantees and project support via technical assistance. A CIV can be structured so that all investors are exposed to the same risk-return profile (flat structure) or its cash flows can be structured in such a way that some investors have subordinated repayment claims compared to more senior debt. Box 5.2 discusses such a cash flow structure through subordination. Both structures may mobilise additional commercial investment at the fund level by shifting the risk and/or the return profile. When collective funds are invested into projects and/or companies, further commercial finance may be mobilised at the project level (see Chapters 6 and 7).

Box 5.2 **Subordination as a tool to mobilise commercial investment**

Subordination is an effective mechanism to create a security that appeals to private investors. The structure shields investors from losses incurred by a commercial entity or portfolio of assets.[8] In the case of *companies*, subordinated debt (which resembles mezzanine finance) as well as junior equity can absorb higher risks and take first losses compared to senior debt and common equity holders, respectively. In the case of *a portfolio of assets*, subordination provides credit enhancement by creating multiple tranches (tranching) with different levels of seniority as relate to the cash flows generated by the special purpose vehicle (SPV) to pay the notes, starting with the most senior notes and only repaying subordinated tranches thereafter. This is the so-called "waterfall structure" (Figure 5.6). In the blended finance context, development finance providers usually hold the first loss piece in order to provide cushion to more senior, commercial investors. An alternative form of credit enhancement in a securitised transaction for development finance providers to provide guarantees on the senior and/or mezzanine tranche of a subordinated transaction rather than taking the first loss positions. The European Investment Bank, for example, offers this kind of guarantee for tranches of credit quality of a minimum rating equivalent to BB/Ba2.

Box 5.2 **Subordination as a tool to mobilise commercial investment** *(cont.)*

Figure 5.6 **Visualising subordination**

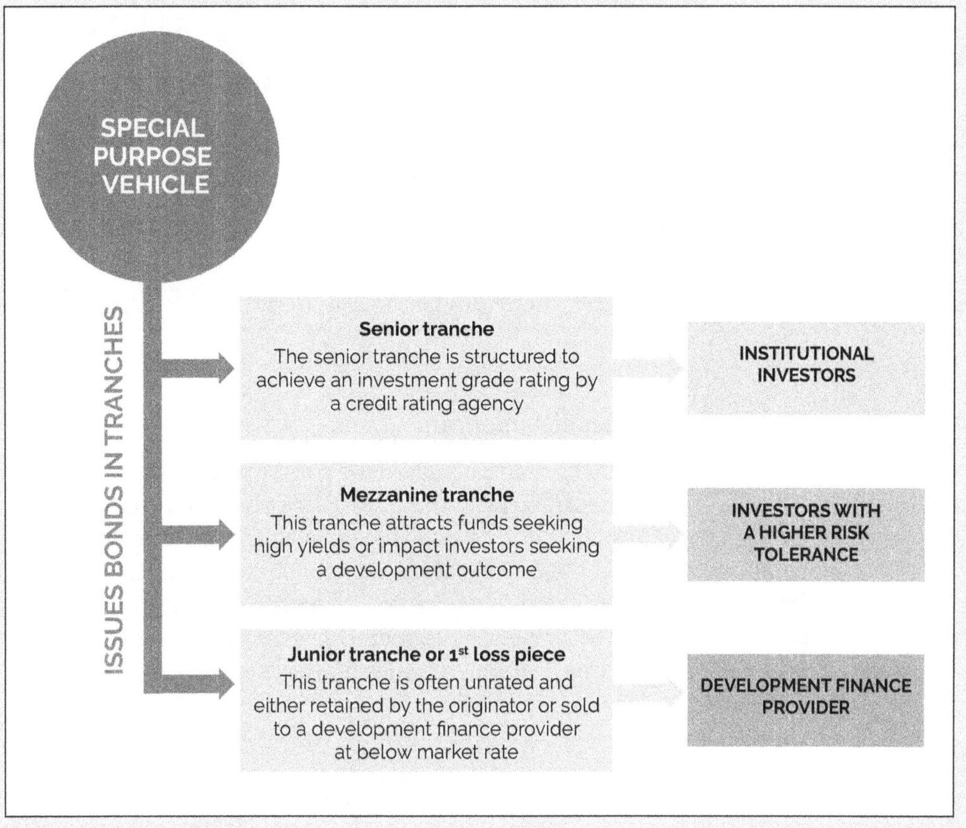

Source: Authors' compilation

Syndicated loans mobilise commercial investment

Syndications mobilise commercial investment by positively strengthening investor confidence in projects or companies and by reducing transaction costs and hence investment barriers for commercial investors. Syndicated loans are provided by a group of lenders, typically a mix from public and private sectors (Bielenberg et al., 2016). Multilateral development banks (MDBs) usually take the role of lead arrangers with the private sector engaging as a B-loan provider (see Figure 5.7). The division of the loan amount leads to risk diversification. The due diligence capabilities and reputation of the public sector arrangers (i.e. the MDBs) boost investor confidence[9] and reduce transaction costs. An example of syndication is the EBRD-arranged loan of USD 100 million for a structured working capital facility with Nibulon SA, a Ukrainian integrated grain/oilseeds exporter and producer. In addition to EBRD's own funds, this mobilised USD 75 million in B loans from ABN Amro, BNP Paribas, Credit Agricole, ING Bank and Rabobank (EBRD, 2017).[10]

Figure 5.7 **Visualising loan syndication**

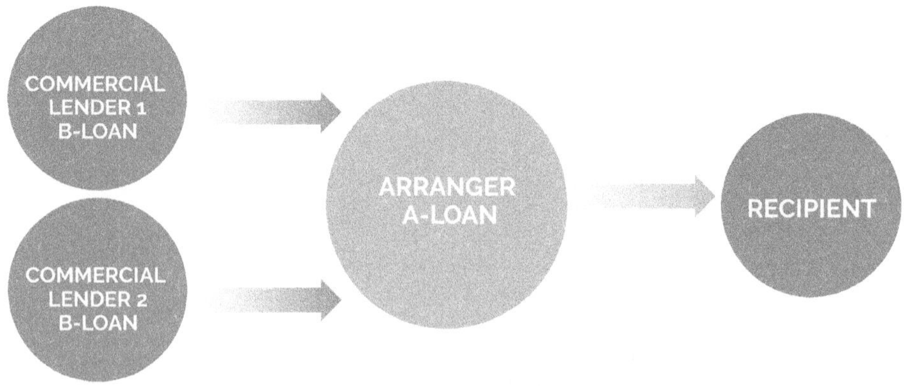

Source: Authors' compilation

Public-private partnerships and blended finance

Public-private partnerships (PPPs) combine blending instruments and as such can constitute a mechanism to crowd in commercial finance. A public-private partnership is defined as a co-operation between a government and private partners in which the latter provide public services for a financial return (OECD, 2008). PPPs thus are collaborations between public and private entities in which risks, returns and financing are negotiated among the partners. As such, PPPs are an institutionalised form of blended finance. However, the role of PPPs in blended finance needs further investigation, given the specificities of this arrangement.

OECD analyses of finance mobilised through selected instruments provides important insights

In order to enrich the picture of official development finance (ODF) flows captured in the OECD Creditor Reporting System (CRS), the OECD has engaged in measuring the amounts mobilised from the private sector by ODF interventions (see Chapter 7 for more details). Methodologies have been developed to track amounts mobilised for selected instruments; these have been piloted among development finance providers through surveys. The results from this exercise provide some insights into the potential of different instruments to mobilise private finance.

In total, USD 81.1 billion were mobilised from the private sector by ODF interventions in 2012-15 through five instruments: guarantees, shares in collective investment vehicles, syndicated loans, direct investment in companies (i.e. equity), and credit lines (Benn, Sangaré and Hos, 2017). This conclusion is based on data collected from 35 bilateral and multilateral institutions working for development; the sample did not include foundations. The majority of financing was mobilised in middle-income countries, with 43% in upper middle-income countries (UMICs) and 34% in lower middle-income countries (LMICs). The remainder of the financing was either mobilised in lower income countries and least developed countries (LDCs), or was unallocated by income group. In terms of regions, Africa accounted for 30% of finance mobilisation followed by Asia with 26%.

Of the different instruments, guarantees were found to have mobilised the largest share of finance across the four years (USD 35.9 billion), followed by syndicated loans (USD 15.8 billion) and credit lines (USD 15.2 billion). Shares in CIVs and direct investment in companies mobilised USD 9.5 billion and USD 4.7 billion, respectively. Guarantees are seen to be driving mobilisation in Africa and Asia and to be the main instrument used to mobilise financing in low-income countries and LDCs. Credit lines and syndicated loans are associated with mobilisation most significantly in Europe and America, respectively. Both these instruments mobilise capital in middle-income countries, although UMICs have a larger share than LMICs (Figure 5.8).

Figure 5.8 **Amounts mobilised per instrument, by income group, USD million**

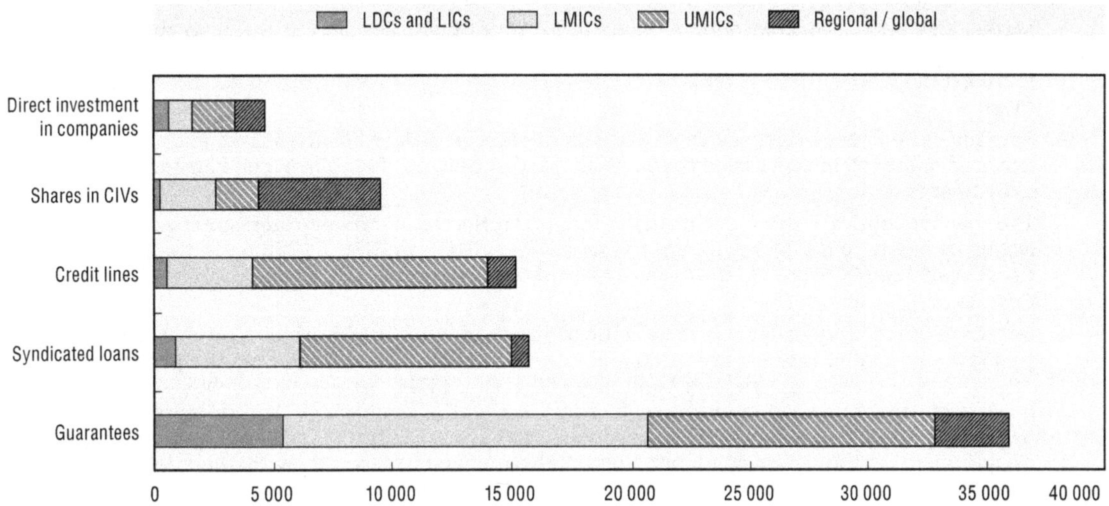

Source: Benn, Sangaré and Hos (2017), "Amounts mobilised from the private sector by Official Development Finance interventions", http://dx.doi.org/10.1787/8135abde-en.

StatLink http://dx.doi.org/10.1787/888933648328

Mobilisation is most pronounced in the banking and financial services sector, reflecting the European Investment Bank's dominance in using credit lines to mobilise private finance (Figure 5.9). In the four-year period 2012-15, USD 27.1 billion were mobilised in the financial sector and USD 20 billion in the energy sector. The health sector accounts for just USD 2 billion of amounts mobilised from the private sector.

Figure 5.9 **Amounts mobilised per instrument, by sector**

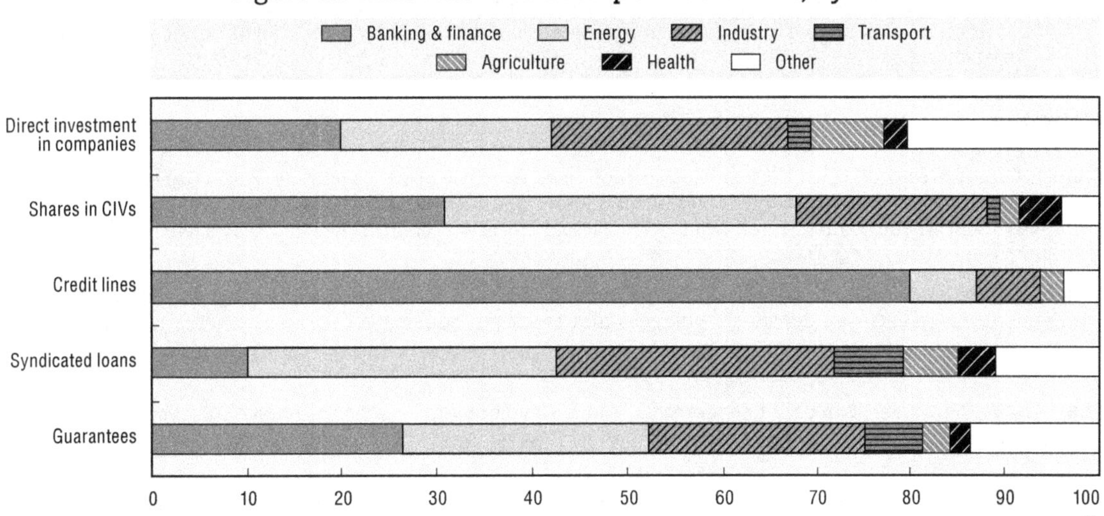

Source: Benn, Sangaré and Hos (2017), "Amounts mobilised from the private sector by Official Development Finance interventions", http://dx.doi.org/10.1787/8135abde-en.

StatLink http://dx.doi.org/10.1787/888933648195

Notes

1. In the aftermath of the financial crisis, for example, competition is emerging among debt providers in the infrastructure sector in creditworthy and stable economies such as those in Europe. As a result, decreasing loan margins undermine profitability of infrastructure investments in Europe. See Moody's (2015).
2. Liquidity risk, for example, is related to exit options available to investors (i.e. that a share in a company cannot be sold) or general financing availability to a project or company.
3. Market risk adds a macroeconomic angle to an investment decision. It refers to the overall economic situation in the country or context where the investment is domiciled, which may manifest in volatile inflation rates or, in the case of a foreign investment, in volatile exchange rates.
4. Singling out currency risks out from other macroeconomic and business risks allows a more nuanced approach in addressing them. A further discussion is found in 5.3 on blended finance instruments.
5. The need for political risk mitigation instruments is reflected in the steep increase of guarantees issued by MIGA, to USD 4.3 billion in the fiscal year 2016 from USD 2.8 billion in the previous fiscal year. See MIGA (2016), *MIGA Annual Report 2016*, www.miga.org/Lists/Feature%20Stories/CustomDisp.aspx?ID=113.
6. Debt instruments typically require periodic payment of interest and principal at maturity, the periodic payment of interest and principal in an amortizing bond, or simply the principal at maturity in case of a zero coupon bond. See OECD DAC (2016). Investors in debt instruments have stronger rights than equity investors in the event of bankruptcy. Equity represents an ownership interest in a company. Equity investors have an ability to influence and direct the management of the company, depending on the ownership interest, with their returns on investment based on the company's success in growing or enhancing profitability. Ownership constitutes a claim on the residual value of the company after all creditors are reimbursed. Mezzanine instruments can take the form of subordinated debt or preferred equity. The claims of subordinated debt holders are inferior to claims of senior debt holders, whereas those of preferred equity holders are superior to common equity holders.
7. For a description of the Sida guarantee, see www.sida.se/contentassets/01c9a3938ab44047809981abd2daaff2/ce49f12a-74e9-47a4-807a-ea5d0a1899dd.pdf.
8. The subordination concept also is used at the fund level, e.g. junior/subordinated capital is applied to crowd in capital in structured or layered funds (see Chapter 6).
9. An underlying assumption is that official investment can help to reduce both political and business risk by circumventing problems related to government intervention or creditworthiness during the lifecycle of the outstanding exposure. The latter for instance would be reflected in higher flexibility in regards to repayments, etc.
10. EBRD lists UniCredit Group, Raiffeisen Bank International and ING Group as its three main commercial B loan partners in loan syndications arranged by the International Financial Institution.

References

Benn, J., C. Sangaré and T. Hos (2017), "Amounts mobilised from the private sector by Official Development Finance interventions: Guarantees, syndicated loans, shares in collective investment vehicles, direct investment in companies, credit lines", *OECD Development Co-operation Working Papers*, No. 36, OECD Publishing, Paris, http://dx.doi.org/10.1787/8135abde-en.

Bielenberg, A. et al. (2016), *Financing Change: How to Mobilize Private-Sector Financing for Sustainable Infrastructure*, McKinsey Centre for Business and Environment, http://newclimateeconomy.report/workingpapers/wp-content/uploads/sites/5/2016/04/Financing_change_How_to_mobilize_private-sector_financing_for_sustainable-_infrastructure.pdf.

EBRD (2017), "European Bank for Reconstruction and Development: Partner of choice", European Bank for Reconstruction and Development, www.ebrd.com/documents/financial-institutions/loan-syndications-update-on-activities.pdf.

IMF (2016a), "Debt: Use it Wisely", *Fiscal Monitor*, October 2016, International Monetary Fund, Washington, DC www.imf.org/en/Publications/FM/Issues/2016/12/31/Debt-Use-it-Wisely.

IMF (2016b), "Development of local currency bond markets: Overview of recent developments and key themes", Staff Note for the G20 IFAWG, Seoul, 20 June 2016, International Monetary Fund, Washington, DC, www.imf.org/external/np/g20/pdf/2016/121416.pdf.

MIGA (2016), *MIGA Annual Report 2016: Insuring Investments, Ensuring Opportunities*, Multilateral Investment Guarantee Agency, World Bank Group, Washington, DC, www.miga.org/Lists/Feature%20Stories/CustomDisp.aspx?ID=113.

Moody's (2015), "A wave of capital for infrastructure, but mismatched with investment opportunities", press release, 28 May 2015, Moody's Investor Services, London, , www.moodys.com/research/Moodys-Despite-wave-of-infrastructure-capital-investment-opportunities-remain-scarce--PR_326366.

OECD (2017), *Investing in Climate, Investing in Growth*, OECD Publishing, Paris. http://dx.doi.org/10.1787/9789264273528-en.

OECD (2015a), *Infrastructure Financing Instruments and Incentives*, OECD Publishing, Paris, www.oecd.org/finance/private-pensions/Infrastructure-Financing-Instruments-and-Incentives.pdf.

OECD (2015b), Mapping Channels to Mobilise Institutional Investment in Sustainable Energy, Green Finance and Investment, OECD Publishing, Paris, www.oecd-ilibrary.org/environment/mapping-channels-to-mobilise-institutional-investment-in-sustainable-energy_9789264224582-en.

OECD (2008), *Public-Private Partnerships: In Pursuit of Risk Sharing and Value for Money*, OECD Publishing, Paris, http://dx.doi.org/10.1787/9789264046733-en.

OECD DAC (2016), "Converged statistical reporting directives for the Creditor Reporting System (CRS) and the annual DAC questionnaire - Addendum 1, Annexes - modules A, B, and C", OECD Publishing, Paris, www.oecd.org/dac/stats/DCD-DAC(2016)3-ADD1-FINAL-ENG.pdf.

OECD/World Bank Group (2015), *Risk and Return Characteristics of Infrastructure Investment in Low Income Countries*, OECD/World Bank Group, Paris/Washington, DC, www.oecd.org/g20/topics/development/Report-on-Risk-and-Return-Characteristics-of-Infrastructure-Investment-in-Low-Income-Countries.pdf.ß

OECD/World Economic Forum (2015), *Blended Finance Vol. 1: A Primer for Development Finance and Philanthropic Funders*, ReDesigning Development Finance Initiative, OECD/World Economic Forum, Paris/Cologny, Switzerland, , www3.weforum.org/docs/WEF_Blended_Finance_A_Primer_Development_Finance_Philanthropic_Funders_report_2015.pdf.

TCX (2017a), "*About the Fund*", The Currency Exchange websites, https://www.tcxfund.com/about-the-fund/ (accessed 13 December 2017).

TCX (2017b), "*M-Kopa connects low income homes to affordable solar energy – fast*", http://climatefinancelab.org/wp-content/uploads/2017/03/M-Kopa-Description.pdf (accessed 13 December 2017)

PART II
Insights from blended finance in practice

Chapter 6

Pooling finance through blended finance facilities and funds

Collective investment or pooled vehicles such as facilities and funds are prominent in the blended finance landscape. This chapter presents results from OECD and Association of European Development Finance Institutions (EDFI) surveys of blended finance funds and facilities carried out in 2015 and 2017. It explores the increasing interest in donor government facilities to pool donor financing for blended finance, highlighting the main trends in the development of these facilities. It also explores blended finance funds that bring together development and commercial investors to invest in projects in developing countries. The chapter also considers to what extent facilities and funds are addressing the SDGs and initial lessons learned.

HIGHLIGHTS

Recent years have seen an increasing interest in facilities that pool donor government financing towards blending. These facilities do not engage private investors directly but rather provide the finance that development banks and other intermediaries can use to crowd in commercial investors. Such facilities are seen to target a range of global issues, geographies and sectors.

In contrast to facilities, blended finance funds bring together development and commercial investors to achieve development and commercial objectives. They also can crowd in private investment within the fund itself or further downstream at the transaction level. Structured funds provide an opportunity for development finance to be used in a first-loss tranche to attract additional investors. Impact funds bring investors together to invest in projects with the aim of generating both financial and developmental returns.

All funds and facilities target the SDGs at a broad level, but some SDGs are targeted more than others. Climate is emerging as a key area for blended finance operations.

Blended finance funds are well suited to attracting additional commercial investors, but efforts are needed to increase private participation in funds and to provide financing in local currency.

Key facts

- Between 2000 and 2016, a total of 167 facilities that engage in blending were launched, with a combined size as measured by commitments of approximately USD 31 billion
- MDBs and DFIs are the main intermediaries managing blended finance facilities, while private asset managers play a greater role in managing blended finance funds
- More than 50% of blended finance funds and facilities in the survey sample targeted eight SDGs: 1 (no poverty), 6 (clean water and sanitation), 7 (affordable and clean energy), 8 (decent work and economic growth), 9 (industry, innovation and infrastructure), 11 (sustainable cities and communities), 13 (climate action), and 17 (partnerships for the goals)

Introduction

Blended finance transactions typically involve a mix of stakeholders and a combination of instruments structured so to crowd in commercial investment for development (Chapter 5). Of the various mechanisms used, collective investment or pooled vehicles, such as facilities and funds, predominate in the blended finance landscape. A survey undertaken through the ReDesigning Development Finance Initiative (OECD/World Economic Forum, 2016) finds pooled vehicles to be a primary channel for blended finance flows. Similarly, a database of blended finance transactions collected by Convergence (2017) shows that 74% of these transactions are facilities and funds and that they account for 64% of mobilised capital (Convergence, 2017). This chapter presents results from OECD and the Association of European Development Finance Institutions (EDFI) surveys of blended finance funds and facilities carried out in 2015 and 2017. It outlines the main types of pooled finance mechanisms in use for blended finance, highlights trends and presents insights on the use of these mechanisms for future blending.

Pooled vehicles: Flagship mechanisms for blended finance

The unique features of pooled vehicles explain in part their prominence among blended finance channels. These include reduced transaction costs from economies of scale and a structure that fosters innovation and is suited to target specific issues and/or geographic areas — features that are particularly useful to blended finance. Facilities and funds, both used for pooling capital for development objectives are anchored in different rationales (Annex B). A facility is an earmarked allocation of public development resources (sometimes including support from philanthropies), which can invest in development projects through a range of instruments including by purchasing shares in collective vehicles such as funds. There is no blending as such within facilities; rather facilities provide finance that supports blending further downstream at the fund or project level. In contrast, funds are pools of private or public-private capital in which blending also can occur at the capital structure level.

Both mechanisms have advantages for development finance providers and private sector actors. For example, contributing to a facility allows bilateral actors to work where their presence is limited; raise the profile and visibility of specific development issues for which investments are suboptimal; and foster increased co-ordination and knowledge exchange. At the same time, investing in a fund offers private investors a number of benefits, such as mitigating portfolio risk via diversification and the possibility to pilot and learn from innovative approaches in a contained environment.

While several recent efforts have attempted to map the blended finance market, none has managed to capture the entirety of activities under way at the level of development finance providers, facilities, funds and other instruments, and projects (Chapter 8). Nevertheless, pooled financing mechanisms are gaining traction among development finance providers, providing the impetus for a new OECD survey on blended finance funds and facilities that built on an earlier, EDFI-commissioned survey (Box 6.1). Annex B presents the methodology of the 2017 OECD survey in greater detail.

Box 6.1 OECD and EDFI surveys of blended finance funds and facilities

The results presented in this chapter are drawn from two surveys on blended finance funds and facilities: an OECD survey carried out in 2017 that builds on the approach and dataset developed by the Association of European Development Finance Institutions (EDFI) in a 2015 survey. The new OECD survey distinguishes between funds and facilities, extends the scope to all Development Assistance Committee (DAC) members, and includes new types of funds such as private equity funds. The 2015 EDFI survey considered 140 funds and facilities in total. The 2017 OECD survey supplemented the EDFI sample and considered 167 facilities and 189 funds, or a total of 356 entities. Desk research was conducted to map these entities and determine their size and shareholders. A targeted questionnaire also was carried out of a subset of facility and fund managers on additional aspects; responses were received from 43 facilities (representing USD 20.3 billion in commitments) and 31 funds (representing USD 9.3 billion in assets under management). The questionnaire covered aspects such as financial, operational and developmental performance; sectoral and geographical coverage; share of portfolio in local currency; Sustainable Development Goal focus; instruments used; shareholding structure, governance and management, strategy; marketing; and exit routes, among others.

Annex B provides more detail on the survey sample and methodology.

Facilities pool development finance towards blending

Facilities are important mechanisms in the context of development finance. The Independent Evaluation Group of the World Bank noted in a 2011 report that, "donor countries generally allocate money to [facilities] from within a fixed aid budget in order to earmark and pool aid for particular countries or issues, or to foster innovations in aid of new issues" (IEG, 2011). In this sense, putting a facility in place can help enable the process of mobilising non-traditional sources of capital and testing new financing approaches that differ from traditional bilateral and multilateral programmes. Through a facility, governments have the ability to influence the allocation of funds to specific issues by development finance institutions (DFIs) and multilateral development banks (MDBs). This fills a gap in the multilateral system, providing financing to issues not covered by these institutions' core budgets.

Facilities can be used to channel financing to blended finance instruments and mechanisms. Such blended finance facilities differ from other donor facilities in their intention to support the mobilisation of private investment.[1] Thus blended finance facilities do not pool public and private capital; rather they provide development capital to be spent with the purpose of crowding in additional private finance further downstream, such as within the context of a project or company. Some examples of issues covered by specific blended finance facilities include climate change mitigation and adaptation (e.g. the Canadian Climate Fund for the Private Sector in Asia II and the United Kingdom's Green Africa Power); development of small businesses (World Bank and the IFC joint Middle East and North Africa small and medium-sized enterprises; employment (IFC Women Entrepreneurs Opportunity Facility); and infrastructure development (the World Bank Global Infrastructure Facility).

Increasing interest in blended finance facilities among development finance providers

Facilities are a popular choice for development finance providers when engaging in blending, as demonstrated by the upsurge in blended finance facilities set up in the last decade. Between 2000 and 2016, a total of 167 facilities that engage in blending were launched, with a combined size as measured by commitments of approximately USD 31 billion.[2] The number of blended finance facilities launched per year increased significantly over this period (Figure 6.1). Peaks occurred in 2012, when the European Union (EU) set up a number of blending facilities including the Caribbean Investment Facility and the Investment Facility for the Pacific, and in 2014 with the establishment of facilities managed by the World Bank, United States Agency for International Development (USAID) and the European Investment Bank (EIB). Another sign of rising interest is that between 2009 and 2016, three times more new blended finance facilities were launched every year than between 2000 and 2008.[3]

Figure 6.1 **Number of facilities that engage in blending launched, 2000 to 2016**

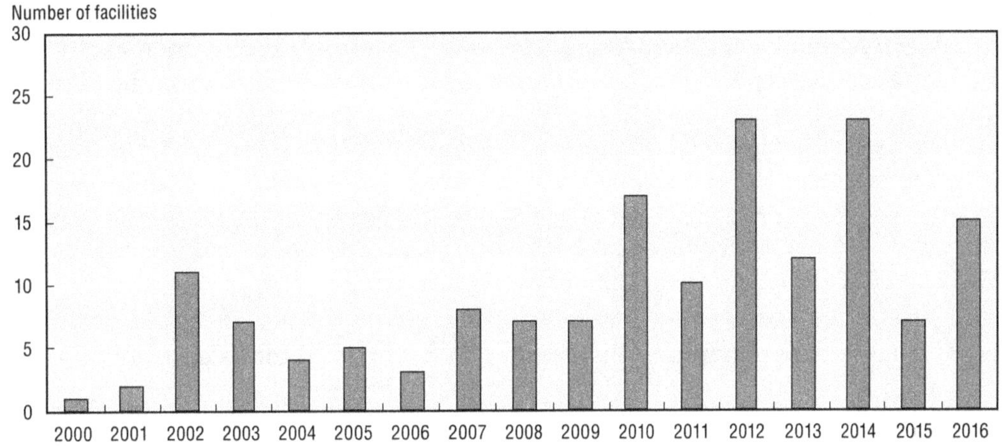

Source: OECD 2017 survey on blended finance funds and facilities (see Annex B); 2015 EDFI survey on blended finance funds and facilities (unpublished)

StatLink http://dx.doi.org/10.1787/888933648176

A granular picture emerges from responses to the 2017 OECD survey from 43 facilities that together account for USD 20 billion in total contributions in 2016. It shows that 86% of capital and contributions came from governments and aid agencies; 12% from MDBs and DFIs; and 2% from foundations. Among governments, the main providers of finance are, in alphabetical order, are the EU, France, Germany, the Netherlands, Sweden and the United Kingdom.

While MDBs and DFIs manage most facilities, some are also managed by donor governments or aid agencies. Examples of this include the EU blending facilities, which the European Commission manages directly, and USAID Power Africa programme. The OECD survey finds the top five facility managers are the IFC (managing 21 facilities), the European Commission (15), the EIB (7), the Asian Development Bank (7), and the African Development Bank (5). Single donor facilities are often managed by bilateral DFIs. For example, the Netherlands Development Finance Company (FMO) manages the Access to Energy Fund on behalf of the government of Netherlands. Some facilities (7%) are also managed by private sector managers. This is the case especially for challenge funds and technical assistance facilities that are attached to an investment fund. For instance, the Responsible and Accountable Garments Sector (RAGS) Challenge Fund is managed by the consulting firm Maxwell Stamp PLC.

Facilities are seen to provide one or more instruments such as grants, loans, equity and guarantees well as technical assistance. For facilities that provide loans or equity, it is unclear how allocation or treatment of reflows occurs at the end of its life. Some donors explicitly stipulate that facility capital should be evergreen and recycled in projects, meaning that the facility can continue its activity for many years. While most of the facilities target private sector projects or recipients, and especially private financial institutions, some facilities also target public financial institutions and other actors.

Blended finance facilities target global issues and many sectors

Almost half of the total commitments to blended finance facilities, amounting to USD 10 billion, went to facilities that are global and target specific issues such as climate change, food security, etc. across several or all continents (Figure 6.2). Facilities targeting Africa and Asia as priority regions received most of the remaining commitments, which respectively accounted for 29% and 15% of total commitments. In terms of geographic priorities, the 2017 OECD survey shows that facilities focusing on a specific geographic area tend to target many sectors such as, inter alia, energy, transport, communications, water and sanitation, banking and financial services, education, and agriculture. For instance, the EU-managed Investment Facility for Central Asia (IFCA) targets energy, transport, communications, agriculture, and environmental protection sectors.[4] On the other hand, facilities with a mandate to tackle a specific issue across several continents are seen to focus on a few sectors. For instance, the IFC-Canada Climate Change Program focuses specifically on energy, the Global Agriculture and Food Security Facility on agriculture, and the Global SME Finance Facility on banking and financial services.[5]

Figure 6.2 **Geographic distribution of facilities, % total contributions**

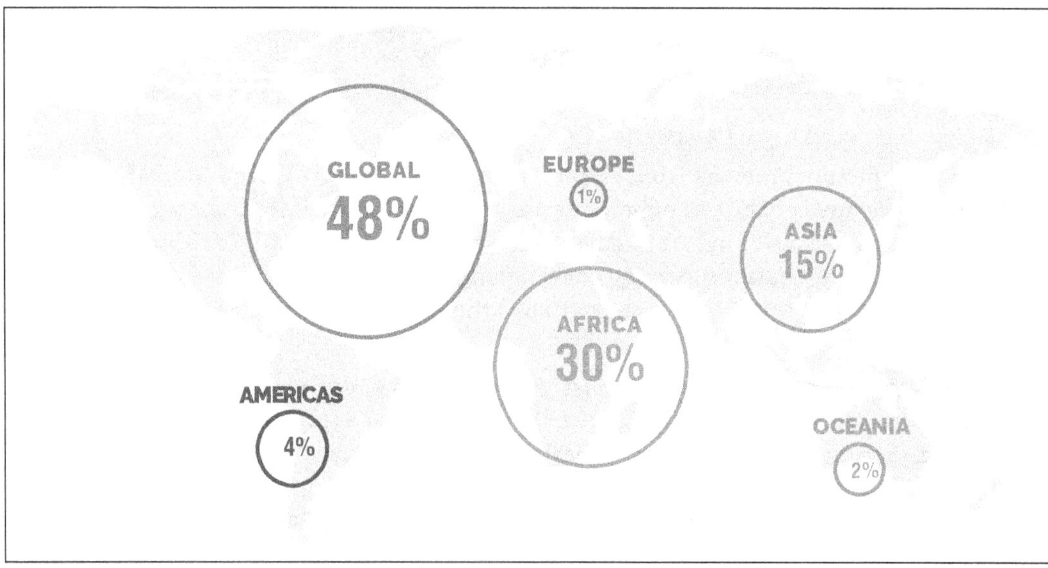

Notes: This figure is based on information received from 42 out of 43 facilities. The percentages were computed by aggregating the total contributions for each facility that identified a certain region as a priority region. When the facilities identified three or more regions, their total contributions were allocated to "global". Likewise, when their priority regions included only Asia and Africa, half of each facility's assets under management were allocated to each continent.

Sources: OECD 2017 survey on blended finance funds and facilities (see Annex B)

Funds crowd in commercial investment at several levels

A fund is a financial vehicle that enables investors to pool their capital together and jointly invest in projects and companies[6] (Chapter 5). They offer a number of advantages: profit-sharing opportunity for investors, access to a wide number of transactions, reduced transaction costs through economies of scale, and focus on a specific investment strategy in terms of geography or sector (interviews in connection with the OECD 2017 survey on blended finance funds and facilities). Funds are required to adhere to precise investment eligibility criteria and governance rules in terms of manager-investor communication, reporting and management. For development finance providers, funds are a testing ground for new approaches to scale up investment for important development outcomes; they work "at the nexus of blended finance and impact investing" (Koenig and Jackson, 2016). Funds offer development finance providers a chance to mobilise capital at multiple levels. Development finance actors can blend their capital with investors in the capital structure of the fund or the fund itself can be used to support blended finance transactions at the project level and crowd in investors for particular projects.

Funds can offer a way to combine commercial and development objectives

Funds can be structured in two ways, either in a flat structure where capital is repaid and returns are allocated equally to all investors or in a layered structure where risks and returns are allocated differently across investors. The layered structure allows development finance providers to take more risk and/or a smaller share of the returns, therefore attracting private investment to the fund. Development finance providers use junior/subordinated capital (longer maturity, concessional terms: lower yield, dividend or return) as their main instrument to crowd in capital in both structured and layered funds.

Research conducted as part of OECD and EDFI surveys found at least 189 funds were launched between 2000 and 2016 that engage in blended finance in some form. This may well be an underestimation as it does not reflect the gamut of private equity funds in which DFIs invest and which also may be considered to engage in blending, depending on whether they mobilise additional commercial capital.[7] According to responses to the 2017 OECD survey from 31 funds, with USD 9.5 billion in total assets under management, structured, or layered, funds account for a greater share of assets under management. In these funds, development-driven shareholders provide some kind of risk mitigation or profit enhancement for more commercial shareholders. In addition, structured funds tend to be larger in size (an average of USD 500 million in the survey sample) and provide guarantees, debt and equity. Most funds responding to the survey also can be classified as debt or guarantee structured funds. Flat funds, on the other hand, are smaller in size (an average of USD 150 million) and provide primarily equity.

Interviews conducted during the 2017 OECD survey reveal additional insights about the two types of funds. While funds can cover a range of risk/return profiles, structured funds may have more potential to attract institutional investors (among other private investors) because they offer a suitable return rate for commercial investors and an investment-grade profile due to low volatility, significant vehicle sizes and the potentially higher liquidity of their assets.[8] On the other hand, flat funds — e.g. seed capital, social impact funds, growth equity funds, infrastructure equity funds, etc. — can provide bespoke long-term financing that is appropriate for illiquid assets such as infrastructure and for industrial capacity investment where capital market flows are insufficient. Flat funds usually attract DFIs, impact investors, philanthropies and high net worth individuals. Concessional finance from donor governments and aid agencies can also provide support for flat funds. This finance may take the form of grants, technical assistance or concessional loans to support the fund's fundraising and operations rather than come from within the fund's capital structure, as is the case in layered/structured funds (Box 6.2).

The OECD survey responses show that the geographic targets of blended finance funds resemble that of blended finance facilities. Africa and Asia are the main recipients, with 27% and 20% respectively of total commitments. The remaining 44% of commitments are directed to funds supporting projects around the world. Like blended finance facilities, global funds target specific sectors. The Global Energy Efficiency and Renewable Energy Fund (GEEREF) exclusively targets the energy sector, for example, and the MicroBuild Fund specifically targets the water and sanitation sector. Several funds that focus on a particular geographic area also tend to focus on a range of sectors. An example is the German Investment Corporation (DEG) up-scaling programme for SMEs, which focuses solely on Africa but targets the energy, communications, banking and financial services, health, and agriculture sectors. Unlike facilities, several funds aim to focus on a specific sector in a particular region (e.g. Microfinance Initiative for Asia, Regional MSME Investment Fund for Sub-Saharan Africa and Armstrong South East Asia Clean Energy Fund).

Box 6.2 **IPDEV 2: An innovative equity sponsor in Africa**

IPDEV 2 is an investment company managed by Investisseurs & Partenaires (I&P) that supports investment teams dedicated to start-ups and early-stage businesses in Africa. While equity is a relevant tool to promote African small-and medium-sized enterprises (SMEs), mainstream investors usually concentrate on larger investments. As a result businesses find it hard to raise the required smaller amounts (ranging from EUR 100 000 to EUR 300 000). It is this so-called "missing middle" that IPDEV2 targets, building on I&P's past experience of investing across developing countries since 2002.

IPDEV 2 includes both public and private investors, and relies on blended finance through the support of patient investors who accept low single digit financial return (e.g. DFIs, foundations). IPDEV 2 sponsors the creation of national funds in Africa. IPDEV 2 covers the initial expenses needed to launch the fund (legal costs, market study, etc.); identifies and selects the first team members for each team; and trains these team members. While national investors provide the majority of the investment capacity of each national fund, IPDEV 2 also provides one-third of the total investment capacity of each fund and supports the team in the fundraising process. Finally, IPDEV 2 provides technical assistance resources to the funds in order to contribute to capacity building at the company level (EUR 7 million TA was secured from donors). As of August 2017, IPDEV 2 has started three African funds in Senegal, Burkina Faso and Niger and is planning to launch ten African funds in total in the coming years.

IPDEV 2 key facts:

- **Mandate:** Sponsor new investment teams dedicated to SME equity investment in West Africa and East Africa
- **Size:** EUR 20 million
- **Target impact:** Create ten African funds and investment teams, support 500 SMEs, generate 500 jobs
- **Target return:** Low single digit
- **Investors:** DFIs (AfDB, Proparco-AFD, BOAD), foundations, high net worth individuals
- **Technical assistance:** USAID, World Bank, Proparco-AFD, Monaco
- **Junior Debt:** AFD provided a EUR 3-million, long-term junior debt to IPDEV 2 covering first losses

Source: Interview with Investisseurs & Partenaires

Mobilisation of private investors in the capital structure of the fund, or capital blending, offers a promising approach

Structured funds offer an opportunity for development finance providers to mobilise private investment in the capital structure of the fund. First loss capital is commonly used to mitigate risk for commercial stakeholders on capital loss, and the first loss portion of capital is generally situated between 20% and 30% of total capital commitments. For funds providing credit guarantees and local foreign exchange guarantees (e.g. The Currency Exchange Fund, GuarantCo and InfraCredit), one or several tranches of loss coverage are paid in capital or placed in callable capital/contingent capital that converts to equity if claimed. The provision of first loss, second loss and third loss tranches by governments and aid agencies contributes to the limitation of risk perception for commercial investors. Private sector investors benefit from the risk coverage, as do other development finance actors such as DFIs or private sector arms of MDBs who are operating on close to market terms. These entities face tighter restrictions than governments and aid agencies on the risk they can take. DFIs, in turn, also contribute to second and third tranches of loss provision to improve risk protection for private sector investors. First loss protection covers beneficiaries of guarantees and ensures other equity shareholders capital protection or some commercial return.

Structured funds providing equity instruments (e.g. GEEREF, InsuResilience Investment Fund, the German Investment Corporation's SME Upscaling Fund, the Danish Investment Fund for Developing Countries' Danish Climate Investment Fund and the Danish Agribusiness Fund) issue junior shares (first loss capital) and senior shares. The remuneration of shares is predefined by a cash distribution waterfall, which can be structured as agreed by investors. For instance, senior share commitments are repaid in priority and receive a preferred return (e.g. 4% on commitment) before junior share commitments are repaid. Senior shareholders may then receive another amount in preferred return (e.g. 6% additional return on commitments, making 10% return received by this share class in total at this stage of the distribution). Finally, all shareholders (senior and junior) share the remaining profit equitably (50% each) (OECD 2017 Survey on Blended Finance Facilities and Funds).

Structured funds providing debt instruments (e.g. Eco.Business Fund, Microfinance Enhancement Facility, Microfinance Initiative for Asia, the Emerging Africa Infrastructure Fund) also issue different classes of notes and shares with different risk-return profiles to best address the needs of various investors. Such a fund can thus issue senior notes (top rank), junior notes, mezzanine, senior shares and junior shares (first loss) (see Box 6.3).

Box 6.3 The Microfinance Initiative for Asia

The Microfinance Initiative for Asia (MIFA) is an example of a blended finance structured debt fund. The USD 175 million, private-public fund is the first fund to exclusively focus on refinancing Asian microfinance institutions that operate sustainably. Germany's Federal Ministry for Economic Cooperation and Development (BMZ), KfW and the International Finance Corporation (IFC) established MIFA. BlueOrchard manages MIFA as a structured fund with the following capital structure (see Figure 6.3):

- The European Union (EU), BMZ (through KfW) and IFC invest in the more junior tranche known as C-shares, which have an unlimited maturity and represent a first-loss tranche fully subordinated to all other classes of securities issued. In 2012, the EU invested USD 9 million in risk capital, investment grants and technical assistance to support MIFA capacity building. The EU capital was channeled through the two European blended finance facilities dedicated to Asia, the Asian Investment Facility and the Investment Facility for Central Asia. The German institutions' contributed USD 30.8 million. IFC's share of capital is USD 16.25 million.

Box 6.3 **The Microfinance Initiative for Asia** *(cont.)*

- Private commercial investors such as pension funds, insurers, etc. are investors in the mezzanine B-shares, which are fully subordinated to A shares and Notes.
- Private investors also subscribe to the senior A-shares and Notes. Notes have a maturity of up to ten years. The target dividends of these shares and notes are only impacted by losses incurred by the fund if those losses exceed the value of the B and C shares.

MIFA targets Tier II and Tier III microfinance institutions (MFIs) to achieve deep outreach in its target markets. The main objectives are to create and enhance institutional capacity for sustainable microfinance delivery in Asia and to strengthen links between domestic and international capital markets. The main instruments used are loans with an average tenor of 18 months. By the end of June 2017, the portfolio reached almost USD 153 million across 14 countries. Half the loans given out were in one of nine local currencies.

Figure 6.3 **Structure of the Microfinance Initiative for Asia (MIFA)**

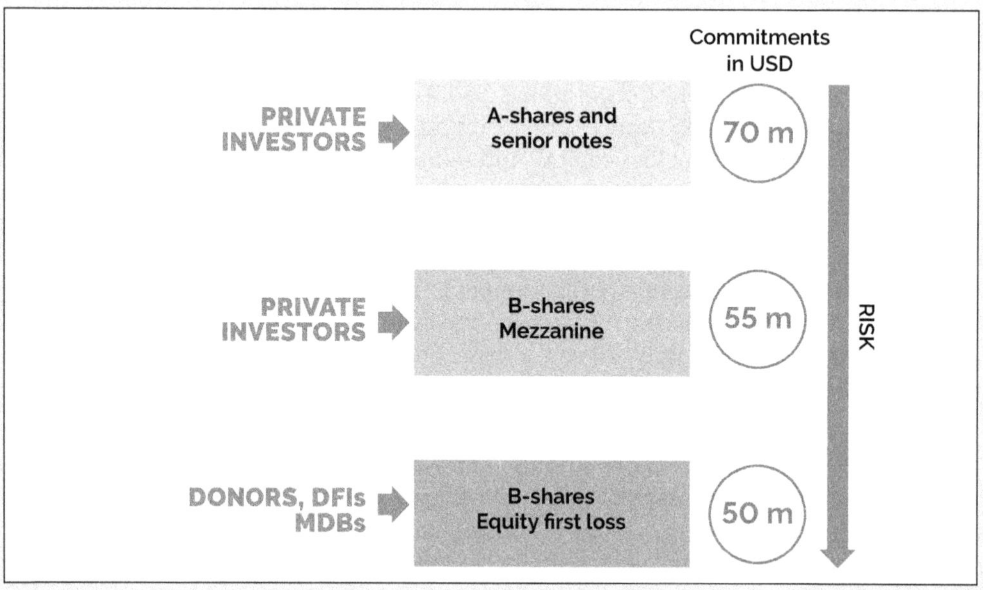

Sources: BlueOrchard (2017), www.blueorchard.com/investment-solutions/customized-mandates/mifa/ (accessed 11 September 2017); European Commission (2012), https://ec.europa.eu/europeaid/blending/structured-microfinance-fund-asia-mifa-debt-fund_en; KfW (2012), www.kfw-entwicklungsbank.de/International-financing/KfW-Development-Bank/KfW-Entwicklungsbank_alt/About-us/Pressemitteilungen/Pressemitteilungen-Details_10073.html.

Funds also can mobilise investors at multiple levels

Funds can support downstream blending by crowding in private investors at the project level or into companies (Chapter 7). Respondents to the OECD and EDFI surveys on blended finance noted funds' advantages in attracting private investment at the project level. These include their signalling/demonstration effect; co-financing opportunities; guarantee instruments with the development of a risk-sharing market, technical assistance capabilities; and co-operation with DFIs and donors in the regions, especially to mobilise local currency financing. Respondents also cited stringent risk management as an advantage of funds in mobilising additional private commercial capital.

Another example of how funds can mobilise private investment at different levels is through a so-called "fund-of-funds" approach. The EIB-managed Global Energy Efficiency and Renewable Energy Fund (GEEREF) is a well-known example. GEEREF, established by the European Commission in 2006 as a public-private partnership, has assets of EUR 222 million under management. It supports the transfer of clean and renewable energy technologies to developing countries by providing equity to specialist private equity funds. These funds, in turn, invest through equity and mezzanine instruments in a broad mix of small to medium-sized projects. The projects focus on renewable energy such as solar, biomass and wind farms and in energy efficiency sectors, focussing on the riskier, early-stage development phase of projects.[9] These sub-funds also mobilise additional commercial capital. Governments provided initial funding to GEEREF of EUR 112 million; these so-called "public seed contributions" then were used to raise EUR 110 million from private sector investors, thereby granting GEEREF a blended capital structure. The fund-of-funds approach further enhances the leveraging effect of the public investment and enables commercial investors to diversify their portfolio by taking part in sizeable funds (Figure 6.4). As of August 2017, GEEREF's portfolio was comprised of 12 funds[10] (GEEREF, 2017). Following the success of this model, EIB is in the process of raising funds for a successor to GEEREF, GEEREF Next, which aims to cover a larger amount of assets under management from commercial investors.

Figure 6.4 **How GEEREF mobilises private investment at multiple levels**

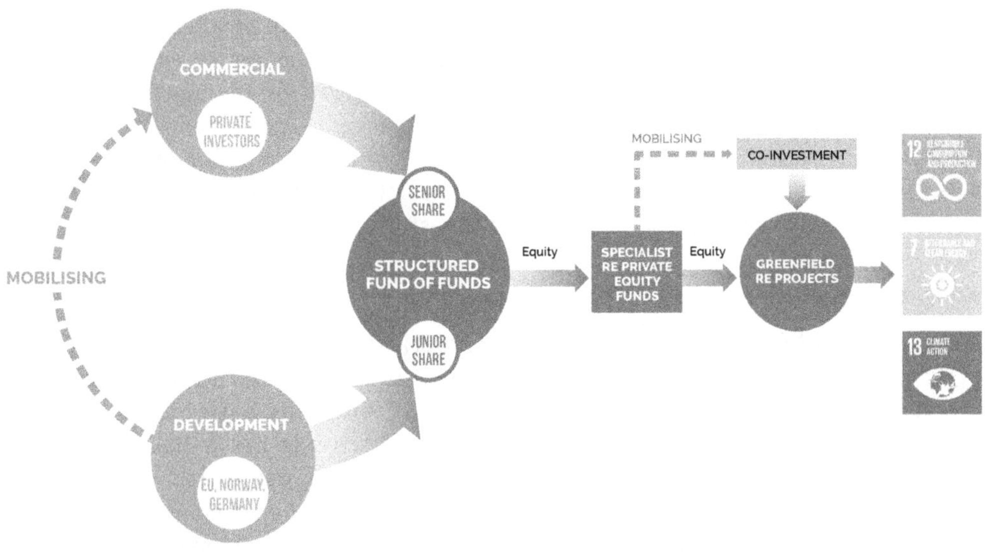

Source: GEEREF (2017), "What GEEREF is", Global Energy Efficiency and Renewable Energy Fund website, http://geeref.com/about/what-geeref-is.html (accessed 11 September 2017).

Funds attract different investors and demand different rates of financial return

The 2017 OECD survey found that only 16 of the 31 respondent funds provide information on financial performance (e.g. internal rate of return, or IRR). The available information suggests that flat funds often are associated with higher expected rates of return (between 12% and 20%) than structured funds, which is to be expected given the relatively high risk profile of equity investment in many developing countries. This finding is in line with IRR observed in developing countries, notably for infrastructure project equity, of 12-19% with a markup.[11] IRR for similar activity in developed countries is 8-9% (Deloitte, 2017). However some flat funds and especially growth equity capital funds, which are associated with more stable cash flows in sectors such as energy production, present lower target rates of return ranging from 8-10% or LIBOR+ 3-6%. For some flat funds such as social impact funds, the targeted net IRR can be as low as 2-5% as they are attracting largely patient capital. On the other hand, among structured funds the IRR depends on types of tranches. For equity, it is 10% for first loss tranche and 12% for the senior tranche. For debt, a typical structure allows a 2.25% return for first loss, 5.5% for mezzanine and 4% for senior tranche (OECD 2017 Blended Finance Survey).

In terms of reflows to shareholders, most flat funds pay out dividends to their shareholders. However, some of these funds can capitalise dividends because their shareholding structure is composed largely of patient capital; structured funds pay dividends to commercial investors but may not pay dividends to more concessional investors.

Anchors or fund managers play a critical role in facilitating investment

Further insights can be drawn from the process by which funds facilitate investment from and engage with private investors. Most funds included in the OECD 2017 survey (68%) are managed by private asset managers. In contrast, only 7% of facilities surveyed are managed by private fund managers. Respondents said anchors or fund managers play a critical role in reaching out to private investors and making them aware of blended finance investment opportunities. Among flat funds, 6 of the 12 respondents said private sector investors are brought in directly and solely as a result of the fund manager reaching out to institutional investors, high net worth individuals and asset managers with no intervention of the public investors.[12] Among structured funds, 11 of the 19 respondents reported that private sector investors are brought in directly and solely by the fund manager reaching out to investors with no intervention of the public investors.[13]

Governance structure depends on capital ownership

While blended finance funds pool public and private capital, the division of capital is not equal. Private commercial investors still hold a limited share in the capital of funds that responded to the 2017 OECD survey (Figure 6.5). All funds have contributions from development finance providers. Those engaged in flat funds are a balance of private development actors (social impact investors such as high net worth individuals and foundations) and public development actors (equally split between governments and DFIs). Those engaged in structured funds are mainly public development finance actors (equally split between governments and DFIs). This division of capital is also reflected in the governance of the funds, where development finance providers usually take part in the funds' investment committee and boards. In flat funds, these are largely DFIs. In structured funds, they are governments, MDBs or aid agencies.

Figure 6.5 **Breakdown of the capital structure of funds**

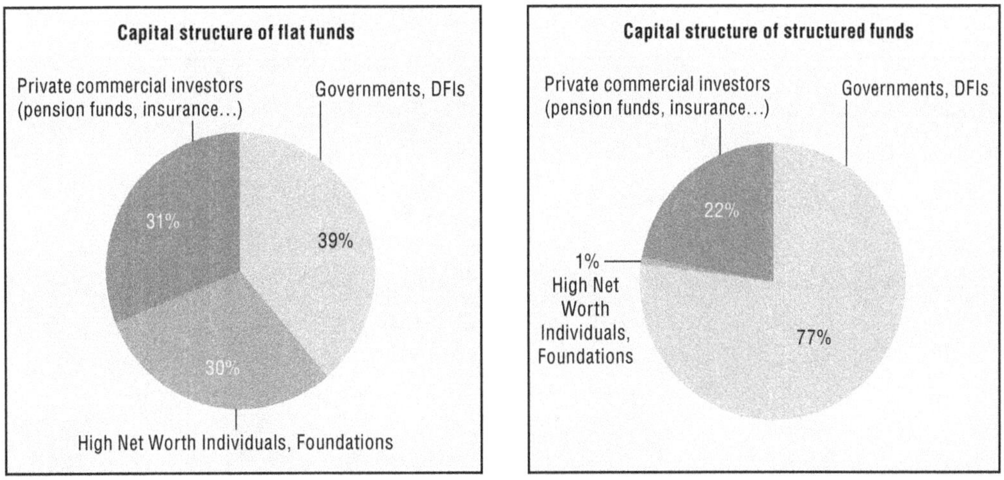

Source: 2017 OECD and 2015 EDFI surveys on blended finance funds and facilities.

Facilities and funds target the SDGs differently

All Sustainable Development Goals are not equal in blended finance

Some trends emerge from analysis of the extent to which the strategies of blended finance funds and facilities align with the Sustainable Development Goals (SDGs) (Figure 6.5). One is the stark discrepancy among SDGs. Eight of the SDGs were targeted by more than 50% of blended finance funds and facilities in the survey sample: SDG 1 (no poverty), SDG 6 (clean water and sanitation), SDG 7 (affordable and clean energy), SDG 8 (decent work and economic growth), SDG 9 (industry, innovation and infrastructure), SDG 11 (sustainable cities and communities), SDG 13 (climate action), and SDG 17 (partnerships for the goals). However, less than 35% of funds and facilities targeted two of the SDGs — SDG 14 (life below water) and SDG 15 (life on land).

The emphasis of funds and facilities on SDG 1 is to be expected, given that all development efforts target poverty reduction as an overarching goal to some extent. The focus on partnerships (SDG 17) also makes sense for blended finance funds and facilities since blending by nature embraces a partnership approach. The nature of blended finance also may explain the relative emphasis on goals pertaining to energy, water, climate change, economic growth, industry and cities. Blended finance tends to focus on sectors in which the private sector already is playing a role and the business case therefore is clearer and the potential for commercial gains more apparent. For projects in sectors linked to these goals, market analysis would be important in order to make sure blended finance approaches effectively crowd in rather than crowd out the private finance.

A second trend highlighted in this analysis is that more blended finance facilities than funds target the SDGs (with the exception of SDG 11), as illustrated by Figure 6.6. This can be explained in part by the different natures of the two types of vehicles: by definition a facility is a more public- and development-oriented financial mechanism. In general, given the potential of blended finance to significantly scale up resources for development by unlocking non-development commercial private sector capital, there is a need for blended finance facilities and funds particularly to extend their reach and target a wider range of issues.

Figure 6.6 **The extent to which funds and facilities target different SDGs**

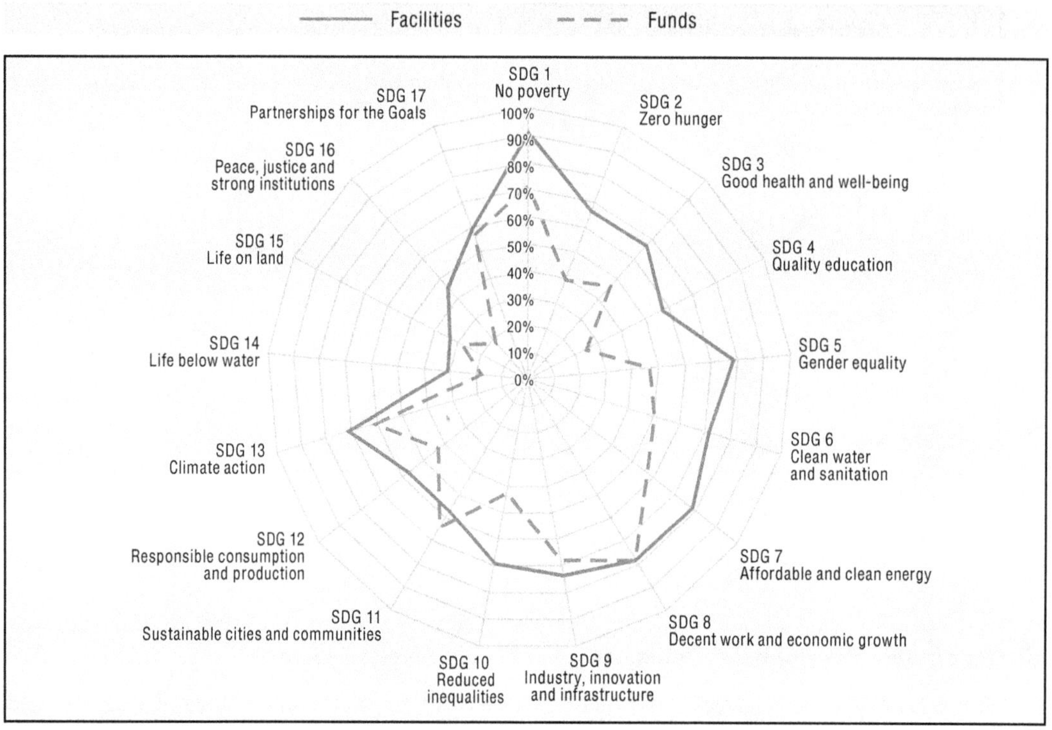

Note: Survey respondents were asked to what extent their development strategy was linked to the SDGs. Three possible responses were presented and respondents could choose only one. The possible responses were 1) "the SDG is explicitly mentioned in our strategy; 2) "We have similar objectives, but the SDG is not explicitly mentioned"; and 3) "the SDG is not at all relevant in our strategy. Figure 6.5 presents the combination of the first and second responses.

Source: OECD 2017 survey on blended finance funds and facilities (see Annex B); 42 of 43 facilities and 28 of 31 funds responded to this question.

StatLink http://dx.doi.org/10.1787/888933648214

Blended finance and climate action

The surveys found a significant level of activity among blended finance facilities and funds related to climate, with 78% of the 69 respondents targeting climate change mitigation and 49% targeting climate change adaptation. The percentage for mitigation can be correlated with the clear potential for returns in the renewable energy sector (see Figure 6.6 above on SDG 7 and SDG 13). The percentage targeting adaptation, however, is more surprising because development co-operation private sector engagement efforts traditionally overlook this sector (Crishna Morgado and Lasfargues, 2017). The creation of several dedicated blended finance facilities and funds for climate change in recent years may explain the relatively strong activity in this regard (Box 6.4).

Box 6.4 **Blended finance for climate change: A surge in climate finance facilities**

Tackling climate change requires a shift to a low-carbon, climate-resilient economy. This will cost trillions of US dollars a year — more than public finance alone can provide. International agreements have recognised that countries have "common but differentiated responsibilities" and that developed countries should "take the lead in combating climate change" and support developing countries to address climate change (UN, 1992). As a result, developed countries in 2009 jointly pledged to mobilise USD 100 billion a year in finance by 2020 for climate action in developing countries. These commitments have led to the creation of several climate funds and facilities that provide such financing. In the context of increasing recognition of the need to address subpar investments from the private sector, these facilities have started using concessional finance to leverage additional private finance for climate action. Many also now provide a dedicated private sector window. Some of the major facilities doing this include:

Global Environment Facility (GEF) is a global facility that brings together 183 countries and 18 agencies including several MDBs and United Nations agencies. It was created around the 1992 Rio Earth Summit to serve as the financial mechanism for the Rio Conventions (UN Framework Convention on Climate Change, UN Convention on Biological Diversity and UN Convention to Combat Desertification), the Minamata Convention and the Stockholm Conventions. The GEF has undertaken several blended finance activities over the years. In 2014, it launched a non-grant instrument pilot, a USD 110-million blended finance facility to address environmental degradation issues.

Climate Investment Funds (CIFs) are a set of facilities – the Clean Technology Fund (CTF) and the Strategic Climate Fund (SCF) – that were designed to help bridge a gap in the international climate finance architecture. They provide finance and support at scale for low-carbon and climate-resilient development; pilot innovative approaches and draw lessons learned for the international community. 30% of CIF's funding – totaling USD 2.4 billion – as of September 2017 has gone to the private sector. CIFs carry out private sector engagement activities directly, via private sector projects specified in CIF investment plans, or through two dedicated blended finance programmes: the CTF Dedicated Private Sector Programs (DPSP) and the SCF "set-asides" for the private sector. CTF DPSP has allocated USD 508.5 million for clean energy projects; the USD 200-million SCF "set-asides" for the private sector, which are in talks of being subsumed into a new SCF Private Sector Facility (PSF).

Nordic Development Fund (NDF) is a multilateral facility whose aim is to facilitate investments to address climate change in lower income countries using grants and other financing instruments. Since its inception, NDF has provided EUR 1 billion in concessional financing (representing 190 ticket items). Consistent with its focus on leveraging investment from the private sector, NDF uses blended finance approaches and has set up the Nordic Climate Facility (NCF) as a challenge fund that provides seed investments for climate change activities.

Green Climate Fund (GCF) is a global facility set up within the UN Framework Convention on Climate Change to combat climate change by providing finance to low-emission and climate-resilient projects in developing countries. In recognition of the important role of the private sector, the GCF has established a private sector facility as one of its key mainstream components. As of September 2017, the GCF Private Sector Facility encompasses pilot programmes to mobilise funding at scale for high-impact projects (allocated USD 500 million) and to fund climate activities of micro-, small- and medium-sized enterprises (allocated USD 200 million).

Sources: GEF (2017), "About us", webpage, Global Environment Facilty, www.thegef.org/about-us (accessed 15 December 2017); CIF (n.d.), "About us", webpage, Climate Investment Funds, www.climateinvestmentfunds.org/about (accessed 15 December 2017); NDF (n.d.), "About", webpage, Nordic Development Fund, https://www.ndf.fi/about (accessed 15 December 2017); GCF (n.d.), "Private Sector Facility", webpage, Green Climate Fund, www.greenclimate.fund/what-we-do/private-sector-facility (accessed 15 December 2017).

Developing local capital markets: Blended finance and local currency

Beyond the mobilisation of additional capital for development, blended finance can complement efforts to strengthen enabling environments and contribute to the development of local capital markets. Doing transactions in local currency, for example by issuing local currency bonds, encourages greater participation from domestic private sector actors. Most respondents to the 2017 OECD survey reported a low exposure to local currency in their portfolio, with 60% of respondents said less than one-fourth of their portfolio is in local currency. This is due partly to the relative ease of borrowing and lending in hard currency. However, when possible, blended finance funds and facilities should try to gradually expand the share of their portfolio in local currency. It is notable that some microfinance fund managers gave two answers in the survey, saying hard currency represents the majority at the fund outflow level but favouring local currency transactions at the microfinance institution level.

Research on blended finance funds and facilities offers insights for future practice

The use of pooled mechanisms to support blended finance is gaining interest and traction in the development community, as demonstrated by the sharp increase in the number of blended finance facilities and funds established in recent years. OECD and EDFI surveys on these mechanisms highlight a number of issues and opportunities that need to be considered further in the context of these specialised mechanisms.

Blended finance facilities and funds offer different opportunities for scaling up blended finance

Blended finance facilities and funds differ in their purpose, structure and mode of engagement and each offers comparative advantages to donor governments, development finance providers and private investors. Facilities enable donor governments to support blending for specific development issues or specific regions and also represent a means for governments to encourage MDBs and DFIs to scale up blending. While facilities do not blend private and public capital at the facility level, they implement blended finance instruments downstream at the project level (including investing in shares in common vehicles, i.e. funds) to finance development projects. Funds, on the other hand, allow the effective partnering between development and commercial finance providers and facilitate blending at multiple levels.

Pooled blended finance mechanisms facilitate the development of innovative solutions

While blended finance facilities have largely used concessional loans and grants as their means of engagement in blended finance projects, more sophisticated mechanisms have emerged involving more guarantee and equity including through specialised private sector windows such as those offered by climate funds. Among funds, innovative approaches are emerging to mobilise private commercial investors including through a signalling/demonstration effect, guarantee instruments with the development of a risk-sharing market and technical assistance. Some of these are exemplified by the IPDEV 2 investment company, which provides financial and technical support to a network of local equity fund managers. The GEEREF fund-of-funds structure is another example of the many ways to leverage private commercial investment at different levels, especially for energy infrastructure projects at early stages of development. This structure offers private investors diversification opportunity in a sizeable portfolio of 12 funds.

Blended finance funds are well-suited to attracting additional commercial investors

Development finance providers use junior/subordinated capital as their main instrument to crowd in capital in structured or layered funds. The higher expected rate of return in flat funds may attract private commercial investors. Governments may provide concessional capital in the form of grants, technical assistance or concessional loans to support the fund's fundraising and operations of the fund and to leverage additional private capital. In interviews about flat and structured funds conducted with stakeholders between March and August 2017, respondents said structured funds offer several potential advantages in mobilising commercial finance including a suitable return rate for commercial investors and an investment-grade profile due to low volatility, significant vehicle sizes and the potential higher liquidity of their assets.

Efforts are needed to increase private participation in funds

The leveraging potential of funds, especially structured funds, is not yet reflected in the capital structure of the funds that responded to the surveys. However, interviews conducted in connection with the surveys suggest that new funds currently in the fundraising phase will target more commercial capital. It will be increasingly important to scale up the participation of commercial finance and private actors in the capital of the funds while also calibrating and learning from experience to find the right balance between additional capital and development focus. Initiatives in which DFIs and MDBs are providing first loss and co-financing for institutional investors are a positive signal for scaling up private sector participation in development projects.

Funds and facilities need to better target a broader range of development issues

As discussed in this chapter, much blended finance activity focuses on SDGs. However, the full spectrum of SDGs is not covered, especially pertaining to key development issues such as quality education and biodiversity. The majority of surveyed pooled vehicles target climate mitigation and climate adaptation. While some blended finance pooled vehicles also aim to develop local currency markets, they have not reached this objective. Sixty percent of survey respondents invest in a maximum share of 25% in local currency projects.

Notes

1. The 2017 OECD and 2015 EDFI surveys included only those facilities that clearly stated an objective to mobilise private investors for development in their strategy or documentation.
2. The size of the facilities is approximated by the total committed amounts by development finance providers since the setup of the facilities.
3. New, significant facilities launched in 2014-16 include Power Africa (managed by USAID, 2014), Dutch Good Growth Fund (managed by Triple Jump, 2014), Women Entrepreneurs Opportunity Facility (IFC/ Goldman Sachs, 2014), Renewable Energy Performance Platform (EIB, 2014), Global Infrastructure Facility (WBG, 2014), Private Sector Credit Enhancement Facility (AfDB, 2015), Leap Fund (Asian Development Bank, 2016), Tropical Landscape Financing Facility in Indonesia (2016), and European Fund for Sustainable Development (European Commission, 2016).
4. There are a few exceptions: Green Africa Power, Middle East and North Africa SME facility, Seed Capital and Business Development (SCBD) Facility, and Responsible and Accountable Garment Sector (RAGS) Challenge Fund each target a specific sector across a particular region.
5. Some facilities target many sectors across multiple geographic areas, although they are a minority. These include the MASSIF fund, Impact Fund, Finnpartnership and Nordic Climate Facility.

6. Private equity funds and private debt funds, which use equity or debt respectively for investment, stand for two specific asset classes of unlisted investments in the financial sector.
7. Further research is being conducted into private equity funds to determine whether any should be considered blended finance.
8. This is particularly true for debt financing in support of private financial institutions where exit opportunities are clearly identified in the occurrence of debt repayment or debt refinancing.
9. The development phase encompasses the issuance of project permits, the signing of project contract and the construction phase.
10. Additional considerations for a fund of funds include the fund's lifetime, especially for infrastructure projects that generally take longer than the lifespan of the sub-funds. For instance, small hydropower or photovoltaic panel projects may take from six months to two years for the construction and one to two years to secure operating permits. The sub-fund thus can sell the asset after four to five years to large corporates or local actors. After the sub-fund has exited its investments, it can repay and distribute return to its shareholders including the fund of funds. In turn, the fund of funds can repay and distribute return.
11. The mark-up accounts for business model premium (+2-4%), currency premium (1-4%) and political premium (1-2%).
12. Of the remaining respondents, three reported they rely on the public sector investors; one relies on a broker or a placement agent; and the two other respondents did not answer the question.
13. Of the remaining respondents, four said they count on a placement agent or a broker; another four said they may on occasion rely on the support of the public investors but also rely on the fund manager directly reaching out to private sector investors; one fund reported relying solely on public investor support; and three fund managers did not answer the question.

References

BlueOrchard (2017), "Investment solutions", website, www.blueorchard.com/investment-solutions/customized-mandates/mifa/. (accessed 11 September 2017).

Convergence (2017), "The state of blended finance", *Working Paper*, for the Blended Finance Breakthrough Taskforce, Convergence, Toronto, https://convergence.finance/knowledge-detail/1qdtFkf5Fq86S4u8U4G8YU.

Crishna Morgado, N. and B. Lasfargues (2017), "Engaging the private sector for green growth and climate action: An overview of development co-operation efforts", *OECD Development Co-operation Working Papers*, No. 34, OECD Publishing, Paris, http://dx.doi.org/10.1787/85b52daf-en.

Koenig, A.N and E.T. Jackson (2016), "Private Capital for Sustainable Development: Concepts, Issues and Options for Engagement in Impact Investing and Innovative Finance", Evaluation Study for Danish Ministry of Foreign Affairs, www.evaluatingimpactinvesting.org/resources/private-capital-for-sustainable-development/.

Deloitte (2017), Insight: Blended finance in the national planning process", Deloitte Development LLC, https://www2.deloitte.com/content/dam/Deloitte/global/Documents/About-Deloitte/gx-blended-finance-in-national-planning-process.pdf.

European Commission (2012), "Structured Microfinance Fund for Asia (MIFA Debt Fund)", Directorate General for International Cooperation and Development https://ec.europa.eu/europeaid/blending/structured-microfinance-fund-asia-mifa-debt-fund_en.

GEEREF (2017), "What GEEREF is", Global Energy Efficiency and Renewable Energy Fund website, http://geeref.com/about/what-geeref-is.html (accessed 11 September 2017).

IEG (2011), *Trust Fund Support for Development: An Evaluation of the World Bank's Trust Fund Portfolio*, Independent Evaluation Group, World Bank Group, Washington, DC, https://ieg.worldbankgroup.org/sites/default/files/Data/Evaluation/files/tf_eval.pdf.

KfW (2012), "BMZ and KfW bolster the Asian microfinance sector with USD 100 million", press release, 28 June 2012, KfW Development Bank website, www.kfw-entwicklungsbank.de/International-financing/KfW-Development-Bank/KfW-Entwicklungsbank_alt/About-us/Pressemitteilungen/Pressemitteilungen-Details_10073.html.

UN (1992), "United Nations Framework Convention on Climate Change", FCCC/INFORMAL/84 GE.05-62220 (E) 200705, UN, New York, https://unfccc.int/resource/docs/convkp/conveng.pdf.

OECD/World Economic Forum (2016), *Insights from Blended Finance Investment Vehicles & Facilities*, ReDesigning Development Finance Initiative, OECD/World Economic Forum, Paris/Cologny, Switzerland, www3.weforum.org/docs/WEF_Blended_Finance_Insights_Investments_Vehicles_Facilities_report_2016.pdf.

Making Blended Finance Work for the Sustainable Development Goals

Chapter 7

Insights from project-level case studies on blended finance

While blended finance is emerging as an area of interest among donor governments, evidence is lacking on the outcomes and implications of blending as one approach in a toolkit of development co-operation approaches. This chapter presents insights from ten project level case studies of blended finance. It describes how blending has been applied in each case, focussing on the sources and terms of financing for each project, the financing structures used, and the project's contribution to achieving the Sustainable Development Goals. The chapter points to implications for donor government policies and raises operational issues that need to be considered.

Case studies suggest several important implications for policies on blended finance. As a collaborative approach between development and commercial actors, blended finance will require a culture change, especially among development finance providers. Established roles and mandates differ among development and commercial actors, as do working modalities.

Development finance providers contribute more than finance to blended finance transactions by playing a role in removing broader market distortions. Sometimes the presence of development finance providers in a transaction can have a mitigating effect on risks.

Blended finance is temporary and needs a clear exit strategy. However, all blended finance activities need a reasonable time horizon to effectively mobilise investment.

Operational insights from the case studies also point towards issues that need to be addressed when designing blended finance. Individual projects require approaches that are specific to their context, but, ensuring scalability will require standardisation of some approaches. Intermediaries are important in blended finance, in part because donor governments lack skill sets and cultures to work with the private sector. Rating agencies also are critical in engaging commercial actors.

Introduction

The catalytic use of development finance including through blended finance instruments and mechanisms is a growing priority for most development finance providers. Yet there is uncertainty about what constitutes blended finance, resulting in the lack of a widespread understanding of how blending can mobilise resources and support development outcomes and impact. This chapter presents insights from ten project-level case studies of blended finance to demonstrate the ways blending may be applied in different contexts. It focuses on how blending is being applied at the project level, complementing the analysis of pooled financing mechanisms presented in Chapter 6. This chapter highlights examples of good practice as well as challenges related to the application of blended finance.

Blended finance applied to projects provides policy and operational insights

Blended finance can be used as an effective tool to mobilise private investment at the project level by using development finance to adjust the risk-return relationship of a project, for instance by mitigating investment risk or structuring cash flows effectively. Each of the ten case studies developed for this report focuses on the sources and terms of financing for the project, the financing structures used, and the project's contribution to achieving the Sustainable Development Goals (SDGs). The case studies were sourced from members of the Development Assistance Committee (DAC) of the Organisation for Economic Co-operation and Development (OECD) and separate research. For each case study, interviews were conducted with development finance actors and other stakeholders, including private actors, where available. The selection of cases for further study focused on including a variety of actors (both development finance and private sector participants in the project), sectors and financial instruments. Table 7.1 provides an overview of the cases explored. Annex C presents the detailed case studies.

Table 7.1 **Case studies of blended finance at the project level**

Case	Sector	Country	Financing sources		Financing structure and instruments used	Potential impact
			Development	Commercial		
1. Providing access to high quality seedlings for export-oriented crops	Agriculture	Ghana	Global Affairs Canada through MEDA	Tree Global and its investors	Concessional loans and grants and technical Assistance	Improving the productivity and incomes of Ghanaian tree crop farmers and value chains
2. Increasing the availability of low-cost renewable energy production (Lake Turkana Wind Power Project)	Energy	Kenya	European Commission through EIB	Private project sponsors and other private investors	Concessional and mezzanine finance	Increased availability of low-cost energy in Kenya through a large-scale wind power plant
3. Empowering households to access renewable energy and lower power costs	Renewable energy	Rwanda	NDF	Private households	Grants	Increased uptake of solar water heaters and development of the solar water heater market
4. Encouraging private sector participation in financing water sector projects	Water and sanitation	Philippines	JICA and USAID through Development Bank of the Philippines	Private financial institutions	Concessional credit line and guarantee	Increased access to private finance for water utilities
5. Enabling municipalities to tap capital markets to fund infrastructure development	Infrastructure	India	KfW and Government of Tamil Nadu	Private bond investors	Concessional loan and equity backing a bond issuance	Increased access to finance for municipal infrastructure projects
6. Establishing the commercial viability of off-grid business models in renewable energy	Energy	India	ADB and Clean Technology Fund	Private equity investors	Equity and concessional loan	Demonstration of the commercial viability of off-grid business models that in turn will improve access to clean energy in rural areas
7. Improving access to affordable, clean energy and digital communication services	Energy	Papua New Guinea	Department of Foreign Affairs and Trade, Australia	Digicel Asia Pacific	Grant	Increased access to clean energy and to digital sources of communication
8. Promoting the participation of untapped investor classes in health care (Elazig Integrated Health Campus project)	Healthcare	Turkey	EBRD and MIGA	Meridiam, Ronesans and bond investors	Liquidity facility and political risk guarantee to enhance project bonds	Improved access to healthcare through a new hospital facility
9. Developing a securitised bond market to expand financing for farmers and entrepreneurs	Financial services	Armenia	USAID	Private bond investors	Securitised loans backed by a guarantee and technical assistance	Increased access to finance for universal credit organisations
10. Constructing a food production plant to improve food nutrition security and support local farmers	Food production	Rwanda	Government of Netherlands and FMO	DSM (Netherlands)	Corporate equity and debt	Reducing malnutrition through the production of improved food using locally source raw materials

Notes: ADB - Asian Development Bank; EIB - European Investment Bank; EBRD - European Bank for Reconstruction and Development; FMO - Netherlands Development Finance Company; JICA - Japan International Cooperation Agency; MEDA - Mennonite Economic Development Associates; MIGA - Multilateral Investment Guarantee Agency; NDF - Nordic Development Fund; USAID - United States Agency for International Development. Source: Adapted from case studies prepared for this report

Both policy and operational insights emerge from the case studies of project-level blended finance presented in this report. Policy insights relate to the application of blended finance at a project level against the ambitions for blending in the international agenda, and suggest issues for development finance providers to consider when situating blended finance in development co-operation strategies. Operational insights derive from lessons learned from the applied side of blended finance transactions, and focus on the sources of finance as well as the technicalities of the underlying financing arrangements.

Emerging policy insights on blending from project level case studies

Mobilising a broad set of private actors is at the heart of blended finance projects

The case studies analysed reflect a clear focus on private sector mobilisation despite the broad variety of blended finance approaches and frameworks in use at the project level. The range of private actors and finance mobilised varies widely. The Elazig hospital project in Turkey and Lake Turkana wind farm Kenya, both infrastructure projects, mobilise international investors including banks and corporations; private financial institutions are involved in scaling up financing for water utilities in the Philippines; and Global Affairs Canada works with an international business providing equity investment and expertise in support of supplying high-quality seedlings to tree crop farmers across Ghana. The Nordic Development Fund's support for solar water heaters in Rwanda mobilises private investment from individual households.

The financial instruments applied also reflect the focus on mobilisation. (Chapter 5 further explores the taxonomy of blended finance instruments.) Private sector instruments play an increasingly important role in development co-operation.[1] All forms of finance, concessional and non-concessional, can be used in a smart and strategic form to catalyse private sector investment.[2] In some cases, guarantees have been used. In cases where grants have been used, development finance providers explicitly aim to mobilise other forms of finance. For example, Global Affairs Canada uses concessional loans to complement grant funding in order to unlock private capital and support value chains for tree crop farmers in Ghana.

Even among development finance providers who in the past have taken a so-called "public-public" approach to blending, the focus on private or commercial finance is increasing. For example, the European Commission gives the private sector greater prominence in its External Investment Plan (EIP) than in the existing EC blending facilities, which provide concessional finance to development finance institutions (DFIs) to blend with their own resources in private sector operations. The EIP includes the European Fund for Sustainable Development, which has more than USD 30 billion in funding to provide guarantees in order to unlock private investment and focuses on Africa and the European Union neighbouring countries (Box 7.1).

Box 7.1 European Commission's External Investment Plan

In September 2016, the European Commission announced the proposal for the External Investment Plan (EIP), which puts the private sector at centre stage in achieving the Sustainable Development Goals. The EIP comprises three pillars that work closely together and leverage their value added. One of these is "mobilising investments through the new guarantee under the External Fund for Sustainable Development", which focuses on actual transactions to mobilise the private sector. A second pillar is "stepping up technical assistance to develop financially attractive and mature projects thus helping to mobilise higher investments", which facilitates the transactions. The third is "improving economic governance, the business environment and engaging with the private sector", which aims to foster a conducive environment for private sector participation in development finance. The objective of EIP is to mobilise at least EUR 44 billion of additional capital for Africa and the EU Neighbourhood.

Source: ADE (2016)

Blended finance approaches need a stronger focus on mobilisation of commercial resources

The aim of blended finance is to increase the amount of available financing for development by mobilising additional capital that does not have a development mandate. Blended finance mechanisms and instruments should unlock this previously untapped capital. For financing to qualify as blended, it should incorporate not only development finance but also mobilised commercial investment.

Some broad insights can be drawn from the ten case studies, outlined in Table 7.1 above. One is that traditional development finance operations targeting the private sector remain of critical importance in meeting financing demands and providing additional financing where no commercial financing alternatives exist. For example, the Australian Department of Foreign Affairs and Trade (DFAT) partnership with Digicel in Papua New Guinea unlocks corporate investments in business expansion. It also serves important development needs including improved access to energy and to digital communication services such as mobile phones and Internet. The investment by the Mennonite Economic Development Associates (MEDA) and Tree Global in a subsidiary in Ghana is another illustration of the value of traditional development finance. Nevertheless, as they move forward, development finance providers should aim to mobilise additional commercial finance, in addition to their own investment, when possible.

The mobilisation of household finance, as in case study 3, does not increase commercial finance flows directed to development outcomes and therefore falls outside the scope of blended finance as defined in this report. However, it should be noted that interventions of this type are critical in catalysing commercial finance at a broader level by helping to build markets (see Chapter 3 for a discussion of the boundaries of blended finance). Overall, blended finance approaches should aim to put development impact as well as the required additional commercial resources at the centre stage of operations.

Co-operation between private and public sector requires a cultural change

While there is consensus around the need for additional financing towards development to come from the private sector, there is no simple blueprint for the effective use of official funds to unlock private sector financing. By reaching out to complementary partners, both public and private actors can overcome weaknesses emerging in the changing investment environment and leverage their new partners' strengths. Partnerships of private and public actors, however, are not necessarily a natural fit. Established roles and mandates differ, as do working modalities. These differences are exemplified by the private sector's need for standardised processes and documentation, low entry and exit barriers, and efficient time management practices to maximise cost/benefit ratios. Stakeholders interviewed in support of the case studies presented in this chapter emphasised that the main issue regarding co-operation is not the technical challenges but the need for a culture change, particularly among development finance providers.[3] Additional challenges related to bringing together local governments and the private sector include a lack of experience.

Development finance providers bring more than finance to blended finance transactions

Blended finance aims at creating viable market opportunities for the private sector by adjusting the risk-return relationship in such a way that the private sector sees sustainable market opportunities and is willing to invest. The case study analyses suggest that the contribution of blended finance to creating market opportunities extend well beyond the mere financial technicalities of a blended transaction.

In that regard, it is widely acknowledged that participation of development finance providers in blended finance should include more than facilitating the transaction and should aim to contribute to removing broader market distortions. For instance, engagement by development finance institutions (DFIs) could address local regulations or content requirements (see e.g. O'Keefe and Moss, 24 May 2017). Another area is political risk coverage, in which the official development finance providers already play a decisive role and are particularly suited to address markets. The Multilateral Investment Guarantee Agency (MIGA) highlights this ability to handle riskier markets in recent strategy report, noting that its access to governments as a member of the World Bank "enhances its ability to mediate on investment disputes and help resolve issues that can occur during the course of the projects it covers" (MIGA, 2015).

Similarly, involvement of the Australian public sector is important for DFAT's private sector engagement. The official participation of the government through the Business Partnerships Platform (BPP) allows private companies to credibly make their business case. The rating agency Moody's, moreover, viewed the involvement of MIGA and the European Bank for Reconstruction and Development (EBRD) in Elazig hospital project in Turkey as "credit positive", given their positive impact and relationship with the Turkish government (Moody's, 2016).[4] Thus the presence and endorsements of particular entities in a project can have a risk mitigating effect. When assessing opportunities to deliver development objectives, consideration should be given to blending as a tool to mobilise additional private finance via appropriate financial structures. The ability of blended finance to mobilise private finance beyond the financing structure of the project also may be taken into account.

Blended finance is temporary but needs a reasonable time horizon

Development co-operation efforts to scale up the use of blended finance are important, but should not lose sight of the fact that blended finance is a means to an end — that is, the goal is to facilitate market building that enables private stand-alone investment (Chapter 3). Put a different way, the ultimate goal of blended finance is to generate development outcomes by making itself redundant. Official flows that aim to mobilise private finance recognise the transitory nature of blended finance. By enabling private investment to build a track record and gather experiencing in uncovered jurisdictions or sectors, official development finance (ODF) contributes to reducing investment barriers stemming from information asymmetries. Blended structures may be needed initially to address the risk-return relationship but also may serve as entry points for future stand-alone private investment. The water sector project in the Philippines provided by the Japan International Cooperation Agency (JICA) and others illustrates the temporary nature of blended finance. The use of blended finance was meant to encourage local private financial institutions to lend to local water and sanitation providers. Once they started engaging in stand-alone activities with these providers, the institutions became less interested in accessing the blending scheme. Other factors such as the overall decrease in interest rates, also certainly contributed to this result. Blended finance should be used as a temporary measure, but the case studies suggest that the transition period can last longer than anticipated and that determining exit points and strategies may be quite complex. The Nordic Development Fund (NDF) solar water heater project, for example, mobilised private sector investment into an untapped market. An accompanying awareness-raising campaign ultimately helped to build the market for solar water heaters, but the campaign took longer than initially expected to have an impact. The KfW project in Tamil Nadu, India successfully mobilised private finance via the issuance of local currency infrastructure bonds. High secondary market activities of these bonds do not only reflect the impact the project had on the local bond market development, but also the sustained high private sector demand in the long-run.

Operational considerations from applying blending to individual investments

Balancing scalability and individualisation is key in blended finance

Blended finance should provide ways of tapping into domestic and international pools of capital, for instance of pension funds and asset managers. Institutional investors prefer standardised financial instruments, which enable investments at large scale (see Chapter 5). The blended finance approaches presented in this report, however, are tailored specifically and deliberately to context-specific needs and development goals. These entail sector- and instrument-specific challenges such as limitations in the project pipelines for infrastructure projects or in the number of credit-viable investee businesses. The case studies highlight additional common limitations in up-scaling or replicating projects. Each project is adapted to the particularities of its geographic or sectoral environment. Some approaches might work in different settings, such as the infrastructure debt fund that was KfW used in its support for the government of India. But the individual terms and conditions have to be adapted and structured to match the risk-return requirements of commercial investors in specific regions.

An example of how standardisation can be achieved is the Netherlands Development Finance Company (FMO)'s support for nutritious food production for children in Rwanda. The joint venture with other DFIs and the private sector company DSM is set up in a way to fund subsidiaries in other jurisdictions beyond Rwanda. Local government engagement in such subsidiaries helps align goals and operations to the individual context.

Transparency is crucial for fair competition in blended finance

The underlying mechanism of blended finance is to target official development interventions effectively so that private investors see an investment opportunity with an adequate risk-return relationship. This goal may be achieved with the use of concessional money, although non-concessional tools also may be effective in structuring financial instruments so as to address private sector investment concerns. With both tools, official development finance interventions must be transparent to ensure fair competition among private sector participants. Transparency is particularly important when it comes to the provision of subsidies.

In the case of infrastructure projects, for example, all private actors including project developers, investors and other consortium members should have access to the same amount of information in terms of blending opportunities available. The same holds for equal access to information for all project recipients. Removing information asymmetries will facilitate fair competition beyond financing terms and conditions when all potential actors are aware of the official investment support available. This is crucial particularly for public-private infrastructure projects where procurement of public services is taking place via private sector investors organised as a consortium, such as the consortia investing in the Lake Turkana Wind Power project in Kenya or the Elazig Hospital Campus project in Turkey. In such projects, different consortia offer different financing packages, making transparency regarding blended finance opportunities decisive in establishing fair competition. More fundamentally, a lack of transparency can undermine the use of blended finance and the potential for the market to grow.

The availability of information on blended finance opportunities ex ante complements the need for blended finance information ex post, for instance in regard to transaction data or development impact data. Chapter 8 explores the issue on data availability in more depth.

Intermediaries are important actors in blended finance

Intermediaries played a critical role in structuring the transaction, bringing together the actors and facilitating the blending. As demonstrated in many of the projects in the case studies, development banks and DFIs such as EBRD, the Asian Development Bank (ADB), FMO and MIGA take on this role. This is in part due to their function and mandates that make them well suited to mobilise the private sector. Other partners such as local financing institutions or non-governmental organisations (NGOs) also can take on this role. For instance, JICA works closely with the Development Bank of the Philippines (DBP) to channel support for the Philippine Water Revolving Fund, a co-financing facility with private financial institutions that on-lends long-term loans to water utilities. In the case of Tree Global in Ghana, Global Affairs Canada works with the international NGO MEDA in implementing blended finance.

This use of intermediaries is a relatively easy way for ministries and aid agencies to engage in blending, particularly those who may not be used to working directly with the private sector to mobilise investment. One of the lessons drawn from a 2016 study of OECD DAC members' private sector engagement is that working with and through the private sector, including blended finance, requires sufficient lead time, capacity and incentives (OECD, 2016). Staff capacities in development finance organisations need to adjust to the increasing focus on the private sector in order to fully exploit the potential of such co-operation. Some DAC members are beginning to work directly with private companies and generating such in-house capacity, as is the case with Australia's BPP, a platform that establishes a direct link to private sector actors.

The private sector should be involved in developing blended finance products

Blended finance transactions bring together partners with a policy mandate and those with commercial objectives. Since potential private sector partners need to see clear value, early involvement of the private sector in the joint development of blended finance solutions can engage these partners and ensure transparency. An example is consultation process between Australia's DFAT and private sector stakeholders in the development of the BPP, which now serves as the interface enabling a direct relationship between the government and businesses. Engaging the private sector early on also ensures that the private sector perspective is represented in the project design. Early engagement of the private sector does not mean that official institutions will have to initiate, develop or lead a project. A private player can effectively propose projects to development partners to gain support and provide the necessary insight to bring a project to fruition. In the Elazig Integrated Health Campus project in Turkey, the global investor and asset manager Meridiam took a leading role in co-ordinating with EBRD to structure a cost-effective transaction that included a guarantee by MIGA, and made the bond offering attractive to international bond investors.

Effectively calibrating the risk-return relationship is critical to mobilising commercial investment

When allocating assets, investors pay attention to the return they expect in compensation for the risk involved in the project or investment fund. Investment opportunities that fail to provide an adequate return for the risks involved will likely fail to attract sufficient capital. Even when investors are aware of risks, they may want a track record of several successful projects before warming to the sector, region or product. This influenced KfW's intervention in India, which allows the state of Tamil Nadu to access the capital markets by providing the capital into a mechanism to de-risk bonds issued on the local capital markets. The KfW use of subordination and India's equity support provided two layers of cushion before any loss would be borne by a private investor. This lowered the yield required by investors allowing for a blended debt service payment that the municipalities could afford.

Another example is the Elazig project in Turkey, which was also successful at incorporating MIGA political risk insurance and unfunded liquidity facilities by EBRD to enable the project bond rating to pierce the sovereign ceiling by two notches. This resulted in a lower coupon payment and longer maturity of the project bonds providing a cost-effective financing source for the project.

Sometimes effectively calibrating the risk-return relationship requires concessional financing

Like all development co-operation, blended finance engagement is driven by a development rationale and so should serve as an enabler of development outcomes. Such a solution-based approach may require the use of concessional finance in order to deliver on development targets. While concessional finance is not a necessary condition for blended finance – market-priced guarantees for instance may serve the purpose of mobilising commercial finance very well in specific contexts (see also Chapter 5) — it may be required to unlock commercial finance and to deliver on intended outcomes.

Two examples from the case studies make the case for using concessional finance to unlock commercial investment and ultimately deliver on development outcomes. In both the Lake Turkana Wind Power project in Kenya and the ADB investment in Simpa Energy India, the use of concessional finance in the blended financing structures emerged during the course of the projects. In the first case, the European Commission stepped in as the financial close of the Lake Turkana Wind Power project was in doubt due to cost increases resulting from a long due diligence process and inadequate financing from debt providers not matching the changing demands. Based on a thorough assessment, the provision of concessional mezzanine finance has been identified as the solution to reach financial closure. While this intervention was initially not foreseen in the project financing structure, the concessional element served its purpose ex post. The Simpa Energy India case also shows that the need for concessionality in development finance may vary over time with market conditions and development goals. ADB has been engaged in the company since 2013, when it provided equity financing in support of Simpa Energy India's business model focusing on solar photovoltaic systems for households. A few years after the initial engagement, the company set up a mini-grid and distributed power generation programme in a move aimed at expanding its operations and thereby addressing electricity gaps in India. This plan was co-funded with concessional debt provided by the Clean Technology Fund and channelled through the ADB. Again, an ex-post assessment of solving electricity challenges led to the conclusion that concessional finance was the most effective mechanism in this case.

Rating agencies remain vital to attracting investment by institutional investors

Large institutional investors manage vast pools of assets. Insurance companies, investment funds and pension funds in OECD countries alone manage assets in excess of USD 85 trillion (OECD, 2015). Institutional investors, especially pension funds and insurance companies, are understandably subject to bylaws and regulatory control to safeguard assets to fund retirements or ensure liquid funds are available for insurance payouts. Rating agencies play a significant role for institutional investors to ensure investment quality. Many institutional investors will not invest in financial products that are assigned a credit rating below investment grade (BBB- by Standard & Poors and Fitch and Baa3 by Moody's). Blended finance engagements have addressed this. For example, the use of innovative financing structures and credit enhancements for the Elazig project in Turkey resulted in the issuance of bonds with an investment grade rating (Baa2 by Moody's) in a country with a sub-investment grade sovereign rating. This was critical to attracting EUR 208 million from bond investors such as Japan's Mitsubishi UFJ Financial Group, Italy's Intesa Sanpaolo, Germany's Siemens Financial Services, France's Proparco, and the Industrial and Commercial Bank of China.

Local engagement enables viability and sustainability of projects

Local ownership is an important principle in development co-operation. Aligning development interventions with national interest and engaging with local actors in development finance transactions are essential to ensure the sustainability needed to build markets. National ownership is a building block of FMO's intervention in Rwanda, for example. The Rwandan government holds 8% of shares in the local operational food production company, which facilitates alignment with national interests.

From a financial perspective, engaging in local currency intervention is another key criterion to enable local investment. It also is fundamental to the financial sustainability of the project in that instruments in foreign currency introduce a layer of risk that can be detrimental to the long-term viability of a project, for instance by introducing a divergence between revenue streams and refinancing currency. Interventions in several successful projects in the case studies understood that mobilising investment in local currency via local capital markets or financial institutions was critical to the sustainability of the project. Moreover, the activity itself serves as a catalyst for developing and deepening local capital markets and the investor base, in addition to enhancing the prospect for follow-on project investments. An example is the USAID project to develop a securitised bond market in Armenia; the USAID bond issuance enables private investors to buy local currency bonds backed with the universal credit association's assets.

Notes

1. The OECD DAC is currently assessing methodologies to better reflect the growing use of private finance in development co-operation in the official development assistance measurement and to offer the right incentives to use such instruments. See www.oecd.org/dac/financing-sustainable-development/modernisation-dac-statistical-system.htm.
2. In the same vein, foundations such as the Ford Foundation are increasingly making use of social impact investing beyond purely grant-based approaches. See www.fordfoundation.org/the-latest/news/ford-foundation-commits-1-billion-from-endowment-to-mission-related-investments/.
3. This is also one of the major findings of the OECD Peer Learning report. See http://dx.doi.org/10.1787/9789264266889-en.
4. More concretely, Moody's (2016: 1-2) states, "We view the EBRD and MIGA involvement in the transaction as credit positive, considering their potential influence on offtake behaviour (owing to their status as preferred creditors and potential deterrence effect) in scenarios where the Government of Turkey may be under strain, ability to intermediate investment disputes, and the extent of their activities in Turkey."

References

ADE (2016), *Evaluation of Blending: Final Report, Volume I – Main Report*, https://ec.europa.eu/europeaid/evaluation-blending_en.

Moody's (2016), " ELZ Finance S.A.: Pre-sale report - Elaziğ hospital PPP exceeds Turkey's sovereign rating with strong multilateral support", Report Number 1048045, *Infrastructure and Project finance*, Moody's Investor Services, London, UK.

Chapter 8

Progress and challenges in tracking blended finance

The growing prominence of blended finance is creating an increased demand for data. The use of public, concessional development finance in the context of commercial investment has raised the need for transparency and accountability, particularly regarding the effectiveness of blended finance. This chapter outlines the main efforts to track and map the blended finance market. It highlights what has been achieved through stand-alone surveys and in the context of existing reporting systems for development finance. The chapter also presents gaps in existing data systems and identifies areas for further work.

HIGHLIGHTS

Blended finance presents special challenges for tracking and information gathering. It features public development finance, private development finance and commercial finance flows in combination. It brings together a greater variety of actors with diverse legal and financial structures, making tracking a complex endeavour.

Currently, there is no single comparable, consistent estimate of the blended finance market covering the entirety of flows.

Several stand-alone surveys by the World Economic Forum, the Association of European Development Finance Institutions and the OECD have helped to shed light on aspects of blended finance, but provide limited information on the overall market. Individual deal-focussed databases also provide insights on aspects of blended finance, especially on infrastructure projects.

Existing development finance reporting systems are adapting to track private sector flows. The work of the OECD Development Assistance Committee in developing methodologies to track private finance mobilised is an important step forward.

Ultimately, the availability of disaggregated, transaction-level data on blended finance will be important to ensure transparency and to enable a better understanding of the efficiency, availability and additionality of blended finance.

Introduction

The growing prominence of blended finance is creating an increased demand for data. This in turn is prompting related calls for further engagement in transparency and accountability regarding a number of issues. How much development finance is being channelled towards blended approaches, for instance? What is being mobilised as a result, how is this financing being allocated in terms of countries and sectors, and what impact is being achieved through blending? Which instruments are most effective in mobilising commercial finance and addressing different Sustainable Development Goals? Different actors understand and define blended finance differently (Chapter 3). The result is a series of different efforts to track blended finance in order to properly answer these, and other, questions. This chapter outlines these efforts, provides an overview of the current landscape of data that can be used to analyse blended finance, and highlights gaps and areas for further work.

Efforts to track blended finance flows require specific, and varied, data and information

The use of public, concessional development finance in the context of commercial investment has raised the need for transparency and accountability, particularly regarding the effectiveness of blended finance (Tew and Caio, 2016). Market information available from non-concessional development finance is critical for the effective pricing of capital and is key to the efficient crowding in of commercial finance. The full spectrum of stakeholders requires data: governments and policy makers, development finance providers and commercial investors, investees, and civil society. Information supports accountability, and builds trust and effective partnerships among all stakeholders (Lonsdale, 06 July 2017). Information at a disaggregated level is needed to better understand and improve blended finance approaches.

Blended finance presents special challenges in terms of tracking and information gathering. The concept of transparency and accountability is well established in development co-operation, standing as a major pillar of development effectiveness principles. Traditional official development finance (ODF) also is subject to established transparency norms and ODF is one of the building blocks of blended finance. However, blended finance is a more complicated ecosystem than traditional donor-driven development finance, with a greater variety of actors with a greater variety of legal and financial structures, making tracking a complex endeavour. Blended finance also features public development finance, private development finance and commercial finance flows in combination. This entails a broad spectrum of financial instruments (Chapter 5). Blended finance also involves intermediaries like funds and facilities between investors and investees (Chapters 6 and 7), so accounting and tracking must be multidimensional. No overarching system now covers and/or connects on these types of flows to properly inform blended finance policies.

A lack of information on the development impact adds to the complexity. While blended finance is considered a tool to increase the finance available for development outcomes, the systematic evidence base to support this understanding is lacking. Impact evidence of blended finance compared to other development finance is especially important given the sensitivities around private sector participation in development co-operation. Therefore, transparency in blended finance is needed in both transaction activity data and impact data (see Chapter 9 for insights into monitoring and evaluation in the blended finance ecosystem).

This section discusses existing data sources on blended finance: stand-alone surveys, systematic efforts under existing statistical systems covering specific financial flows, and stand-alone deal databases that cover a specific market angle.

Stand-alone surveys provide useful but limited market information about blended finance

Several stand-alone surveys in recent years have helped to shed light on blended finance. Results of different surveys are not directly comparable because blended finance is defined differently. While entry points for surveys differ, their focus has been on pooled financing for blending such as funds and facilities.

Three major surveys have focused on blended finance facilities and funds, including the OECD survey carried out in 2017 that is introduced in this report. One is the World Economic Forum (WEF) review of 74 blended finance vehicles launched between 1999 and 2016, undertaken under the WEF-OECD ReDesigning Development Finance Initiative (World Economic Forum/OECD, 2016). The survey sample was selected through the WEF network, desk research and stakeholder analysis, and included funds and facilities that received public and private development finance. Commons Consultants, on behalf of Association of European Development Finance Institutions (EDFI), conducted a second survey in 2015. It aimed to analyse how concessional financing from donor governments was leveraging private sector investment and covered 140 vehicles launched between 1986 and 2014, including both funds and facilities (as defined in Chapter 5). Due to its focus on concessional finance, the sample excluded vehicles that received support at market rates. The OECD conducted a third survey in 2017 that builds on the two earlier surveys. It is presented in this report (see Chapter 6).

Stand-alone surveys have provided useful insights on blended finance. However, their focus on pooled finance vehicles means such surveys do not provide information on how blending is occurring outside of funds and facilities. Another issue is that donor governments set up facilities that may in turn invest in funds, so surveys that do not differentiate between the two could result in double counting. Moreover, these surveys were conducted as stand-alone exercises and as such do not provide a picture of how the market is changing over time.

Existing development finance reporting systems are adapting to track private sector flows

Collective efforts to track blended finance can leverage existing systems that track official development finance. This offers a number of advantages. Building on existing statistical systems helps to ensure open access as well as the use of mutually agreed definitions, robust accounting systems, and mechanisms to avoid double counting (OECD, 2017).

The OECD DAC Creditor Reporting System (CRS), particularly through its activity-level reporting, tracks all resource flows to developing countries including concessional and non-concessional public flows, private flows at market terms, and private grants and private philanthropy (Box 8.1). As mandated by the 2014 and 2016 High Level Meetings, the DAC has been working to develop an international standard for measuring the amounts mobilised by official development finance interventions including guarantee schemes. This work is carried out in consultation with multilateral and bilateral development finance institutions and in close collaboration with the OECD-led Research Collaborative on tracking private climate finance.[1] This work also contributes to the ongoing development of a broader measurement framework, total official support for sustainable development (TOSSD) and the DAC work stream on blended finance.

To initiate this work, instrument-specific methodologies have been developed in collaboration with development and climate experts, and piloted through surveys. The most recent survey finds that during 2012-15, USD 81.1 billion were mobilised from the private sector by official development finance interventions in the form of guarantees, syndicated loans, shares in collective investment vehicles, credit lines and direct investment in companies (Benn, Sangaré and Hos, 2017; see also Chapter 4). This data also have been used as a proxy in analyses of blended finance (Tew and Caio, 2016a).

In addition, starting in 2017, the regular DAC statistical system is collecting data on amounts mobilised from the private sector (starting with 2016 flows). By mid-2017, DAC methods and data collection were covering guarantees, syndicated loans, shares in collective investment vehicles, direct investment in companies, and credit lines. Work is underway on methodologies for measuring the mobilisation effect of other instruments and mechanisms — among them stand-alone grants and loans — as well as more complex financing schemes such as private-public partnerships (PPPs) and project finance.

The methodologies underlying these efforts are well aligned with this report's definition of blended finance (Box 8.2). Going forward, reporting according to these methodologies will result in project-level data in the CRS, enabling ongoing assessment of mobilisation and putting private investment into the context of official development finance flows.

Another existing system is the International Aid Transparency Initiative (IATI), which also facilitates the publishing of data on development finance flows. More than 500 organisations have submitted raw data, building on IATI's common open data standard and covering aid, development, and humanitarian flows at the transaction level. Among the reporting organisations are development finance institutions such as the CDC Group and the International Finance Corporation that engage in the mobilisation of private finance. Londsdale (2016) argues that the IATI reporting initiative is useful in the context of blended finance data.

Box 8.1 **The OECD DAC statistical system and the new development finance architecture**

The Creditor Reporting System (CRS) database is a long-established data collection system that tracks official development finance flows including official development assistance (ODA) and other official flows (OOF). DAC members are increasingly engaging in development finance with and through the private sector, for instance by using private sector instruments as guarantees (see also Chapter 5). The modernisation of the ODA measure that is underway will better reflect the changing landscape in the development finance architecture.

The CRS system traditionally has been flow-based, thereby undermining tracking of donor engagement in guarantees. As part of the modernisation process, the DAC is working to better reflect the donor effort in the use of private sector instruments such as guarantees and to track the amounts mobilised from the private sector by such guarantees. Beyond existing measures, the OECD, under the auspices of the United Nations, also is working on developing a broader measure of total official support for sustainable development (TOSSD) with the aim to cover all official financial flows and interventions including and beyond ODA in support of the Sustainable Development Goals.

Source: OECD (2017), "Getting development finance data right", in *Development Co-operation Report 2017: Data for Development*, OECD Publishing, Paris. http://dx.doi.org/10.1787/dcr-2017-11-en

Parallel to the OECD mobilisation measurement efforts, a task force of multilateral development banks (MDBs) is engaging in measuring and reporting aggregate amounts of finance mobilised by their interventions. In 2017, this task force published first results for 2016, covering private co-financing of the private sector alongside MDB investment (World Bank 2017a; World Bank, 2017b). They show that private direct mobilisation is estimated at USD 49.9 billion in 2016. The MDB approach differs significantly from the OECD mobilisation methodology in that it does not take into account the roles played by bilateral DFIs or domestic governments in mobilisation; all finance mobilised is attributed to MDBs exclusively. Another major difference is the definition of private mobilisation. In the MDB approach, it refers to commercial finance that may include public money extended on commercial terms (e.g. DFI investments) and thus may lead to double counting.[2] The individual MDBs also are continuing to regularly report to the DAC using the OECD DAC methodology.

Box 8.2 **Tracking blended finance through the OECD DAC statistical system**

The OECD DAC statistical system tracks official development assistance (ODA) and other official flows (OOF). The system will track data on amounts mobilised by the private sector starting from 2017. As blended finance combines development finance and private finance, data on these elements can help in understanding of blended finance. Several issues are salient to evaluating the extent to which data from this system will be able to reflect blended finance, as defined in this report.

Definitions and methodology. Blended finance is defined as strategic use of development finance for the mobilisation of additional finance towards sustainable development in developing countries (Chapter 3). Private finance mobilisation is defined as the "direct causal link between private finance made available for a specific project and an official intervention" (Benn et al., 2016). In terms of determining and tracking mobilisation, the OECD methodology rests on three main principles (see also OECD DAC, 2014):

- Demonstrating a causal relationship (causality) between the official intervention and the private finance mobilised, i.e. would the private financier have invested in the project without the official investment?
- Attributing mobilisation of private capital between official investors if more than one is engaging in an activity. In doing so, the instrument-based mobilisation methodology associates a risk-based and volume-based estimate for amounts mobilised to the official institutions.
- Framing the boundaries of mobilisation in order to maintain causality and avoid double counting at the international level, the mobilisation methodologies capture the intention to mobilise private finance at the time of the commitment of the ODF.

Differences between blended finance and mobilisation. The objectives of blended finance and mobilisation — increasing the overall finance resources available to deliver development impacts — are clearly aligned. Central to both is the notion that this additional money would not have been invested without the driving force of development finance. However, there are differences between the two that are relevant to blended finance tracking.

In terms of measuring causality, the OECD mobilisation methodologies refer to the first level of mobilisation, i.e. the direct outcome of the instruments. Direct mobilisation can refer to an official investor investing in the equity of a company and mobilising additional commercial debt in the same financing round. The rationale behind only considering the first level of mobilisation is to avoid double counting and ensure the measurement approach is feasible to implement. Blended finance, as defined in this report can go beyond the first level of mobilisation and also include approaches at the second level.

Box 8.2 Tracking blended finance through the OECD DAC statistical system *(cont.)*

A concrete example is the project in India described case study 5 (see Chapter 7). In the project to enable municipalities to tap into capital markets for infrastructure development funding, KfW engaged in the mobilisation of commercial bondholders. KfW extended a concessional loan to the Indian government, which channelled the funds into backing the subordinated tranche of the bond issuance of a special purpose vehicle. In the mobilisation methodology, this blended finance deal is considered as a government loan in the first level and as such is not covered, since the mobilisation is taking place at a second level.

A conservative picture. Overall, the data provided by the OECD methodologies as they stand today on tracking amounts mobilised from the private sector can provide a useful, if conservative, picture of blended finance.

Sources: Benn, J., C. Sangaré, T. Hos and Semeraro, G.M. (2016), "Amounts Mobilised from the Private Sector by Official Development Finance Interventions: Guarantees, syndicated loans and shares in collective investment vehicles", OECD Development Co-operation Working Papers, No. 26, OECD Publishing, Paris. http://dx.doi.org/10.1787/5jm3xh459n37-en; OECD DAC (2014), "Measuring mobilisation in an international statistical system", DAC Note, OECD Publishing, Paris, www.oecd.org/dac/stats/principles-for-mobilisation.pdf.

Deal databases highlight detailed information on selected aspects of blended finance

Databases focusing on projects also provide insights on aspects of blended finance. The Investment Network, a database of deals launched by Convergence, is an online "matchmaking platform"[3] that aims to connect private, public and philanthropic investors to participate in blended finance for development. The database includes basic information about transactions that are reported by registered institutions and that have an overall deal size of at least USD 5 million.[4] In terms of deal size, no differentiation is made between the catalytic public or philanthropic investment and the private finance mobilised. Convergence used the data in a recent effort to analyse the blended finance market for the Blended Finance Breakthrough Taskforce led by the Business and Sustainable Development Commission (Convergence, 2017). This analysis looked at 187 deals that were defined as blending when they employed junior/subordinate capital, guarantees and risk insurance mechanisms, donor-funded technical assistance facilities, or the design or preparation of grant funding. It found blended finance funds and facilities were involved in 74% of the deals analysed (see Chapter 6) and at the project level (Chapter 7). The blended finance transactions, the analysis found, directed a total USD 51.2 billion towards the Sustainable Development Goals through, catalytic public or philanthropic funds as well as private finance mobilised (Convergence, 2017).

Another database is the World Bank's Private Participation in Infrastructure Project Database, which provides data on more than 6 000 infrastructure projects in low- and middle-income countries. These include data on investment volumes and sources for projects that have a level of private participation of at least 20%. As such, the database provides insights into how private finance is mobilised at the activity level for the infrastructure sector. Public-private partnerships are a combination of financial instruments that aim to establish a risk-return profile attractive enough to draw the private sector investment (Chapter 5).

Several commercial databases also capture data on the infrastructure sector that can provide useful insights for blended finance. Given the interest of large-scale private investors in such alternative investments, companies including Bloomberg or IJGlobal are tracking infrastructure deal flows. IJGlobal Transactions provides an overview of infrastructure projects starting in 2010; covers transport, power and water sectors; and currently covers more than 12 000 transactions.[5] The Bloomberg New Energy Finance database provides insights into renewable energy transactions, coving transactions in the wind, solar, bioenergy and nuclear sectors, among others; the database also covers newly built infrastructure, refinancing deals, and mergers and acquisitions in the sector. Both databases cover corporate and project infrastructure finance. Inclusion in the databases and access are restricted to subscribers (see also OECD, 2017). Blended finance transactions are not filtered.

Several data gaps continue to hamper an assessment of the blended finance market

The need for evidence in blended finance is evident, given its importance in financing the SDGs. While initial efforts to build an evidence base are shedding light on blended finance, crucial information such as the total market size and potential is not available. It is even more important to make available disaggregated, transaction-level data that would enable policy makers, governments, research organisations, private and public sector investors, and investees to better understand the efficiency, availability and additionality of blended finance. This would be especially useful if the data include development finance institutions' own funds, concessional windows, and commercial flows. Three issues from analysis of existing evidence on blended finance that also define what is important going forward:

- *Lack of a common framework of blended finance.* Initial data efforts build on divergent views and definitions of blended finance. For instance, concessional flows must be involved for a flow to be considered blended finance in some datasets while others, including the 2017 OECD survey presented in this report, consider blended finance to include any of the forms of official development finance (ODF). This difference inhibits the comparability of figures and studies.
- *Lack of transparency on the commercial dimension of blended finance.* ODF tracking is well established through the CRS and efforts are underway to implement track of other development-mandate flows such as philanthropy.[6] However, tracking private financial flows for development raise sensitivities and so is relatively underdeveloped. If it is tracked at all now, private finance is disclosed in data aggregates rather than at the activity level. Understanding individual transactions, however, is crucial if scarce development-mandate resources are to be used most effectively. It is important, therefore, to strike a sensible balance between confidentiality issues and the need for transparency, guidance and insights.
- *Lack of alignment and harmonisation.* Valuable efforts are being made to track blended finance specifically and private participation in development finance generally. While stand-alone surveys serve their purpose and help to investigate and better understand specific aspects of blended finance, they are of limited value from a macro perspective. Comparing specific survey results is challenging since their underlying frameworks of blended finance vary and they focus on different instruments and sectors. Future data-gathering efforts related to blended finance should align and leverage existing efforts, rather than building new systems.

Opportunities to better co-ordinate data gathering efforts emerge. Going forward, data efforts should build on a common understanding of blended finance. This publication makes the case for an OECD view on blended finance (see Chapter 3), which may shape future tracking approaches. In addition, the current level of transparency is inconsistent with expectations of and demand for the increasing importance of blended finance for development. The OECD DAC Blended Finance Principles strongly emphasise the need for transparency. Understanding the mechanisms of blended finance by looking at transaction as well as performance data, including the development impact, is crucial to effectively navigate the investment gap associated with the SDGs.

Notes

1. The Research Collaborative brings together stakeholders to share information and knowledge on how to track publicly mobilised, private climate finance. Its work is designed to address information needs under the United Nations Framework Convention on Climate Change including in relation to the commitment made by developed countries to mobilise USD 100 billion per year by 2020 in support of climate action in developing countries. See www.oecd.org/env/researchcollaborative.
2. For a full overview of similarities and differences between the approaches, see page 13 of the MDB Reference Guide, http://documents.worldbank.org/curated/en/495061492543870701/pdf/114403-PUBLIC-PrivInvestMob-Ref-Guide-Aug-14-2017.pdf.
3. See https://convergence.finance/press-detail/rhWu3d265iQMWSOMKAIuo.
4. The deal information includes name, sponsor, a short description, type of instrument, region, sector and the volume.
5. See https://ijglobal.com/data
6. The OECD has launched a survey on private philanthropy for development. See www.oecd.org/development/stats/beyond-oda-foundations.htm.

References

Benn, J., C. Sangaré and T. Hos (2017), "Amounts mobilised from the private sector by Official Development Finance interventions: Guarantees, syndicated loans, shares in collective investment vehicles, direct investment in companies, credit lines", *OECD Development Co-operation Working Papers*, No. 36, OECD Publishing, Paris, http://dx.doi.org/10.1787/8135abde-en.

Benn, J., C. Sangaré, T. Hos and Semeraro, G.M. (2016), "Amounts Mobilised from the Private Sector by Official Development Finance Interventions: Guarantees, syndicated loans and shares in collective investment vehicles", OECD Development Co-operation Working Papers, No. 26, OECD Publishing, Paris. http://dx.doi.org/10.1787/5jm3xh459n37-en.

Convergence (2017), "The state of blended finance", *Working Paper*, for the Blended Finance Breakthrough Taskforce, Convergence, Toronto, https://convergence.finance/knowledge-detail/1qdtFkf5Fq86S4u8U4G8YU.

Tew, R. and C. Caio (2016a), *Blended Finance: Understanding its Potential for Agenda 2030*, Development Initiatives, Bristol, UK, http://devinit.org/post/blended-finance-understanding-its-potential/.

Lonsdale, C. (2016b), "Aligning blended finance with the Busan principles of development effectiveness", *Discussion Paper*, Development Initiatives, Bristol, UK, http://devinit.org/wp-content/uploads/2016/10/aligning-blended-finance-with-the-busan-principles-of-development-effectiveness_di_discussion-paper.pdf.

Lonsdale, C. (06 July 2017), "Why transparency and accountability should be a principle of good blended finance", Development Initiatives blog, http://devinit.org/post/transparency-accountability-blended-finance/.

OECD (2017), *Investing in Climate, Investing in Growth*, OECD Publishing, Paris. http://dx.doi.org/10.1787/9789264273528-en.

OECD DAC (2014), "Measuring mobilisation in an international statistical system", DAC Note, OECD Publishing, Paris, www.oecd.org/dac/stats/principles-for-mobilisation.pdf.

World Bank (2017a), "Joint MDB reporting on private investment mobilization: Methodology reference guide", *Working Paper*, 114403, World Bank Group, Washington, DC, http://documents.worldbank.org/curated/en/495061492543870701/Joint-MDB-reporting-on-private-investment-mobilization-methodology-reference-guide.

World Bank (2017b), "Mobilization of private finance by multilateral development banks: 2016 joint report", *Working Paper*, 114433, World Bank Group, Washington, DC. http://documents.worldbank.org/curated/en/860721492635844277/Mobilization-of-private-finance-by-multilateral-development-banks-2016-joint-report.

World Economic Forum/OECD (2016), *Insights from Blended Finance Investment Vehicles & Facilities*, ReDesigning Development Finance Initiative, OECD/World Economic Forum, Paris/Cologny, Switzerland, www3.weforum.org/docs/WEF_Blended_Finance_Insights_Investments_Vehicles_Facilities_report_2016.pdf.

Chapter 9

Monitoring and evaluation in the context of blended finance

Monitoring and evaluation (M&E) are essential to assessing the performance of blended finance and raising awareness on its effectiveness in achieving development outcomes. This chapter presents an overview of existing M&E systems for private sector engagement in development co-operation and highlights implications for blended finance. It reviews governance of M&E as well as challenges and issues relating to monitoring and the importance of evaluation. The chapter presents the main areas that need to be addressed in order to strengthen M&E for future blending.

HIGHLIGHTS

Increasing fragmentation in the governance of blended finance presents a challenge for monitoring and evaluation (M&E). Results frameworks must meet the needs of all partners, and several layers of intermediation can hamper information flows.

The quality and completeness of monitoring information collected in blended finance need to be improved. Results of the 2017 OECD survey of blended finance funds and facilities demonstrate that monitoring is not always conducted at the project level and ex-ante data collection is not mandatory in all reported funds and facilities.

Evaluation is critical for blended finance but many evaluation strategies have yet to fully address its specificities. Many bilateral development finance institutions that engage in blended finance lack a formalised evaluation strategy and even where one is in place, it may not explicitly address the relatively new field of blended finance.

Many donor governments have not yet adopted guidelines on how blended finance should be monitored or evaluated, in contrast to other tools in their development co-operation strategies. Impact is not properly measured, yet it is key to establishing evidence of proven success for blended finance.

Shortcomings on monitoring and evaluation will need to be addressed as the blended finance market matures and continues to grow in scale. These include balancing between performance indicators and impact observed on end beneficiaries, testing the causal link and integrating the results of M&E into decision making on blended finance.

Key facts

- 22% of the blended finance funds and facilities surveyed for this report have no formalised internal M&E function
- For 77% of the surveyed funds and facilities ex ante data collection is mandatory on all projects. Data collection differs significantly at the closure stage, when 93% of the surveyed facilities but only 48% of funds require final updates.
- Evaluation practice vary greatly depending on the vehicle, with 81% of the surveyed blended finance facilities reported having undertaken at least one evaluation compared to 56% of funds. Less than half of final evaluation reports from surveyed facilities and funds are made public.

Introduction

Effective deployment of blended finance is hindered by the lack of a robust evidence base on what works and what does not work in mobilising commercial finance and delivering development results. Monitoring and evaluation (M&E) are essential to assessing the performance of blended finance and building such an evidence base. This chapter looks at existing M&E systems for private sector engagement activities among development finance providers and highlights implications for blended finance. It presents an overview of existing M&E frameworks, discusses monitoring of blended finance, outlines the role of evaluation in fostering learning at the policy and practitioner levels, and highlights remaining challenges. The analyses presented in this chapter draw primarily from the 2017 OECD survey of blended finance facilities and funds (Chapter 6), a literature review, and interviews with experts from development finance organisations.[1]

Why monitoring and evaluation are needed in blended finance

While closely interrelated, monitoring and evaluation (M&E)[2] are distinct functions that aim to produce different sets of information and influence different decision-making processes. Monitoring includes but is not limited to transactional data. It should also gather information on the non-financial performance of an intervention, i.e. related to the outputs and possibly the outcomes towards sustainable development. Evaluation builds on the available monitoring information and collects additional primary data. By cross-analysing different sources, evaluation is meant to produce robust evidence on the relevance, efficiency, effectiveness, impact and sustainability of a development intervention.[3]

Monitoring and evaluation is key to reporting and to effective implementation

Development finance providers need sound monitoring and evaluation (M&E) to report their contribution to achieving the Sustainable Development Goals (SDGs). The OECD DAC Blended Finance Principles confirm the importance of monitoring blended finance results in order to agree on performance and result metrics from the start; track performance and development results throughout the intervention; and dedicate appropriate resources for monitoring and evaluation (OECD DAC, 2017).

Most donor countries identify private sector mobilisation as a priority in their development co-operation policies, but few have yet defined a specific strategy on blended finance (Chapter 3). In those countries that have such a strategy, the stated objectives in terms of development outcomes clearly underpin the need for a solid and robust reporting system. In the United Kingdom, for instance, blended finance instruments are expected to reach a sustainable and systemic development impact and also must be commensurate to the use of concessionality.[4] Evaluating the performance of blended finance against such standards would require a refined tracking system, able to relate the level of disbursed subsidies to the results actually observed in the field. Given the increasing prominence of blended finance in the context of global discussions on development, it is becoming ever more important for development finance providers to capture and communicate their contributions to the progress on SDG indicators.

Apart from the international agenda, blended finance operations also must measure their performance against stated development goals for strategic stakeholders, taxpayers and investors. M&E also is crucial for decision making at the operational level. Indeed, blended finance funds and facilities responding to the 2017 OECD survey use monitoring information to support decision making on project approval and renewal, in communications with governing boards and investors, and for wider public dissemination (Box 9.3).

Only effective monitoring and evaluation systems can address concerns about blending

A number of concerns have been raised about the impact and effectiveness of blending. Ensuring that robust M&E systems are in place will be essential for the scaling up of effective blended finance (Vaes and Huyse, 2015; Commons Consultants, 2015; Savoy, Carter and Lemma, 2016; Boyd, R. et al., 2017). Little reliable evidence has been produced linking initial blending efforts with proven development results. This has exacerbated fears of potential misuse of public support and/or market distortion. Moreover, there is a greater need for blending practices to prove their leveraging effect and in particular their development additionality, i.e. the development results that could not have been achieved without the mobilisation of commercial capital. Since complex experimental techniques have never been applied at scale in this field, meta-evaluations may be needed to pull together sufficient evidence to that effect (Paniagua and Denisova, 2013). Finally, development finance providers have a diverse understanding of what development impact is and how it should be assessed.

Monitoring and evaluation systems for blended finance are evolving

Governance of blended finance influences the monitoring and evaluation function and tools

The formalisation of M&E systems is a critical step to establish clear lines of responsibility within the corporate structure of blended finance mechanisms, especially when relying on independent vehicles such as funds, and to promote the visibility of the M&E function internally and externally. The governance of M&E systems will often mirror the complex and multi-layered architecture of blended finance instruments (Figure 4.3 in Chapter 4), as each individual instrument must adapt its results framework to meet the needs of all partners, as well as of the investment. Lessons from the OECD DAC on private sector engagement suggest that, to promote ownership and buy-in from staff on blended finance operations, government institutions should ensure that M&E provisions are established at the outset of partnerships and that allocated resources are proportionate to the size of investments (OECD, 2016).

Development finance providers usually have internal, but not necessarily independent, teams in charge of M&E. This ensures compliance with the monitoring requirements and requires evaluations as part of the wider institution's learning approach. Multilateral development banks, in response to requirements of their member countries, have well established M&E systems for both public and private sector operations. For example, the monitoring and evaluation policy of the International Finance Corporation (IFC) is fully aligned with that of its sister organisation, the World Bank. MDBs also usually track blending operations as part of their overall portfolio. The IFC does so through its Development Outcome Tracking System, one of the oldest and most advanced in the field. Other MDBs have set up their own corporate tools and may make separate arrangements for specific financing instruments. For instance, the Canadian Climate Fund for the Private Sector in Asia, a single-donor trust fund managed by the Asian Development Bank, is integrated with the design and monitoring framework of the Clean Energy Financing Partnership Facility. Another example is the World Bank-run Global Environment Facility (GEF), which has its own M&E policy.[5]

The monitoring and evaluation function for bilateral development finance providers is validated and closely overseen by the government since ministries or aid agencies generally manage development co-operation. Responses to the 2017 OECD survey of blended finance funds and facilities suggest that donor-led facilities are more likely to identify internal M&E responsibility within the organisational chart than funds, which generally are managed by development finance institutions, multilateral development banks or private fund managers (Box 9.1). Most development finance institutions have established proprietary monitoring and evaluation systems. A leading example is the Corporate Policy Project Rating, developed by the German Investment Corporation (DEG) as an internal decision-making tool and now used by 15 other DFIs. Building on this experience, and guided by the 2030 Agenda for Sustainable Development, the DEG currently is piloting a new monitoring system that also will be proposed to European DFIs.

Monitoring and evaluation arrangements differ according to the managing organisation

Blending instruments led by a multilateral or bilateral public investor can rely on pre-existing M&E resources, as described above. Private managers, however, must build such competency in house. The OECD 2017 survey finds that privately managed blended finance vehicles usually comply with the M&E requirements of their main investor[6] or, in the most mature cases, have set up their own ad hoc monitoring system, often in compliance with the IFC Performance Standards.[7] The more impact-oriented companies generally identified a person in charge of environmental, social and governance (ESG) standards and so-called "impact" reporting.[8]

Box 9.1 **Responsibility for monitoring and evaluation in blended finance funds and facilities**

The 2017 OECD survey of blended finance funds and facilities included questions concerning their monitoring and evaluation (M&E). Responses were received by 43 facilities (USD 20.3 billion in commitment in-flows) and 31 funds (USD 9.3 billion in assets under management). Annex B provides details on the survey methodology. The following are some of the key takeaways on these questions:

- More than 88% of the facilities and 74% of funds responding have a formalised M&E function. In the majority of these, the organisation chart clearly identifies a team or unit responsible for M&E. Overall, 22% of the respondents have no formalised internal M&E function and the responsibility for such activity lies with each investment or project manager. The survey responses were not correlated to the age or size of the blending instrument. Funds were more likely to make M&E a line management responsibility. Facilities tend to have an independent M&E function reporting directly to the board of directors or equivalent body. Structured and private equity funds are least likely to have an internal M&E function.
- A majority (87%) of donor-managed blending instruments have clearly identified M&E resources. This drops to 75% for those managed by private companies and 50% for development finance institutions. When a multilateral development bank or other multilateral organisation manages the instrument, the M&E function usually lies with the main investor.
- Most respondents have established a monitoring system to track progress towards the achievement of their objectives. Of the blended finance funds, 55% have developed their own monitoring system; 32% use the monitoring system of their main investors or an adaptation thereof. Of the facilities, 72% have defined their own monitoring system.

Private sector operations in DAC member countries have an array of governance arrangements. These influence how monitoring and evaluation of blending is framed and conducted (Box 9.2, see also Chapter 4). For example, M&E obligations may differ significantly from those of other development co-operation actors where the development finance institution or export credit agency is directly managed by one or more ministries and is governed by separate institutional arrangements. Where the development finance institution is embedded in a development bank or an export credit agency,[9] ministries may lose sight of what information is available and to what extent individual activities contribute to the overall development co-operation strategy.

The DFI's sensitivity to public accountability will depend on its ownership, which may be fully in the government's control; delegated to a development bank, aid agency or export credit agency; or under the partially control of private shareholders as is the case with most European DFIs. At times, a government ministry may only hold a seat on the institution's governing board. In these cases, there is a need for governments to take on a stronger co-ordinating role if they wish to understand the contribution of blended finance to the overall national development co-operation policy. Unless satisfactory oversight and accountability mechanisms are put in place to ensure communication of results to the wider public in both developed and developing countries, private engagement in development finance will continue to be met with suspicion.

Box 9.2 **Widening the range of European blending operations and its implications for monitoring**

In the European Union blending framework, responsibility for the monitoring of blended operations is delegated to the lead financial institution. A 2016 evaluation commissioned by the European Commission (EC) found that "the supervision and the monitoring of physical and financial project progress by the [international financial institutions] or their agents [have] been thorough" (ADE, 2016). However, it should be noted that during the period evaluated, implementation of the seven EC blending facilities was delegated to a relatively small number of well-established development banks. In fact, over 90% of blending was done with four major partners: the European Investment Bank, KfW, the French Development Agency and the European Bank for Reconstruction and Development.

The 2016 evaluation recommended increasing the number of financial partners and using special risk cushions to crowd in private funding. In response, eligible counterparts have been broadened to include private law entities from Member States or partner countries with adequate financial guarantees. The reform introduced in the 2014-2020 European Fund for Sustainable Development is intended to increase its attractiveness to the private sector, improve flexibility and maximise the impact of the investments. However, as the delegated partners are progressively diversified, the European Commission will need to make a major effort in terms of capacity building and oversight to ensure that the minimum monitoring and evaluation requirements are met.

Source: ADE (2016), Evaluation of Blending: Final Report, Volume I – Main Report, https://ec.europa.eu/europeaid/evaluation-blending_en.

Monitoring of blended finance activities need to be aligned

Efforts to harmonise monitoring practices are under way

Recent studies have highlighted the many differences in monitoring and reporting processes among multilateral and bilateral development banks that make data comparisons difficult (Lemma, 2015; Savoy, Carter and Lemma, 2016; Boyd et al., 2017). Development finance providers have made efforts to harmonise monitoring and evaluation practices and to expand co-ordination on information sharing at the multilateral and bilateral levels. In 2013, 25 development banks agreed to work towards harmonising their development result indicators with the aim of reducing variations in data, the reporting burden on clients and facilitating lesson learning.[10] Another example is the the Mutual Reliance Initiative[11] agreed by the European Investment Bank, the French Development Agency and KfW, which allows these institutions to use each other's supervision and monitoring systems and reduce the administrative burden on partner countries. Private managers are also converging towards standardised metrics, especially for social impact investing.[12]

Development practitioners widely recognise the interest of a broad alignment, on a set of core indicators at a minimum, to ensure the consistency and comparability of data produced while preserving the opportunity for elective adaptations depending on the instrument's specificities. Ultimately, the usefulness of such efforts hinges on the availability of commensurable data, on the accuracy of data collection, and on the willingness of development finance providers to publicly engage in such comparisons.

The quality of monitoring information needs to be improved

The quality of project monitoring is instrumental to improve implementation (ADE, 2016). Nonetheless, there is wide divergence in development finance providers' support for and engagement in M&E. The quality and completeness of monitoring data for private sector operations also vary widely and this, in turn, influences the accountability of blended finance overall. The 2017 OECD survey points to a number of quality issues relating to monitoring of blended finance. First, project level reporting can be cumbersome, leading some blended finance managers to deploy their M&E system only at the portfolio level rather than for individual projects (Box 9.3). This is the case in 35% of surveyed blended finance funds. Furthermore, as shown in the survey responses, ex-ante data collection is not mandatory for all projects (Figure 9.1). More commonly, managing organisation will perform an interim data collection, half way through the investment lifetime, in the interest of checking progress and making adjustments. Less than half of the surveyed funds will systematically update monitoring indicators at investment closure.

Box 9.3 **Diverse monitoring processes in blended finance funds and facilities**

The 2017 OECD survey of blended finance funds and facilities finds significant differences is monitoring across funds and facilities.

- **Type of information collected:** Quantitative targets to track performance against objectives were identified by 80% of the surveyed funds and 53% of the surveyed facilities. In terms of the types of indicators used, funds are significantly more likely to define economic, social and environmental targets and corresponding indicators. Governance indicators are less frequently used across both funds and facilities. 91% of the facilities apply these targets at the project level compared to 55% of the funds, which tend to monitor them only at the portfolio level.
- **Use of monitoring information:** Monitoring information is used by 80% of the surveyed funds and facilities for decision making on project approval or renewal; for initiating project amendments, where necessary (45%); to inform reporting for all investors (73%); in communications to the governing board (57%); as evidence for internal or external evaluation (68%); and for public dissemination (59%). Private managers, multilaterals and development finance institutions are significantly more likely to use monitoring data for external dissemination.
- **Frequency and timing of data collection:** For 77% of the surveyed funds and facilities, ex ante data collection is mandatory on all projects (Figure 9.1). Mandatory interim updates are required by 84% of facilities and 74% of the funds. Data collection differs significantly at the closure stage, when 93% of the surveyed facilities but only 48% of funds require final updates. Only 20% of the surveyed funds and facilities systematically collect information one year or more after the investment.

Figure 9.1 **Mandatory data collection at the project level across blended finance funds and facilities**

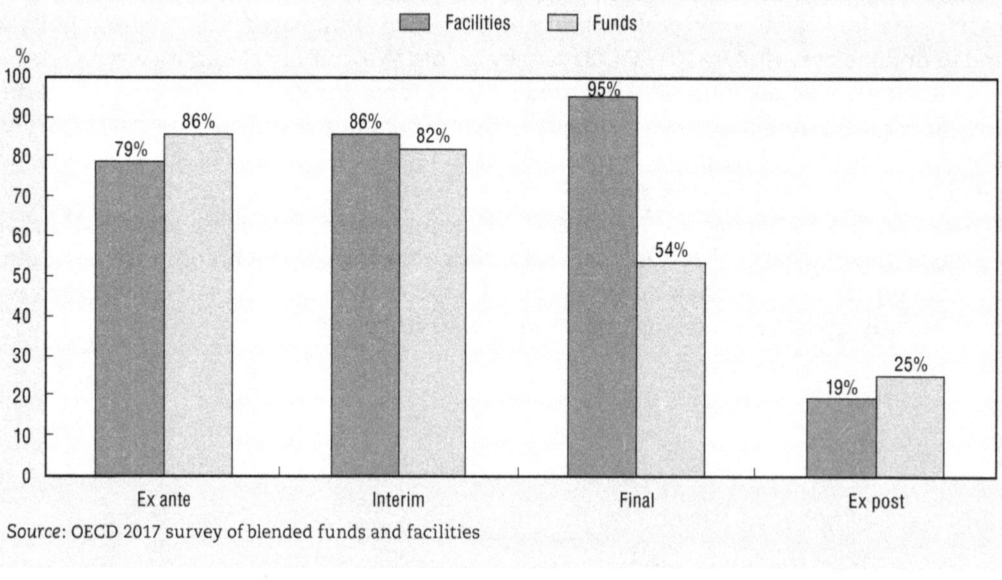

Source: OECD 2017 survey of blended funds and facilities

In addition to the frequency and the granularity of indicators, the manner in which monitoring information is collected is also important. Monitoring indicators for private sector operations are usually filled by internal officers, based on the client's declarations and under the supervision of M&E units.[13] This practice could potentially introduce a conflict of interest, as the same team that agrees to the investment also rates projects, creating potential bias in their judgement, and client declarations are quality checked by the same officers. Besides appropriate quality checks, a financier's ability to generate accurate data thus heavily depends on awareness raising and capacity building amongst operational staff and clients.

Blending operations are not always earmarked in the corporate M&E system or tracked in harmonised manner with other official development flows, presenting additional difficulties in gathering performance data (Chapter 7). For instance, in the GEF Project Management Information System, private sector engagements are not easily retrieved and improvements are needed to ensure systematic tagging (GEF, 2017). As such, the development results that might possibly be tracked cannot be isolated just for blended finance activities. The same issues arise for national development finance institutions. The public contribution to the Netherlands Development Finance Company (FMO) operations, for example, cannot be separately identified, making it difficult to assess how the FMO portfolio is complementing Dutch development programmes (OECD, 2017).

Monitoring information does not cover impacts (nor should it be expected to)

By design, monitoring rarely continues beyond the end of the project implementation, when the impact occurs and can be identified. This is true for blended finance, as it is for most development co-operation. Based on the 2017 OECD survey, only 20% of blended finance funds and facilities systematically collect information one year or more after the investment (see Box 9.3 above). A review mandated by the European Commission also found great variation in the degree to which socio-economic, transition and development impacts are monitored across the seven European blending facilities, which the authors described as a weakness (ADE, 2016).

Evaluation is a more appropriate tool for assessing impact beyond the life of the intervention. Monitoring data will typically capture outputs or, at best, immediate outcomes.[14] A 2013 report by the World Bank Independent Evaluation Group noted that the Development Outcome Tracking System (DOTS) provides little information on results for end beneficiaries:

DOTS tracking is based on "proxy" figures from the financial institutions' portfolio, such as number of loans given to a targeted business segment and the quality of that portfolio. IFC has limited knowledge about the underlying results on its end-beneficiaries, and any claims would be difficult to attribute to the IFC intervention (IEG, 2013)

The impact data quality of European blending instruments has been rated as medium to low, with the exception of DFI impact funds.[15] Impact reporting, when it draws uniquely from the monitoring system, is often based on estimates rather than actual, verified data. While the reported quantitative impacts often converge on similar categories (employment, government revenues, consumer reach, environment, private sector development), their calculation methodology is not yet harmonised across institutions.[16] Moreover, the same development finance provider may use different measurements for the same variable on ex-ante and ex-post assessments.

Evaluation is critical to improve blended finance efforts

Evaluation is essential to ensure evidence-based decision making in order to continuously improve the way resources are allocated and projects managed. The governance arrangements of the blended finance vehicle largely determine how evaluations are conducted. They can be undertaken at the institutional level, when the scope of the evaluation covers the overall development co-operation policy or blending approach of a development finance provider. An evaluation can be conducted for a specific vehicle, i.e. a blended finance fund or facility, ideally to inform decisions on its replenishment. Evaluation may also take place the project level, although these often take the form of light assessments made by monitoring staff during field visits. The choice of when and where to position the evaluation often entails a trade-off between promoting institutional learning for the finance provider and ensuring local ownership of the process.

Many evaluation strategies have yet to fully address the specificities of blended finance

Formalising a multi-year M&E strategy may help ensure synchronisation of evaluation activities and decision making. Establishing a formal evaluation policy is different from setting up a monitoring system and practices will again vary according to the development finance provider. While bilateral DFIs and export credit agencies have monitoring systems, many may lack a formalised evaluation strategy.[17] Even where donor governments and MDBs have an evaluation strategy, it may not explicitly address the relatively new field of blended finance. As a consequence, the specificities of private sector mobilisation rarely are taken into account.

The 2017 OECD survey highlights some preliminary issues related to the evaluation of blended finance (Box 9.4). Overall, evaluations practices appear to be more mature for those blended finance vehicles that are managed by donor governments. Blended finance facilities, for instance, are more often required to carry out evaluations, conduct them periodically, and mandate them to external (and presumably independent) consultants. Some donors may also perform tailored evaluations of their positions in a given blended finance instrument.[18] The survey also finds that blended finance facilities are more likely to make the results of their evaluations public. Additionally, some facilities may publish management responses or lessons learned (e.g. the German DeveloPPP programme and the United Kingdom's Responsible and Accountable Garments Sector facility). It remains unclear, however, whether blended finance evaluations have prompted internal action plans for the implementation of their recommendations. Effective knowledge management systems are needed to ensure good practices drawn from evaluations actually feed into strategic planning processes and subsequent activities (OECD, 2016).

Despite some notable examples, the survey also suggests that external accountability of blended finance vehicles is weak. Although some respondents recognised that evaluations can increase legitimacy, more than half do not make their evaluation reports publicly available. This is at odds with common practice in the development co-operation field. Most often, in the absence of a legal obligation for public dissemination, the blended finance funds and facilities only share such reports internally within management or with their financing partners.[19]

The OECD survey also finds that almost all reported evaluations are theory based and make use of a mixed-methods approach encompassing qualitative and quantitative data analysis.[20] End beneficiaries are often consulted but rarely in an exhaustive (or at least statistically representative) manner. This may be due to budgetary constraints; difficulties identifying the individuals concerned, as is typical for long delivery mechanism; and/or difficulties in reaching beneficiaries, which is often the case in developing countries.

Box 9.4 Evaluation practices vary in blended finance funds and facilities

The 2017 OECD survey finds a diversity of evaluation practices among blended finance funds and facilities.

Level and frequency: Of the surveyed blended finance vehicles, 81% facilities and 56% of funds reported having undertaken at least one evaluation. Donor-led instruments are almost systematically evaluated (93%), but the same does not apply to the ones managed by DFIs (80%), by private entities (79%) and even less for MDBs (75%). For 7% of the surveyed vehicles, evaluation has never been performed, nor it is planned in the near future. This finding mainly concerns privately managed facilities and structured funds. Overall, 70% of respondents reported they undertake recurring evaluations. Among donor-led vehicles, 85% reported that evaluations are conducted regularly.

Motivation for evaluations: Evaluations were performed out of contractual obligations by 65% of the facilities and 23% of the funds. Donor-led vehicles are the most likely to perceive the evaluations as compulsory. Privately managed funds reported most of their evaluations to be voluntary and self-initiated (i.e. not required by investors).

Responsibility for evaluations: Almost 70% of reported evaluations were carried out by external consultants. Funds are more likely to conduct in-house evaluations through internal staff, whereas facilities will most often contract them out to external consultants (84%). Where private managed funds are concerned, 43% of the evaluations are performed by internal M&E staff, identified as part of line management, raising doubts about the robustness and impartiality of results..

Dissemination of evaluation reports: About 40% of surveyed funds and facilities publish their final evaluation reports. The percentage is much higher for donor-led instruments (75%) compared to 29% for vehicles that are privately managed, 24% for multilateral blended finance vehicles, and 13% for DFIs. The dissemination of evaluation results is similar across funds and facilities, but flat funds are the least likely to fully disclose evaluation reports, which most often are shared only with investors (60%).

Evaluation data collection: Evaluations performed by or for the surveyed funds and facilities mostly rely on monitoring data, interviews with clients and end beneficiaries, and benchmarking. Facilities use more varied data collection tools and are more likely to consult end beneficiaries. Almost all reported evaluations featured client interviews (90%), sometimes with the help of surveys (11%). About 70% of the evaluations also included data collection with end beneficiaries, but the use of surveys was extremely limited (4%). This could partially be explained by the novelty of these instruments, whereby long- term impacts are not yet observable on end beneficiaries. MDBs, donors and private managers are the most likely to mandate evaluations addressing end beneficiaries.

Source: OECD 2017 survey of blended finance funds and facilities.

Evaluation is hampered by the lack of a common vocabulary and understanding concerning development results

There is no shared understanding among blended finance actors regarding the definition or assessment of development results. Development finance providers have different practices, and often use the terms "results", "outcomes" and "impacts" interchangeably.[21] Evaluation reports, for example, are sometimes confused with implementation, monitoring, impact or sustainability reports. In the 2017 OECD survey, some privately managed blended finance funds confuse "activity reports", which are solely based on monitoring information, with "impact" reporting, which should pertain to evaluation. Development results, if available, can be presented as part of annual implementation reports, in separate impact studies, reviews and/or independent evaluations. In financial vocabulary, "evaluation" often is used to describe the ex-ante financial appraisal of investment opportunities. Furthermore, external communication on blended finance does not always draw a clear distinction between estimated and observed impacts. The confusion of terms and the lack of methodological rigor undercut efforts to properly assess and promote development results.

In addition, the blended finance community is still debating whether the mobilisation of private finance can, in itself, be considered as an impact. Hartmann, Gaisbauer and Vorwerk (2017) note, for example, that some blended finance actors are questioning whether co-operation with the private sector "represents added value in itself", apart from related development results. From the M&E perspective, and depending on where and when the private sector mobilisation has occurred, this could at best be classified as an outcome.[22] As shown in Figure 9.2, development impacts are socio-economic changes in society or the environment and go beyond changes to financial flows.

Figure 9.2 **Monitoring data versus evaluation evidence along the delivery chain**

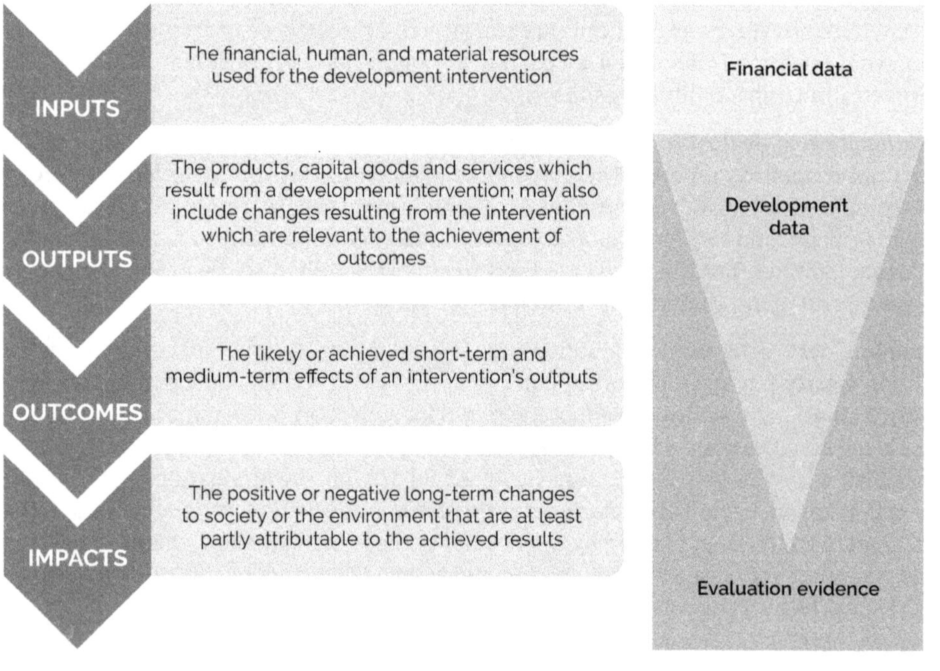

Source: Adapted from OECD (2002), "Glossary of key terms in evaluation and results based management", https://www.oecd.org/dac/evaluation/2754804.pdf.

Impact assessment techniques for blended finance and the attribution problem

While MDBs have performed extensive evaluations (e.g. World Bank, 2001), significant knowledge gaps still exist on the development impact of development finance institutions at the macro level (Lemma, 2015; Savoy, Carter and Lemma, 2016). This is the case particularly for poverty reduction, productivity and climate change (Massa, Mendez-Parra and te Velde, 2016) and other distinctive features of blended finance such as additionality, crowding out and value for money.

From a methodological point of view, the main obstacle remains the absence of counterfactual evaluations. When quantitative impact estimations are attempted, the contribution of the blended finance instrument will be considered proportional to the share of blended investments over the total budget. But in a more complex environment, the actual contribution is affected by numerous other factors, which in the absence of a control group cannot be isolated and controlled for in a statistically robust manner. Experimental approaches may produce a more accurate quantification of the observed impacts, but they are quite resource consuming. Theory-based evaluations instead will validate the underlying assumptions of the public intervention against the observed (qualitative and quantitative) outcomes by analysing the causal mechanisms, possible unintended effects and the specific context in which they work.

Blending instruments generally are aimed at wider macroeconomic development rather than "grass root targeting of poorest" (ADE, 2016). Their outcomes should thus conceivably be assessed as changes at the market level rather than through individual data collection. Different estimation methods (e.g. multiplier analysis, input-output models and micro-econometric analysis) are applied, making horizontal comparisons impossible.[23] Econometric models provide only estimates based on industry averages and different levels of data reliability, and pose the risk of double counting between direct and indirect effects. In addition, these methods do not provide an indication as to when the impacts will (supposedly) occur. Most importantly, economic impact estimates fail to take into account considerations such as environmental and social costs.

Monitoring and evaluation in blended finance faces several challenges

Many donor governments have not yet adopted guidelines on how blended finance should be monitored or evaluated, in contrast to other tools in their development co-operation strategies. As the blended finance market matures and continues to grow in scale, some shortcomings will need to be addressed:

- **Dominance of performance indicators and limited impact observed on end beneficiaries:** The development impact of blending often is assessed based on purely financial indicators, such as return on invested capital and return on equity, or on estimates made by staff and investees that may not have been updated during the life of the investment. End beneficiaries are rarely engaged with before the final evaluation, if there is one.
- **The causal link is rarely tested**: Most evaluations reveal the difficulty in attributing observed results to the blending operation or measuring its net contribution. This limits the learning potential for decision makers, both at the operational and at the strategic level.
- **Weak evidence-based decision making**: Ex-ante appraisals do not systematically occur before project approval or renewal, prompting criticism on the transparency of the investment allocation. Ex-post evaluation is seldom applied to the whole population and its findings rarely feed back into the system. Multi-annual evaluation strategies, which would allow better synchronisation with the decision-making cycle, are not yet common practice.

Impact measurement is the key to address existing criticism on the lack of accountability. A culture of learning must be actively promoted, recognising that various tools of evaluation can help inform policy makers, development finance providers and the public on the results achieved. In the long run, the international community may benefit from adopting a learning agenda on blended finance to guide the development of monitoring and evaluation practice. In adopting the OECD DAC Blended Finance Principles for Unlocking Commercial Finance for the SDGs, DAC members have committed to monitoring development results of their blended finance operations (OECD DAC, 2017). For some key players on the blended finance market, a culture shift is on the way.

Notes

1. These included 18 interviews conducted with experts from multilateral development banks, OECD DAC member ministries, aid agencies, bilateral development banks and development finance institutions.
2. OECD DAC Quality Standards define monitoring as "a continuing function that uses systematic collection of data on specified indicators to provide management and the main stakeholders of an ongoing development intervention with indications of the extent of progress and achievement of objectives and progress in the use of allocated funds." These standards define evaluation as the "systematic and objective assessment of an on-going or completed development intervention, its design, implementation and results". In the development context, evaluation refers to the process of determining the worth or significance of a development intervention. See OECD (2010), "Quality standards for development evaluation", www.oecd.org/development/evaluation/qualitystandards.pdf.
3. For more information on OECD DAC criteria for evaluating development assistance, see www.oecd.org/dac/evaluation/daccriteriaforevaluatingdevelopmentassistance.htm.
4. Based on the 2017 OECD survey of DAC members on Blended Finance (Annex A)
5. For details on the policy, see www.thegef.org/documents/monitoring-and-evaluation-policy
6. The Infrastructure Crisis Facility Debt Pool managed by Cordiant Capital, for example, uses the KfW reporting system.
7. Examples include GCPF, VitalCapital, Armstrong Asset Management, responsibility and Inspired Evolution Investment Management (Pty) Ltd. Often these ad hoc systems are designed to comply with the International Finance Corporation's Performance Standards.
8. Private managers of blended finance instruments with clearly identified personnel in charge of the M&E function typically also engaged on impact investment. Examples include Triple Jump, GroFin, Investisseurs et Partenaires, BlueOrchard, Finance in Motion and Maxwell Stamp. Others, such as Armstrong Asset Management, may have designated a resource person for compliance with environment, social and governance (ESG) standards,. Private asset managers where no public reference to monitoring or evaluation could be found in their organisational structure include Dolma Fund, Innpact Sarl, Symbiotics, Cordiant Capital, Inspired Evolution Investment Management (Pty) Ltd, ARM-Harith Infrastructure Investment Ltd and Incofin Investment Management.
9. This situation applies to three DAC countries: Austria, France and Germany. Canada will soon have the same situation.
10. For more on the Harmonized Indicators initiative, see https://indicators.ifipartnership.org/.
11. For more information, see www.eib.org/products/blending/mri/index.htm.
12. For instance, IRIS, an initiative led by the Global Impact Investing Network, proposes a free online taxonomy on how to measure the social and environmental performance of investments. These definitions underpin the Global Impact Investment Rating System, an impact ratings tool that assesses companies and funds on the basis of their social and environmental performance (e.g. VitalCapital). See https://iris.thegiin.org/.
13. This is mentioned in several M&E internal guidelines. See, for example, IFC (2011) Development Outcome Tracking System, www.ifc.org/wps/wcm/connect/5fd0a7004a57bb0bb346bf8969adcc27/DOTS+Handout+2011.pdf?MOD=AJPERES; IFC (2014), www.ifc.org/wps/wcm/connect/9f1a20804fb4c8d7a6b4ee0098cb14b9/IFC+Development+Impact+Fact+Sheet?MOD=AJPERES; and IEG (2013) report of evaluation systems of IFC and MIGA, https://ieg.worldbankgroup.org/sites/default/files/Data/reports/broe_eval.pdf.
14. In the most mature cases, some qualitative considerations may be integrated to the investment scoring system, e.g. in the DEG Development Effectiveness Rating (DERa), a job created will be weighed by the duration of the labour contract (KfW DEG, 2017).
15. Based on an unpublished study mandated by the EDFI: Common Consultants, 2015, *ODA for Blended Finance in Private Sector Projects*, Final report, 3 February 2015.

16. A notable exception is climate metrics. MDBs have put a lot of efforts into calculating greenhouse gas (GHG) reductions from projects in a harmonised way, driven in part by stringent monitoring requirements imposed by global environmental facilities. See www.ifc.org/wps/wcm/connect/518623004dc5f53c8e36aeab7d7326c0/IFI+Harmonisation+Framwwork+for++GHG+Accounting_Nov+2012.pdf?MOD=AJPERES.
17. To address this issue, some countries have set up an independent centre for the evaluation of development co-operation. An example is the German Institute for Development Evaluation (DEval).
18. For instance, The Currency Exchange Fund was randomly drawn by KfW as part of the project sample for ex post evaluation in 2012 (KfW, 2012)
19. Sometimes, selected evaluation conclusions may be included in other external communications. For instance, an external evaluation mandated by the Asian Development Bank of the Clean Energy Financing Partnership Facility, which includes the Canadian Climate Fund for the Private Sector in Asia, was shared with the financing partners. The evaluation has not been made public, although its conclusions are briefly summarised in the Bank's 2016 annual implementation report.
20. The few exceptions identified are quasi-experimental impact evaluations initiated by Oxfam Novib and Triple Jump on two microfinance institutions (VisionFund Ghana and Attadamoune Morocco, financed by the ASN Novib Microfinance Fund) in 2013. The drawbacks of a purely quantitative approach are clearly mentioned in the reports, as further qualitative research would be needed to interpret the results of the surveys and identify unexpected outcomes. Although the two evaluations reached similar conclusions, the learning opportunity for management was fairly limited, mainly due to the weakness in data reliability (based on the client's self-perception) and to the missing causal link between observed impacts and the products offered.
21. The OECD (2002) glossary of key terms in evaluation and results based management is widely used by development co-operation actors, but this is not yet the case in blended finance.
22. If one of the stated objectives of the blended finance mechanism is to mobilise private finance, then possibly it could be evaluated as part of the effectiveness criterion, but it would certainly not relate to impacts.
23. The pros and cons of different economic impact models, for instance, on job creation effects of DFIs, have been extensively investigated. Examples in the literature include 2011 and 2013 papers by Massa. They are available, respectively, at www.odi.org/sites/odi.org.uk/files/odi-assets/publications-opinion-files/7312.pdf www.odi.org.uk/publications/7370-brief-review-role-development-finance-institutions-promoting-jobs-productivity-change.

References

ADE (2016), *Evaluation of Blending: Final Report, Volume I – Main Report*, commissioned by the European Commission, Analysis for Economic Decisions (ADE), Louvain-la-Neuve, Belgium, https://ec.europa.eu/europeaid/evaluation-blending_en.

Boyd, R. et al. (2017) *The Productivity of International Financial Institutions' Energy Interventions*, Climate Policy Initiative, https://climatepolicyinitiative.org/wp-content/uploads/2017/03/The-Productivity-of-International-Financial-Institutions%E2%80%99-Energy-Interventions.pdf.

Commons Consultants (2015), *The Pitfalls of Innovative Private Sector Financing: Emerging Lessons from Benchmarking of Investment Funds Supported by Aid Agencies*, Summary Report, Commons Consultants, Copenhagen, www.norfund.no/getfile.php/134022/Bilder/Publications/Pitfalls%20of%20Innovative%20Private%20Sector%20Financing_Commons%20Consultants_final_150826.pdf.

DEG (2017), "Development effectiveness rating (DERa)", German Investment and Development Company (DEG), Cologne, www.deginvest.de/DEG-Documents-in-English/About-us/What-is-our-impact/Policy-brief_EN_final.pdf.

GEF (2017), *Evaluation of GEF's Engagement with the Private Sector*, Volume 1, Independent Evaluation Office of the Global Environment Facility, Washington, DC, www.thegef.org/council-meeting-documents/evaluation-gefs-engagement-private-sector.

GroFin (2015), *GroFin Impact Report 2015*, GroFin, Bambous, Mauritius, https://issuu.com/grofin/docs/grofin-impact_report-2015.

Hartmann, C., F. Gaisbauer and K. Vorwerk (2017), *Evaluation of the develoPPP.de Programme*, German Institute for Development Evaluation (DEval), Bonn, www.deval.org/files/content/Dateien/Evaluierung/Berichte/DEval_develoPPP_Bericht_EN_web_final.pdf.

IEG (2013), *Assessing the Monitoring and Evaluation Systems of IFC and MIGA: Biennial Report on Operations Evaluation*, Independent Evaluation Group, World Bank Group, Washington, DC, https://ieg.worldbankgroup.org/sites/default/files/Data/reports/broe_eval.pdf.

IFC (2014), *IFC's Development Impact: Learning from results, adding value for clients*, International Finance Cooperation, www.ifc.org/wps/wcm/connect/9f1a20804fb4c8d7a6b4ee0098cb14b9/IFC+Development+Impact+Fact+Sheet?MOD=AJPERES.

IFC (2011), "Development Outcome Tracking System", International Finance Corperation, www.ifc.org/wps/wcm/connect/5fd0a7004a57bb0bb346bf8969adcc27/DOTS+Handout+2011.pdf?MOD=AJPERES.

KfW (2012), "Ex-post Evaluation Brief:: TCX subordinated convertible debt facility", KfW Development Bank, Frankfurt, www.kfw-entwicklungsbank.de/Evaluierung/Ergebnisse-und-Publikationen/PDF-Dokumente-A-D_EN/Afrika_TCX_2012_E.pdf.

Lemma, A.F. (2015), "Development impact of DFIs: What are their impacts and how are they measured?", Overseas Development Institute, London, https://assets.publishing.service.gov.uk/media/57a08992e5274a27b200014f/Development-Impact-of-DFIs.pdf.

Massa, I. (2011), "The impact of multilateral development finance institutions on economic growth", Overseas Development Institution, London, www.odi.org/sites/odi.org.uk/files/odi-assets/publications-opinion-files/7312.pdf.

Massa, I. (2013), "A brief review of the role of development finance institutions in promoting jobs and productivity change", Overseas Development Institution, London, www.odi.org.uk/publications/7370-brief-review-role-development-finance-institutions-promoting-jobs-productivity-change.

Massa, I., M. Mendez-Parra and D.W. te Velde (2016), "The macreconomic effects of development finance institutions in sub-Saharan Africa", Overseas Development Institution, London, www.odi.org/sites/odi.org.uk/files/resource-documents/11182.pdf.

OECD (2017), *OECD Development Co-operation Peer Reviews: The Netherlands 2017*, OECD Publishing, Paris, http://dx.doi.org/10.1787/9789264278363-en.

OECD DAC (2017), "Blended Finance Principles for Unlocking Commercial Finance for the SDGs", Annex to the DAC High Level Communiqué,31 October 2017, www.oecd.org/dac/DAC-HLM-2017-Communique.pdf.

OECD (2016), *Private Sector Engagement for Sustainable Development: Lessons from the DAC*, OECD Publishing, Paris, http://dx.doi.org/10.1787/9789264266889-en.

OECD (2010), "Quality standards for development evaluation", *DAC Guidelines and Reference Series*, OECD Publishing, Paris, www.oecd.org/development/evaluation/qualitystandards.pdf.

OECD (2002), "Glossary of key terms in evaluation and results based management", OECD Publishing, Paris, https://www.oecd.org/dac/evaluation/2754804.pdf.

Paniagua, G. and A. Denisova (2013), "Meta-evaluation on job creation effects of private sector interventions, summary of preliminary findings, Assessing Private Sector Contributions to Job Creation, *IFC Open Source Study*, International Finance Corporation, Washington, DC, www.ifc.org/wps/wcm/connect/74b157804aebadb88e46fe888d4159f8/IFC_DOTS_factsheet_MetaEvaluation_FINAL.pdf?MOD=AJPERES.

Savoy, C.M., P. Carter and A. Lemma (2016), *Development Finance Institutions Come of Age: Policy Engagement, Impact and New Directions*, Center for Strategic & International Studies, Washington, DC, https://csis-prod.s3.amazonaws.com/s3fs-public/publication/161005_Savoy_DFI_Web.pdf.

te Velde, D.W. (2011), "The role of development finance institutions in tackling global challenges", Overseas Development Institute, London, www.odi.org/sites/odi.org.uk/files/odi-assets/publications-opinion-files/7310.pdf.

Triple Jump (2016), *Impact Report 2016*, Triple Jump http://triplejump.eu/wp-content/uploads/2016/09/Triple-Jump-Impact-Report-2016.pdf.

Vaes, S. and H. Huyse (2015), "Mobilising private resources for development: Agendas, actors and instruments", *Working Paper*, No.2, Belgian Policy Research Group on Financing for Development (BeFind), KU Leuven, , Leuven, Belgium, , www.befind.be/Documents/WPs/WP2.

World Bank (2001), *IDA's Partnership for Poverty Reduction (FY94-FY00): An Independent Evaluation*, Operations Evaluation Department, World Bank, Washington, DC, http://documents.worldbank.org/curated/en/894111468350146295/IDAs-partnership-for-poverty-reduction-FY94-FY00-an-independent-evaluation.

Annex A.
Summary of findings from a survey of OECD DAC members on blended finance

			Systems in place		Current and future plans for blending		
Country	Summary of blended finance activity	Main institutions involved	Strategy/ guidance in place for blended finance	Specific monitoring of blended finance	Current status	Importance of increased understanding of blending?	Future priorities
Australia	Blending is carried out through 1) bilateral and regional programmes where grants and technical assistance are used to help businesses or projects become investment ready or to blend with private capital for investment in business growth and 2) partners, where non-grant instruments (guarantees, equity and debt) are used to leverage commercial investment.	MDBs and other multilateral entities such as Private Infrastructure Development Group (PIDG).	Work in progress	Work in progress	Early stage	Important	Expand range of instruments in use for blending
Austria	Blending is carried out through grant-based support to business partnership programmes and through a range of instruments (debt and equity) at close-to-market conditions to support private investment.	Aid agency (Austrian Development Agency) and bilateral DFI (OeEB).	No	No	Established	Not important for now	Continue at current level
Belgium	Blending is carried out indirectly by using technical assistance and non-concessional investments.	Bilateral DFI (BIO)	Work in progress	Work in progress	Established	Important	Expand blended finance by developing a strategy, operational guidance and monitoring system
Canada	Blending is based on a history of mixed credits and pilots using equity, first loss guarantees, repayable contributions and investment in collective vehicles. Grants are used to provide partial protection against investment risks. Concessional finance is used to facilitate other products such as loans, equity, guarantees and insurance by external partners. Canada also invests in platforms to facilitate more blending.	MDBs and in the future through the new Canadian DFI.	Work in progress	Yes	Established	Important	Continue to deploy blended finance experimentally across sectors
EU	Blending is carried out by combining EU grants with loans or equity from public and private financiers to attract additional financing by reducing exposure to risk. Blending can include 1) investment grants and interest rate subsidies; 2) technical assistance; 3) equity and quasi-equity risk capital; and 4) guarantees.	Bilateral DFIs and EIB as well as a broader range of development actors.	Yes	Yes	Established	Important	Continue to deploy blended finance through dedicated facilities and new External Investment Plan
Finland	Blending is being initiated and operationalised.	Bilateral DFI (FinnFund)	Work in progress	No	Early stage	Important	Initiate blending programme
France	Blended finance has been mainly carried out through the use of concessional loans and technical assistance, either directly with companies or through financial intermediaries.	Bilateral development bank (AFD) and DFI (Proparco)	Yes	No	Established	Important	Expand the range of instruments in use for blending
Germany	Blending is carried out through 1) interest rate subsidies; 2) loan guarantees; and 3) grants including investment grants, grants for project preparation and grants for equity participation. Structured funds and financial intermediaries are used to involve private investors.	Bilateral development bank (KfW) and DFI (DEG)	Yes	Yes	Established	Important	Continue blended finance and target to underserved areas

			Systems in place		Current and future plans for blending		
Country	Summary of blended finance activity	Main institutions involved	Strategy/ guidance in place for blended finance	Specific monitoring of blended finance	Current status	Importance of increased understanding of blending?	Future priorities
Italy	Blending is carried out by mixing grants (national and European) with concessional loans in order to enhance concessionality and mobilise private finance; providing technical assistance; and taking equity stakes in investment funds.	Bilateral DFI (CDP)	Yes	No	Early stage	Important	Expand the range of instruments in use for blending
Japan	Blending is carried out through concessional loans channelled through financial intermediaries, financing to private sector projects (including debt and equity) at market rates, and technical assistance for project development and feasibility studies.	Bilateral technical co-operation agency (JICA)	No	No	Established	Important	Continue to use a range of instruments in blended finance activities
Korea	Blending is carried out through political risk guarantees and loans targeting PPP projects (through the Korean Economic Development Co-operation Fund) and seed funding to support early stage financing for entrepreneurs.	Bilateral technical co-operation agency (KOICA) and Korea EXIM (ECDF)	No	No	Early stage	Important	Expand the range of instruments in use for blending
Netherlands	Blending is carried out using a range of instruments: - grants, loans and guarantees.	Bilateral DFI (FMO) and other multilateral funds	Yes	No	Established	Important	Expand the range of instruments and thematic areas
Norway	Blending is carried out through a limited, untied, mixed credits programme and a private sector grants facility which mitigates investment risks.	Bilateral DFI (Norfund)	No	No		Important	Continue at current level (scale down mixed credits)
Portugal	Blending is being initiated, with grants being proposed as the main instrument at initiation.	Aid agency (IP Camoes) and bilateral DFI (SOFID)	No	No	Early stage	Important	Initiate programme
Spain	Blending has been carried out through the use of loans through partners.	Aid agency (AECID) and bilateral DFI (COFIDES)	No	No	Early stage	Important	
Sweden	Blending is carried out through a guarantee instrument, grant co-financing linked to market financed lending, technical assistance and public-private development partnerships.	Aid agency (Sida), bilateral DFI (SwedFund) and MDBs	No	Yes	Established	Important	Expand blended finance operations
UK	Blending is carried out by mixing grants and commercial resources to bring projects to viability.	Bilateral DFI (CDC) and MDBs	Yes	No	Established	Important	Expand blended finance operations

Note: This table excludes the six countries that responded to the survey but did not have any blended finance activities to report: Czech Republic, Greece, Hungary, Iceland, Poland and Slovakia. Seven DAC members did not respond to the survey: Denmark, Ireland, Luxembourg, New Zealand, Slovenia, Switzerland and the United States. Early stage programmes are those that have been described as such in the survey responses or those that have come into being since 2014.

Annex B.

Methodology for surveys on blended finance funds and facilities

Mapping funds and facilities

Two categories were identified for the purpose of this research: funds and facilities (see Table A2.1 for characteristics of each). An initial mapping was conducted to identify funds and facilities launched between 2000 and 2016, building on surveys by the Association of European Development Finance Institutions (EDFI) and World Economic Forum conducted in 2015, and on OECD surveys of amounts mobilised from the private sector by official development finance interventions (see Chapter 5). The mapping identified 356 blended finance vehicles that were set up in this time period, 167 of them facilities and 189 funds. Facilities are earmarked pools of development resources for blended finance; in contrast, funds always include commercial capital. Within the funds, a distinction was made between structured funds and flat funds. Structured funds allow actors with different risk/return profiles to invest in different tranches. In flat funds, all shareholders hold the same return and bear the same risk as the other.

Structured funds encompass a measure of concessionality, as development finance providers (especially governments) bear higher risk and/or receive lower returns than commercial investors. Among these are the Global Climate Partnership Fund, Global Energy Efficiency and Renewable Energy Fund (GEEREF) and SANAD Fund for MSME. In particular, development finance providers use junior/subordinated capital as their main instrument to crowd in capital in structured or layered funds. These feature longer maturity and subordinated, concessional terms such as lower yield, dividend or return.

In flat funds, all equity investors are treated equally. The measure of expected return may vary according to the funds from 2% to 20% annually. Some examples are The Small and Growing Businesses Fund, Rural Impulse Fund (RIF) II and Vital Capital Fund. Investors in a flat structure, with an expected return at 2%-5%, are patient investors who invest on concessional terms (e. g. IPDEV 2) and take more risk for a lower expected return than market rate. However, such cases are the exception; most flat funds are invested on non-concessional terms, meaning that investors expect a market-rate return for their capital invested at risk. Investors include development finance providers such as development finance institutions (DFIs), private foundations, high net worth individuals and commercial investors such as banks and pension funds. Flat funds target both financial and substantive development returns.

Table B.1 Comparing funds and facilities

	Facilities	Funds
Context	Public development finance	Financial sector
Definition highlights	Vehicles for channelling donor resources from development finance providers	Vehicles for pooling capital from different types of investors
Funders	Solely development-oriented (mostly governments and development banks)	Both development and commercially-oriented, with at least one of the funders being commercially-oriented
Detailed objectives	1) Earmark and pool donor resources for particular countries or issues 2) Foster innovation in donor financing and approaches 3) Increase policy coherence, coordination and synergies among donors	1) Benefit from diversification effect of portfolio to limit risk 2) Benefit from economies of scale by reducing transaction costs and engaging fund professional management services
Capital source instruments	N/A	Development funders: grants, loans, equity, guarantee Commercial funders: loans, equity
Investment instruments	Grants, loans, equity, guarantee	Loans, equity (rarely grants and guarantee)
Financial return requirement	Unclear	Yes
Governing rules	Customized financing and governance arrangements fitting donor needs	Market standards for alternative investment, private equity and venture capital
Advantages for investors	Multi-donor facilities/trust funds bring more visibility and influence for donor governments, reduce transaction costs, and allow targeting of finance towards countries and issues where bilateral presence is limited.	Pooling effects and economies of scale : 1) hire professional fund managers to implement the adequate risk-return strategy and reach higher return 2) lower transaction costs 3) diversify the investment portfolio and reduce unsystematic risk

Source: Adapted from IEG (2011) and interviews with fund and facility managers

Survey sample vs. mapping sample

Based on the initial mapping described above, a targeted survey was sent to 152 entities. Together these entities represented nearly USD 40 billion in total assets under management, which equate to approximately 65% of the total assets under management identified in the initial mapping work. The targeted vehicles were facilities and funds although compared to the sample identified in the mapping exercise, a slightly higher share of facilities and a slightly lower share of funds were contacted. This can be explained by the OECD's enhanced rapport and familiarity with public sector actors, which made access to information on facilities easier.

Of the 152 entities contacted, 74 responded. Survey respondents represent USD 29.6 billion in total assets under management, which is roughly 50% of the total assets under management identified in the initial mapping exercise. The split of facilities and funds in the responses reflected largely the split in the entities targeted by the survey. Within the 74 respondents, the average response rate per question was 84% with a standard deviation of roughly 16 percentage points.

Methodology

All reported amounts from the survey results were converted to USD dollars using OECD 2015 exchange rates (competitiveness indicators). Since some answers were given for a group of entities (e.g. European Union blending facilities), additional desk research was conducted to disaggregate some of the data (e.g. regional focus). Similarly, given the availability of the information, most information on assets under management and launch dates of the entities was compiled using the EDFI survey and desk research. To classify the regional focus of the respondents in percentage of assets under management (Africa, Asia, Europe, America or global), the survey team allocated 50% to each region when two regions were reported, and allocated 100% when one region was reported, and 100% to global when more than two regions were reported. Where no response was provided, desk research and information available on line were used.

Survey responses received

Table B.2 **Survey sample details**

Name of the fund or facility	Type	Structure (for funds only)	Size (USD million)	Launch Date
The African, Caribbean and Pacific Group of States Investment Facility	Facility		4022	2003
Access to Energy Fund	Facility		59	2006
African Development Bank Private Sector Facility	Facility		505	2013
Africa50 Infrastructure Fund	Fund	Structured	830	2013
ARM-Harith Infrastructure Fund	Fund	Flat	250	2013
Armstrong Southeast Asia Clean Energy Fund	Fund	Structured	164	2012
ASN Novib Microfinance Fund	Fund	Flat	265	1999
Canadian Climate Fund for the Private Sector in Asia II	Facility		151	2017
Clean Resources Asia Growth Fund	Fund	Flat	200	2009
InsuResillience Investment Fund	Fund	Structured	77	2015
Climate Investment Funds - Clean Technology Fund	Facility		509	2012
Climate Investment Funds - Strategic Climate Fund	Facility		219	2012
DEG SME Up-Scaling Fund	Fund	Structured	66	2013
The develoPPP.de programme	Facility		365	1999
Dolma Impact Fund	Fund	Flat	26	2014
Eco.business Fund	Fund	Structured	105	2014
Emerging Africa Infrastructure Fund	Fund	Structured	951	2002

Table B.2 **Survey sample details** *(cont.)*

Name of the fund or facility	Type	Structure (for funds only)	Size (USD million)	Launch Date
Employment for sustainable development in Africa (E4D)	Facility		133	2015
EU blending facilities (9 facilities) – Neighbourhood Investment Facility, Africa Infrastructure Trust Fund, Caribbean Investment Facility, Investment Facility for the Pacific, Investment Facility for Central Asia, Asia Investment Facility, Latin America Investment Facility, Agriculture Financing Initiative, Electrification Financing Initiative	Facility		3856	2007
European Fund for Southeast Europe	Fund	Structured	1251	2006
Evolution One Fund	Fund	Flat	94	2010
Finnpartnership	Facility		22	2007
Fonds d'investissement et de soutien aux entreprises en Afrique	Facility		276	2009
Global Environment Facility Non-grant Pilot	Facility		110	2014
Global Agriculture and Food Security Program	Facility		309	2009
Global Climate Partnership Fund	Fund	Structured	305	2009
Global Energy Efficiency and Renewable Energy Fund	Fund	Structured	245	2008
Global Innovation Fund	Facility		208	2014
Global Resilience Partnership	Facility		150	2014
Global SME Finance Facility	Facility		916	2012
Grassroots Business Investors Fund	Fund	Structured	49	2004
Green Africa Power LLP	Facility		163	2013
Green for Growth Fund	Fund	Structured	453	2009
GuarantCo	Fund	Structured	406	2006
Infrastructure Crisis Facility Debt Pool	Facility		650	2009
International Development Association (IDA) Private Sector Window Blended Finance Facility	Facility		600	2017
Infrastructure Development Fund	Facility		461	2002
IFC Catalyst Fund	Fund	Flat	418	2012
IFC-Canada Climate Change Program	Facility		335	2011
Impact Accelerator	Facility		54	2012
Impact Fund	Facility		162	2014
Infracredit	Fund	Structured	200	2014
Investisseur & Partenaire pour le Développement 2 (IPDEV2)	Fund	Flat	11	2015
Lives and Livelihoods Fund	Facility		375	2016
Micro and Small Enterprise Fund (MASSIF)	Facility		476	2006
Middle East and North Africa SME Facility	Facility		430	2013
MicroBuild Fund	Fund	Flat	100	2012
Microfinance Enhancement Facility	Fund	Structured	695	2009
Microfinance Initiative For Asia	Fund	Structured	175	2010
NN-FMO Emerging Markets Loan fund	Fund	Flat	150	2012
Nordic Climate Facility	Facility		26	2009
Oxfam Novib Fund	Fund	Flat	55	1998
Power Africa	Facility		2807	2014
Regional MSME Investment Fund for Sub-Saharan Africa	Fund	Structured	150	2010
Responsible and Accountable Garment Sector Challenge Fund	Facility		5	2010
Results-Based Financing for Low Carbon Energy Access Facility - Energising Development Programme	Facility		54	2013
Rural Impulse Fund II	Fund	Flat	127	2007
SANAD Fund for micro, small and medium enterprise	Fund	Structured	241	2011
Seed Capital and Business Development Facility - Dutch Good Growth Fund Investment Funds Local SMEs	Facility		44	2014
Small and Growing Businesses Fund	Fund	Flat	150	2014
Smallholder Finance Facility	Facility		50	2008
Sustainable Development Goals Fund	Facility		70	2014
The Currency Exchange Fund	Fund	Structured	740	2007
Tropical Landscapes Finance Facility	Facility		1100	2016
Vital Capital Fund	Fund	Flat	350	2011
Women Entrepreneurs Opportunity Facility	Facility		600	2014

Table B.3 **Facilities launched, by date of launch, 2000-2016**

Launch date	Names of facilities
2001	Business Linkages Challenge Fund; Developing Enterprises in South Asia (DESA) Facility
2002	Business Edge (BE); Energy and Environment Partnership (EEP) Central America; FEMIP trust fund; Infrastructure Development Fund (IDF); North Africa Enterprise Development Facility (NAEDF); OCT Investment Facility; PIDG trust (excl. sub-funds); Renewable Energy and Energy Efficiency Partnership (REEEP) for Latin America and the Caribbean; Renewable Energy and Energy Efficiency Partnership (REEEP) Southern African Secretariat; Renewable Energy and Energy Efficiency Partnership (REEEP) East Asia Regional Secretariat; Renewable Energy and Energy Efficiency Partnership (REEEP) South Asia Regional Secretariat; South Asia Enterprise Development Facility (SEDF)
2003	AFD DBSA Project Preparation and Feasibility Study (PPFS) fund; DevCo; Investment Facility for Africa Caribbean and Pacific countries (IF ACP); Investment Facility for Overseas Countries and Territories (IF OCT); Iraq Small Business Finance Facility (ISBFF); Program for Eastern Indonesia Small and Medium (SME) Assistance (PENSA)
2004	Balkans Infrastructure Development Facility (BID Facility); Business Sector Advocacy Challenge Fund: Ghana; PIDG Technical Assistance Facility (TAF); SME Finance Innovation Challenge Fund
2005	ACP-EU Energy Facility Pooling Mechanism; Energising Development Partnership (EnDev); Fund for African Private sector Assistance (FAPA); InfraCo Africa; NEPAD Infrastructure Project Preparation Facility
2006	Access to Energy Fund (AEF); Global Village Energy Partnership (GVEP); MASSIF
2007	EU - Africa Infrastructure Trust Fund (EU - AITF); Facility for Investment Climate Advisory Services (FIAS); FinnPartnership; FPM ASBL; FPM SA - Fonds pour l'inclusion financière en RDC; The Palestinian Loan Guarantee Facility (PLGF);West Bank/Gaza Loan Guarantee Facility (LGF)
2008	Africa Enterprise Challenge Fund (AECF); Carbon Capital Fund Morocco; Neighbourhood Investment Facility (NIF); Norwegian Microfinance Initiative (NMI) Professional Assistance Facility; Smallholder Finance Facility; Technical Cooperation Special Fund
2009	Energy and Environment Partnership (EEP) Mekong; FISEA; Global Trade Liquidity Program (GTLP Phase 2 - Agriculture); Infrastructure Crisis Facility - Debt Pool (ICF-DP); Microfinance Growth Facility (MiGroF);Nordic Climate Facility (NCF); Strategic Climate Fund (private sector); Western Balkan Investment Framework (WBIF)
2010	Asia Investment Facility (AIF); Beira Agricultural Growth Corridor (BAGC) Catalytic Fund; Energy and Environment Partnership (EEP) Africa; Energy and Environment Partnership (EEP) Andes; GAFSP Private sector window; Global Climate Partnership Fund (GCPF) TA Facility; Greater Anatolia Guarantee Facility; Green Climate Fund's private sector facility; Green for Growth Fund (GGF) TA Facility; InfraCo Asia; Investment Facility for Central Asia (IFCA); Latin America Investment Facility (LAIF); Responsible and Accountable Garment Sector Challenge Fund (RAGS); Turkey Mid-size Sustainable Energy Financing Facility
2011	ADB CP3 Asia; Africa Agriculture and Trade Investment Fund (AATIF) TA Facility; Canada Climate Change Program (CCCP); Energy and Environment Partnership (EEP) Indonesia; FEFISOL Microfinance Fund; Innovations Against Poverty (IAP); Phatisa/African Agriculture Fund (AAF) - TA Facility (AAF TA); Regional MSME Investment Fund for Sub Saharan Africa (REGMIFA) TA Facility; SANAD TA Facility; SIDA Innovations Against Poverty (IAP); Voxtra East Africa Agribusiness Fund TA facility
2012	Afghanistan Business Innovation Fund (ABIF); Africa Clean Energy Finance Initiative (ACEF); African Guarantee Fund for SME (AGF); African Guarantee Fund for SME (AGF) Capacity Development Trust; African Local Currency Bond Fund (ALCB); Caribbean Investment Facility (CIF); Clean Technology fund (private sector); Climate Finance Initiative; Fund for Internet Research and Education (FIRE) - SEED Alliance; Geothermal Risk Mitigation Facility (GRMF); Global SME finance facility; IADB MIF Public Private Partnership Program (Under GEF PPP Program); Information Society Innovation Fund (ISIF) Asia - SEED Alliance; Investment Facility for the Pacific (IFP); IRENA/ADFD Project Facility; Municipal Infrastructure Development Fund (MIDF); Peak II (Providing Employment and Knowledge); Powering Agriculture - An Energy Grand Challenge for Development; Regional Fund for Digital Innovation in Latin America and the Caribbean (FRIDA) - SEED Alliance; Sunref; Sustainable Energy Fund for Africa (SEFA); The Jordan Loan Guarantee Facility (JLGF); The Tunisian Credit Guarantee Facility (TCGF); The U.S.-Africa Clean Energy Finance Initiative (ACEF) ; Trademark East Africa Challenge Fund (TRAC); Vietnam Business Challenge Fund
2013	Beyond the Grid Solar Fund; Canadian Climate Fund for the Private Sector in the Americas (C2F); World Bank/MIGA Conflict-Affected and Fragile Economies Facility (CAFEF); European Investment Fund Social Impact Accelerator (SIA); Inter-American Development Bank (ADB) Energy Efficiency Finance Facility; IADB/IIC Energy Efficiency Guarantee Mechanism (EEGM); Girls' Education Challenge (GEC); Green Africa Power (GAP); MENA SME Facility; Private Sector Credit Enhancement Facility (PSF); The Canadian Climate Fund for the Private Sector in Asia
2014	Africa Sustainable Energy Facility (ASEF); Amplify: Collaborative Challenge Fund; DFID Impact Fund; DFID Impact programme TA facility; Dutch Good Growth Fund; Dutch SME Investing; Global Environment Facility 6 - Private sector; Global Infrastructure Facility - Infrastructure Loan Refinancing Facility (ILRF); Global Infrastructure Facility - Downstream Financing window - Capital market catalytic facility; Global Infrastructure Facility - Downstream Financing window - The contingent refinancing facility; Global Infrastructure Facility - Downstream Financing window - The counterparty risk-cover facility; Global Infrastructure Facility - Downstream Financing window - The FX liquidity facility; Global Innovation Fund (GIF); Global Resilience Partnership; JFJCM japan fund ; Logistics Innovation for Trade Fund; OPIC "Portfolio for Impact" program; Power Africa; Rockfeller/IFC development facility supporting private sector-led infrastructure projects ; SDG Fund; Seed Capital and Business Development (SCBD) Facility - Dutch Good Growth Fund (DGGF) Investment Funds Local SMEs ; The Climate-smart Agriculture Fund for Latin America and the Caribbean (CSAF); The Malawi Innovation Challenge Fund (MICF); The Renewable Energy Performance Platform (REPP); Women Entrepreneurs Opportunity Facility
2015	Africa Investment facility (AfIF); Climate Investor one - Development fund; Employment for Sustainable Development in Africa (E4D) ; Global financing facility (GFF) trust fund; Global Financing Facility in Support of Every Woman, Every Child (GFF); Indonesia Climate Change Trust Fund
2016	Agriculture Financing Initiative – AgriFI; Electrification Financing Initiative – ElectriFI; European Fund for Sustainable Development (EFSD); IFC InfraVentures - Global Infrastructure Project Development Fund; LEAP FUND ; Lives & Livelihoods Fund (LLF); Local Currency Facility (LCF); Madagascar Sustainable Landscapes Fund (MSLF); MENA SME Guarantee Fund ; Miga Guarantee Facility (MGF); Revolving Fund for Development Cooperation; Risk Mitigation Facility For Infrastructure (RMF); Scaling off-grid energy grand challenge for dev.; Tropical Landscape Financing Facility in Indonesia

Annex C.

Project-level case studies of blended finance

Case study 1: Providing access to high-quality seedlings for export-oriented crops

Official institution: Global Affairs Canada (GAC)

Blending partners: Mennonite Economic Development Associates (MEDA) and Tree Global Inc. (TG)

Challenge: Ghana's tree crop subsector and cocoa in particular accounts for a substantial 16% of gross domestic product and more than one-third of the country's foreign exchange earnings, while sustaining over 1.6 million families (Mennonite Economic Development Associates (MEDA) 2017). In recent years, tree crop production has declined significantly because of decreasing yields of farmers' aging and diseased trees.

Solution: GAC determined that financial incentives and risk sharing are needed to induce so-called "first-mover" companies and entrepreneurs who appreciate the market potential to invest in and develop these markets and supply chains. Under the Farmers' Economic Advancement Through Seedlings (FEATS) project, Global Affairs Canada provided funding of CAD 10.75 million to MEDA, a well-established international economic development non-governmental organisation, to design and implement a project to bolster Ghana's tree crop subsector over six years from August 2015-21. MEDA partnered with TG, an international tree nursery company, to invest in establishing modern, commercial-scale production and distribution nurseries to grow and supply high-quality seedlings to tree crop farmers across Ghana. The grant funding from Global Affairs Canada has successfully crowded in additional financing, including CAD 1.6 million investment from MEDA (sourced from private donors) and CAD 9.91 million from TG and other organisations (both cash and in-kind). In addition to this project contribution to implement critical complementary activities, Global Affairs Canada and MEDA together are making CAD 2.18 million of blended finance investments in TG in the form of structured, concessional loans.[1] In turn, these grants and concessional loans incentivise and enable TG, the project's key private sector partner, to raise low-cost, long-term finance and to invest CAD 5.1 million in establishing a new operating subsidiary in Ghana, installing commercial production capacity, and meeting its initial working capital requirements including for business development.

Impact: The project aims to contribute to improving the productivity and incomes of Ghanaian tree crop farmers and value chains by supplying 20 million quality seedlings of cocoa, cashew, rubber and shea to 100 000 smallholder farmers, both men and women. Productivity as well as incomes will be increased. The project will contribute to Sustainable Development Goal (SDG) 8 (decent work and economic growth) and SDG 5 (gender equality).

Case study 2: Increasing the availability of low cost renewable energy production (Lake Turkana Wind Power project)

Official institution: EU-DEVCO via the Africa Infrastructure Trust Fund (EU-AITF)

Blending partners: European Investment Bank (EIB); a consortium comprising KP&P Africa B.V. and Aldwych International as co-developers; Investment Fund for Developing Countries (IFU); Vestas Eastern Africa Limited; Finnish Fund for Industrial Cooperation Ltd. (Finnfund); KLP Norfund Investments AS (KNI); and Sandpiper. Vestas and Google have signed a share purchase agreement under which Google will acquire Vestas' shares in the project upon it's upon completion in 2017.[2]

Challenge: The Lake Turkana Wind Power project is unique, and is the largest wind power plant in Kenya and one of the largest private investments in the Kenya's history (EIB, 2011). Once completed, the wind park is expected to produce 310 MW of wind energy, the equivalent of 15% percent of Kenya's current installed energy production. The main sponsors, private companies and several development finance institutions, signed a power purchase agreement in 2010 with the Kenyan Power Company that set a fixed feed-in tariff over a 20-year period based on the project cost at that time. However, the financial close of the wind park was in jeopardy due to cost increases resulting from a long due diligence process and inadequate financing from debt providers.

Solution: EU-DEVCO stepped in via the EU-AITF along with blended concessional financing and with other non-concessional financing from European Investment Bank (EIB) to make the project viable again and reach financial close. The EU-AITF engaged as a public investor and provided special equity of EUR 25 million in the form of cumulative redeemable preference shares. The concessional financing was priced at below-market rates, subordinated in cash flows, and only repaid after all senior debt holders had been reimbursed. Potential dividends will be used for the financing of rural electrification or social projects within the local community. The EIB structured and is managing the financial instrument. It also is part of the senior lender group in the project with commercial investors. In order to avoid agency conflicts, two distinct teams within EIB are managing the two exposures.

Impact: Upon completion, the Lake Turkana Wind Power project will displace 16 million tons of carbon emissions during its lifetime and reduce Kenya's fuel imports by an estimated EUR 120 million annually. Hence, the project will result in an increased availability of low cost energy in Kenya and reduced carbon emissions and oil imports. It will contribute to SDG 9 (industry, innovation and infrastructure), and SDG 7 (affordable and clean energy).

Case study 3: Empowering households to access renewable energy and lower power costs

Official institution: Nordic Development Fund (NDF)

Blending partners: Global Environment Facility (GEF) via the World Bank Group and Rwandan households

Challenge: The demand for electricity is expected to increase across all sectors in Rwanda. Although the government has implemented an ambitious electrification programme connecting households to the electricity grid, it will face several challenges in meeting the increasing demand. Currently, electricity demand, particularly in peak times, exceeds the available capacity in Rwanda. Generally, water heating is one of the major sources of electricity demand. As a consequence, hot water supply is not ensured throughout the day.

Solution: NDF determined that the implementation of solar-operated heaters would address shortages in capacity and have the added benefit of lowering households' energy cost. NDF provided EUR 4 million in grant funding to the local project implementation unit, Rwanda Energy Group. The Global Environment Facility (GEF) provided an additional USD 300 000 in grant funding via the World Bank Group. Through the project's design and implementation, the actual blending takes place at the household level because grant funding mobilises household private contributions. A household pays 25% of the cost of a solar water heater upfront; a grant channelled through the Rwanda Energy Group covers another 25% of the cost; the remaining half is covered by disbursement of a non-interest bearing loan with a 24 month maturity, which is deducted from the energy bill issued by the national electricity utility. The repayment scheme allowed for an immediate net gain, which aims at incentivising private finance of 25% per solar water heater. The contributions of NDF and the Global Environment Facility back the grant, the loan element of the solar water heater purchase programme, and the initial programme design and awareness campaign.

Impact: The project resulted in the purchase of 1 370 solar water heaters; a baseline assessment estimated that only 100 such heaters were in use. This success has encouraged market development and led to a substantial reduction in greenhouse gases. One solar water heater reduces CO2 emission by one to two tonnes per year when it replaces an electric water heater; the actual solar heaters installed thus save an equivalent of 1 370 to 2 740 tonnes per year. As such, the project contributes to SDG 7 (affordable and clean energy).

Case study 4: Encouraging private sector participation in financing water sector projects

Official institution: Japan International Cooperation Agency (JICA)

Blending partners: United States Agency for International Development (USAID), Development Bank of the Philippines (DBP) and private financial institutions

Challenge: While the Philippines has made meaningful progress in installing pipe water systems, it continues to experience water shortages and water pollution (JICA, 2008). The DBP initiated the Philippine Water Revolving Fund (PWRF) project as a response to these issues by enabling private sector financing and thus decreasing the dependence on limited public funding (Paul, 2011). Nevertheless, private investment remained inadequate.

Solution: JICA allocated an initial JPY 1.5 billion concessional loan to the DBP with a 30-year maturity (inclusive of a 10-year grace period), which was co-financed with private financial institution funds that were loaned to both public (i.e. local governments and water districts) and private water service providers. The financing mix between DBP and the private financial institutions is set at 3:1 of the approved loan amount. The initial loan allocation subsequently was increased to JPY 7.6 billion, which has been fully disbursed. Concurrently, private financial institutions apply for a credit risk guarantee covering a maximum of 85% of their exposure. The Local Government Guarantee Corporation, a private entity, issues this guarantee. The USAID Development Credit Authority provided a co-guarantee facility that backs the guarantee, leading to a reduction in the credit risk exposure of the private financial institutions.

Impact: For the water sector, the PWRF project resulted in approximately 216 872 additional households being connected to water services as of January 2017. JICA is scheduled to conduct an external, ex-post evaluation in 2019. The intervention has enabled private financial institutions to engage in the water and sanitation sector by improving their confidence in lending to water service providers. The PWRF facility of DBP saw financing terms improve with tenors increasing from an average of 7 years to up to 20 years at lower fixed interest rates. This allowed water service providers to reduce borrowing costs and better manage their debt capacity. Although initiated and closed under the Millennium Development Goals, this long-term impact affects clean water and sanitation access, captured in SDG 6, and decent work and economic growth (SDG 8) by providing access to finance to municipalities.

Case study 5: Enabling municipalities to tap capital markets to fund infrastructure development

Official institution: KfW

Blending partners: Government of India, government of Tamil Nadu and private investors

Challenge: Municipalities in the state of Tamil Nadu lack access to finance to undertake local infrastructure investments. The government of Tamil Nadu created Tamil Nadu Urban Infrastructure Financial Services Limited (TNUIFSL), an asset manager it owned jointly with private financial institutions, to access private capital markets to finance infrastructure investments at the local level. Nevertheless, tapping capital markets to fund infrastructure projects remained challenging, especially for smaller projects.

Solution: KfW disbursed a concessional loan of EUR 10 million to the government of India. The loan was channelled to fund the subordinated tranche (35%) of the Water and Sanitation Pooled Fund, a special purpose vehicle managed by TNUIFSL that was designed to disburse loans to urban local bodies[3] (see Figure A3.1). The KfW-funded tranche was combined with the equity support by the government of Tamil Nadu as cash collateral (10%) to provide an additional cushion against potential losses. The special purpose vehicle issued two bonds, in 2012 and 2013, mainly to institutional investors at the local and state levels including public and private pension funds. The combination of the KfW concessional loan (with an interest rate of 0.75%) and interest on the bonds (the first bond issued at 10.6%) permitted on-lending on a revolving basis to municipal projects at a sustainable level. In early 2017, a third bond was issued with an additional support from KfW of EUR 5 million for the subordinated tranche.

Figure C.1 **Structure of the Water and Sanitation Pooled Fund**

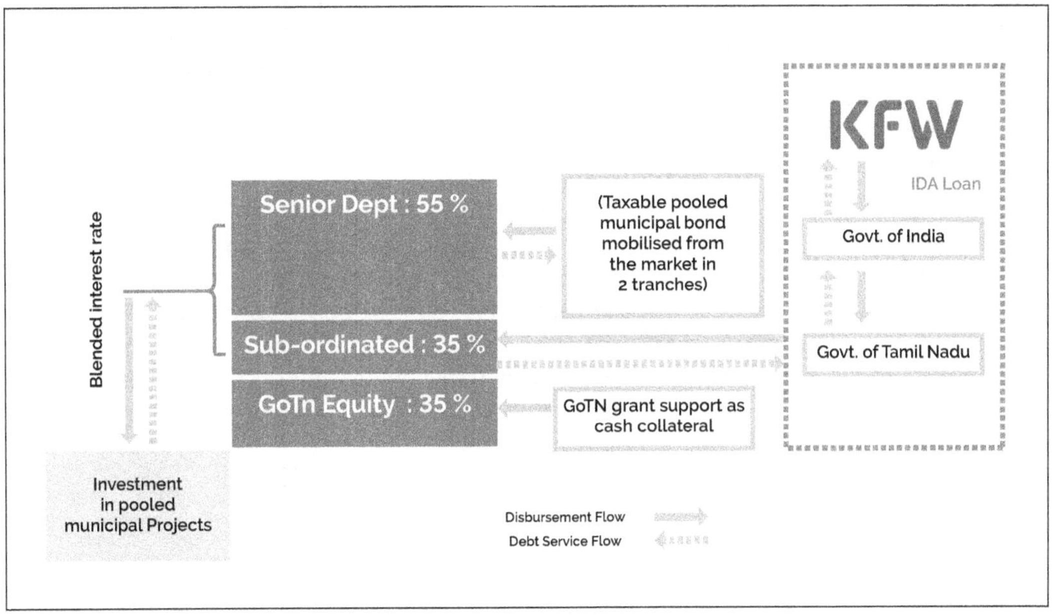

Source: Adapted by authors from unpublished project documentation

Impact: The intervention achieved meaningful outcomes. The ex-ante assessment projects a strong development impact of local infrastructure projects funded with loans from the Water and Sanitation Pooled Fund. In terms of longer-term impact, the issuance of bonds via the special purpose vehicle has enhanced the local bond market. This was measured by high secondary market activity indicating liquidity of the issuances and a positive impact on local currency bond market development. In sum, the project contributed to delivering SDG 9 (industry, innovation and infrastructure) and SDG 8 (decent work and economic growth) by providing municipalities access to finance.

Case study 6: Establishing the commercial viability of off-grid business models in renewable energy

Official institution: Asian Development Bank (ADB)

Blending partners: Clean Technology Fund (CTF) and Simpa Energy India

Challenge: It is estimated that 240 million people in India lack access to electricity (IEA, 2015). While transmission and distribution networks are being expanded, India's grid is not expected to satisfy the full growth in demand. In particular, access to electricity in many rural and remote areas of India is poor. Off-grid sources of renewable energy such as solar are important alternative means to expand access to electricity. However, private sector off-grid power projects in India often face difficulties raising capital due to their profile of perceived high risk.

Solution: ADB identified Simpa Energy India as an investment target to provide affordable solar home systems to rural households in some of India's poorest states. The company's business model focuses on solar photovoltaic systems, which are purchased by households with a small initial down payment. Customers pay a fee for their power using prepaid mobile phone payment services; this fee goes to cover the consumption of electricity and to amortise the purchase price of the solar systems. ADB provided an equity investment of USD 2 million in 2013 to support the growth of the company. ADB followed its equity investment by establishing a mini-grid and distributed power generation programme funded by the Clean Technology Fund, a funding facility capitalized by 14 donors that aim to scale up innovative and successful approaches for low-carbon technologies by funding them from an early stage.[4] Under this program, ADB provided a USD 6 million concessional loan from the CTF to Simpa Energy India when the need for additional capital became evident. This loan was part of a financing plan for the company involving other lenders and equity providers.

Impact: The following outcomes are expected: improved access to electricity particularly in rural areas not covered by the national grid; reduced greenhouse gas emissions due to the use of solar energy; and improved indoor air quality and related health benefits. Another expected benefit is increased income-generating opportunities, especially for female customers, as the programme is marketed directly to women via referral coupons. The programme also aims to demonstrate the commercial viability of off-grid business models. The ADB foresees potential for the scale-up in the off-grid sector in India following the demonstration of a range of successful transactions. In doing so, the intervention tackles SDG 7 (clean and affordable energy) as well as SDG 5 (gender equality).

Case study 7: Improving access to affordable, clean energy and digital communication services

Official institution: Australian Department of Foreign Affairs and Trade (DFAT)

Blending partner: Digicel Asia Pacific

Challenge: Only 10% of the population of Papua New Guinea (PNG) is connected to the electric grid. For the vast majority of the population who are off grid, access to low-quality energy sources, such as kerosene, is associated with high upfront and recurring costs. While 90% of the PNG population have access to mobile phone services, limited access to electricity affects their access to digital services via smart phones and laptops (DFAT, 2016).

Solution: DFAT is working with Digicel, the largest telecommunication provider in the Pacific, to improve access to affordable and reliable solar energy solutions for off-grid households and small businesses in PNG. DFAT is working through its Business Partnerships

Platform (BPP), which is establishing partnerships with businesses to address development challenges in the Indo-Pacific region. DFAT provides grants that are matched one for one by businesses, with business investment occurring first in order to ensure its commitment. In PNG, DFAT will provide of AUD 500 000 grant funding to Digicel and Digicel will invest AUD 1.037 million to increase access to sustainable, cost-effective and environmentally friendly alternatives to current costly and inferior energy sources and to enable better access to, and connection with, the digital economy. The initial term of the partnership is 18 months. Partnering on this initiative through the BPP will also allow Digicel and DFAT to determine whether there are potential opportunities to partner in other countries or activities.

Impact: The partnership, which began in mid-2016, is expected to substantially decrease the recurring energy expenditures of rural households and small businesses in PNG; enhance their access to and connection with the digital economy (e.g. via mobile phones, smartphones and laptops); and improve health and safety by reducing indoor air pollution and the risk of fires from candles and oil lamps. In the SDG framework, this project contributed to SDG 7 (affordable and clean energy), and SDG 9 (industry, innovation and infrastructure).

Case study 8: Promoting the participation of untapped investor classes in the healthcare sector through the Elazig Integrated Health Campus project

Official institutions: European Bank for Reconstruction and Development (EBRD) and Multilateral Investment Guarantee Agency (MIGA)

Blending partners: Meridiam, Ronesans and bond investors

Challenge: Turkey has made great strides in healthcare in the 21st century. One example is universal coverage, achieved in 2003 (OECD, 2014a); another is the dramatic drop in infant mortality rates, with life expectancy at birth now similar to that of the United States. Nevertheless, health outcomes remain stubbornly worse than the OECD average. Under-investment plays an important role: health expenditure as a percentage of GDP and the number of hospital beds in Turkey both are substantially below the OECD average (OECD, 2014b).

Solution: Turkey put in place the Health Transformation Programme to improve, modernise and expand healthcare services across Turkey through the hospital facilities management public-private partnerships (PPP) programme developed by the Ministry of Health, which aims to deliver up to 29 new hospital facilities totalling 42 000 high-quality hospital beds from 2017 onwards. The Elazig Integrated Health Campus project is a EUR 360-million greenfield project structured as a PPP that handles the design, construction, finance and maintenance and with the ministry solely responsible for the core medical services. The Elazig project deployed innovative financing structures and credit enhancements resulting in the issuance of bonds with an investment grade rating (Baa2 by Moody's) two notches above Turkey's sovereign rating (Moody's, 2016). This rating was possible thanks to the combination of MIGA political risk insurance and EBRD's unfunded liquidity facilities. The financing comprised senior debt of EUR 288 million and equity of EUR 72 million, reflecting an 80:20 gearing ratio. ELZ Finance, which is owned by Meridiam and Ronesans, issued senior debt in the form of bonds and the proceeds were on-loaned to the project company. The euro-denominated fixed rate project bonds included EUR 83 million in 18-year, senior secured A1A bonds; EUR 125 million in 20-year, senior secured A1B bonds; and EUR 80 million in 20-year, senior secured A2 bonds. The bonds were issued as deferred draw feature bonds, enabling the issuer to draw the funds gradually to lower financing costs. The A1 bonds have the benefit of EBRD liquidity facilities and the MIGA political risk insurance guarantee. Bond investors include Mitsubishi UFJ Financial Group (Japan), Intesa Sanpaolo (Italy), Siemens Financial Services (Germany), Proparco (France), the Netherlands Development Finance Company (FMO), and the Industrial and Commercial Bank of China. The International Finance Corporation underwrote the A2 bonds, which remained unenhanced.

Impact: The Elazig PPP aims to deliver an integrated health facility with 1 038 beds that includes a general hospital, a women/maternity and paediatrics hospital, a psychiatric hospital, and a dental health clinic serving eastern Anatolia with a population of 1.6 million people. On the financial impact side, the financing arrangement has attracted widespread attention in the financial industry due to its potential applicability for emerging market infrastructure. It has a strong potential to be repeated in markets where certain underlying project risks cannot be fully borne by capital markets and investors. Concretely, the project contributes to SDG 3 (improved access to healthcare, good health and well-being).

Case study 9: Developing a securitised bond market to expand financing for farmers and entrepreneurs

Official institution: United States Agency for International Development (USAID)

Blending partners: Central Bank of Armenia, universal credit organisations (UCOs) and bond investors

Challenge: The development of rural areas is an important priority for the government of Armenia. The micro, small and medium-sized enterprises who play a critical role in rural areas are constrained by the lack of available lending capital to invest in their businesses. UCOs, an Armenian legal form of microfinance institutions, are well established in Armenia to potentially provide additional capital. However, they are not permitted to take deposits and have difficulty borrowing from local banks, thus limiting their ability to raise the necessary capital to meet the demand (U.S. Embassy in Armenia, 2016).

Solution: In partnership with the Armenian government, USAID first provided technical assistance to establish a framework to issue securitised bonds backed by a portfolio of loans originated by UCOs. This required working with regulators to create a legal framework to structure and issue a securitised bond. A special purpose vehicle, Loan Portfolio Securitization Fund I, was established as the legal entity with the sole purpose of securitising the loans. More than 1 000 loans were selected from five participating UCOs, utilising a conservative approach when evaluating their credit quality. This process reduced by half the number of loans eligible for the securitisation, which had the effect of improving the credit characteristics of the underlying portfolio. To further catalyse interest from local investors, two credit enhancements were deployed. First, the participating UCOs purchased a subordinated tranche providing a 10% first loss cushion. Second, USAID's Development Credit Authority provided a 50% guarantee of bond principal on the senior tranche (USAID, 2016). The senior bonds were issued in both local currency and US dollars with a maturity of three years. At a cost of USD 229 500 to USAID, the transaction crowded in USD 5 million in private investment derived from local pension funds and banks.

Impact: As a direct outcome, the influx of funds will provide the necessary capital to finance at least 800 new loans for rural entrepreneurs. Further, the transaction establishes a new financial product to raise capital. The UCOs participating in the inaugural offering now have the ability to offer a follow-on issuance to raise additional capital. Ultimately, the transactions will impact the development of rural areas by supporting farmers in expanding production and entrepreneurs in starting businesses in rural villages via the improved availability of financing from the UCOs. In doing so, the project contributes to

SDG 8 (decent work and economic growth) by providing access to finance to UCOs, which is ultimately generating access to finance for farmers.

Case study 10: Constructing a food production plant to improve food nutrition security and support local farmers

Official institution: Netherlands Development Finance Company (FMO)

Blending partners: Governments of the Netherlands and Rwanda, International Finance Corporation (IFC), Royal DSM NV (DSM), and CDC Group; project enabler is the Clinton Health Access Initiative and project partner is the World Food Programme (WFP)

Challenge: The government of Rwanda actively engages in combatting malnutrition, acknowledging that the first 1 000 days of a child's life are decisive for physical and mental development. The food deficit has progressively improved to 230 kilocalories per person from 360 over the last ten years (World Bank 2017). Nevertheless, there is a scarcity of nutritional food for the population, especially in rural areas.

Solution: To address malnutrition in East Africa, the Clinton Health Access Initiative set up African Improved Foods holding (AIF) to produce high-quality food that would be channelled through the World Food Programme and the Rwanda government. The company is a joint venture between public and private partners. The main equity sponsors are the private Dutch company DSM (47%) the IFC (20%), the CDC Group (20%) and the FMO (13%). In addition to FMO's equity stake of USD 4 million, it has outstanding debt with the holding of USD 4 million. AIF represents a departure for FMO, which normally would not engage in both equity and debt financing in the same project. FMO, which as a development finance institution, disburses debt at market rates. This is blended with high-risk Dutch government money invested as equity through FMO via the Global Agriculture and Food Security Programme (GAFSP) of the AIF. Local ownership has been a central aspect in developing the corporate and financial structure. The government of Rwanda owns an 8% equity stake of the operating company in Rwanda, with the remainder held by the AIF holding. The government also is a major contractor of the products, with the World Food Programme.

Impact: Africa Improved Food Holding in Rwanda will help to reduce malnutrition and increase the economic base and capabilities of the local economy, creating 230 direct jobs and establishing security of outlet to 10 000 farmers by locally sourcing raw materials. Beyond the local impact, the holding envisions expanding its operating companies from Rwanda to Ethiopia and further in the region. To that end, the WFP already plans to distribute the final product in the broader region. In doing so, the project contributes to SDG 2 (zero hunger).

Notes

1. This is an interest-free loan to TG from Global Affairs Canada of CAD 936 000. TG is obligated to repay CAD 250 000 of the loan; the remaining CAD 686 000 is forgivable subject to TG meeting certain performance conditions, upon which this amount is deemed a grant. MEDA's contribution of CAD 1.25 million is a convertible loan at a concessionary interest rate.
2. See www.vestas.com/en/media/~/media/38a166a7ec1e4892a28b32d9beb79af5.ashx.
3. The World Bank has pioneered use of this structure.
4. The CTF is one of two financing windows operating under the Climate Investment Funds, which channel donor funding to private and public sector projects that address the challenges of climate change. The CTF has USD 5.6 billion under management, provided by 14 donor countries. The CTF implementing multilateral development banks include the ADB, African Development Bank and European Bank for Reconstruction and Development.

References

EIB (2011), "Updated environmental and social impact assessment summary: Lake Turkana Wind Power project, Kenya", European Investment Bank, www.eib.org/infocentre/register/all/53222536.pdf.

JICA (2008), "Ex-ante evaluation", Japan International Cooperation Agency, www.jica.go.jp/english/our_work/evaluation/oda_loan/economic_cooperation/c8h0vm000001rdjt-att/philippines01.pdf.

Paul, J. N. Jr. (2011), "Making water reforms happen: The experience of the Philippine Water Revolving Fund", *Background Paper* for the OECD Global Forum on Environment, 25-26 October, 2011, OECD, Paris, www.oecd.org/env/resources/48925373.pdf.

IEA (2015), *India Energy Outlook*, World Energy Outlook Special Report, OECD/International Energy Agency, IEA Publications, Paris, www.iea.org/publications/freepublications/publication/IndiaEnergyOutlook_WEO2015.pdf.

DFAT (2016), "Connecting communities to clean energy and the digital economy in PNG", Business Partnerships Platform, Australian Department of Foreign Affairs and Trade, Canberra, http://dfat.gov.au/aid/who-we-work-with/private-sector-partnerships/bpp/Documents/factsheets/digicel.pdf.

Moody's (2016), " ELZ Finance S.A.: Pre-sale report - Elaziğ hospital PPP exceeds Turkey's sovereign rating with strong multilateral support", Report Number 1048045, *Infrastructure and Project finance*, Moody's Investor Services, London, UK.

OECD (2014a), *OECD Reviews of Health Care Quality, Turkey 2014: Raising Standards*, OECD Publishing, Paris, http://dx.doi.org/10.1787/9789264202054-en.

OECD (2014b), "OECD Heath Statistics", OECD website, www.oecd.org/els/health-systems/oecd-health-statistics-2014-frequently-requested-data.htm.

U.S. Embassy in Armenia (2016), "NASDAQ OMX Armenia announces the listing of the first UCO securitized bonds in Armenia", press release, 27 January 2016, https://am.usembassy.gov/nasdaq-omx-armenia-announces-listing-first-uco-securitized-bonds-armenia/.

USAID (2015), "Microfinance securitization: Raising new sources of capital through local bond markets", Development Credit Authority, USAID, Washington, DC, www.usaid.gov/sites/default/files/documents/1865/dca_dealcard_2016_armeniav16.pdf.

World Bank (2017), World Bank data - "Depth of the food deficit (kilocalories per person per day", World Bank, Washington, DC, https://data.worldbank.org/indicator/SN.ITK.DFCT?locations=RW (accessed 14 December 2017).

ORGANISATION FOR ECONOMIC CO-OPERATION AND DEVELOPMENT

The OECD is a unique forum where governments work together to address the economic, social and environmental challenges of globalisation. The OECD is also at the forefront of efforts to understand and to help governments respond to new developments and concerns, such as corporate governance, the information economy and the challenges of an ageing population. The Organisation provides a setting where governments can compare policy experiences, seek answers to common problems, identify good practice and work to co-ordinate domestic and international policies.

The OECD member countries are: Australia, Austria, Belgium, Canada, Chile, the Czech Republic, Denmark, Estonia, Finland, France, Germany, Greece, Hungary, Iceland, Ireland, Israel, Italy, Japan, Korea, Latvia, Luxembourg, Mexico, the Netherlands, New Zealand, Norway, Poland, Portugal, the Slovak Republic, Slovenia, Spain, Sweden, Switzerland, Turkey, the United Kingdom and the United States. The European Union takes part in the work of the OECD.

OECD Publishing disseminates widely the results of the Organisation's statistics gathering and research on economic, social and environmental issues, as well as the conventions, guidelines and standards agreed by its members.

OECD PUBLISHING, 2, rue André-Pascal, 75775 PARIS CEDEX 16
(43 2018 02 1 P) ISBN 978-92-64-28875-1 – 2018

www.ingramcontent.com/pod-product-compliance
Lightning Source LLC
Chambersburg PA
CBHW080756150926
51501CB00045B/1255
9789264288751